Dreamweaver 8
Design and Construction

Dreamweaver 8
Design and Construction

 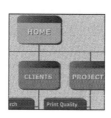 

Marc Campbell

O'REILLY®

BEIJING · CAMBRIDGE · FARNHAM · KÖLN · PARIS · SEBASTOPOL · TAIPEI · TOKYO

Dreamweaver 8 Design and Construction

by Marc Campbell

Published by O'Reilly Media, Inc., 1005 Gravenstein Highway North, Sebastopol, CA 95472.

O'Reilly books may be purchased for educational, business, or sales promotional use. Online editions are also available for most titles (*safari.oreilly.com*). For more information, contact our corporate/institutional sales department: 800-998-9938 or *corporate@oreilly.com*.

Print History:

January 2006:   First Edition.

Editor: John Neidhart

Production Editor: Genevieve d'Entremont

Copyeditor: Derek DiMatteo

Proofreader: Carol Marti

Indexer: Julie Hawks

Compositor: Ron Bilodeau

Cover Designer: Linda Palo

Interior Designer: David Futato

Cover Illustrators: Mike Kohnke and Linda Palo

Illustrators: Robert Romano, Jessamyn Read, and Lesley Borash

RepKover™   This book uses RepKover™, a durable and flexible lay-flat binding.

0-596-10163-5
[C]

Contents

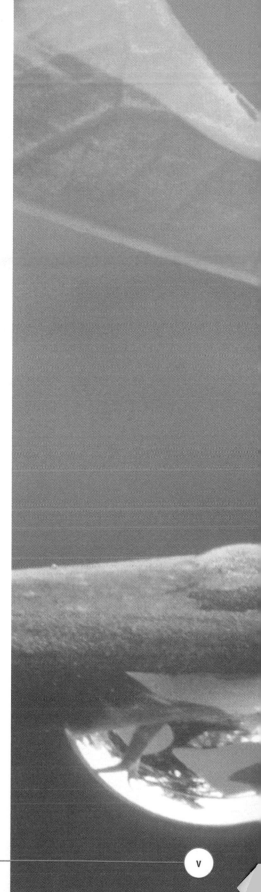

Part II: Designing Your Site

Part III: Building Your Site

Part V: Appendixes and Glossary

Introduction

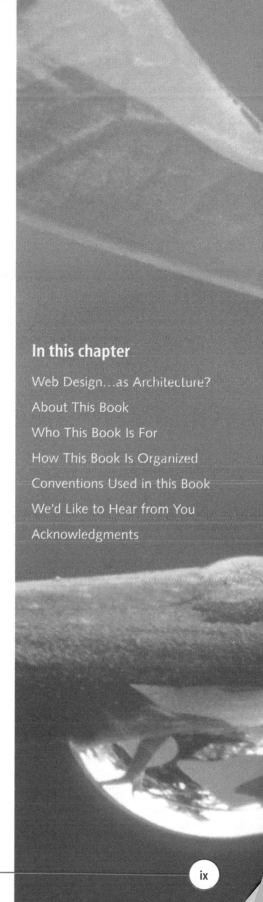

Web Design...as Architecture?

It's a curious notion, but not exactly a new one. Web designers often pull out the architecture metaphor to expound upon the virtues of a good web site. "A good web site feels like a physical space," they say. "It's like a house with many rooms and doors." The rooms, of course, are the pages of the site, and the doors are the links from one to another.

Then there's information architecture, a kind of specialty field in the world of web site construction. Information architects hone the structure of a site—call it the floor plan—so that the visitors don't get lost as they wander around.

Architecture must have been on somebody's mind from the very beginning, because we call these things *sites,* not resources, pools, objects, or quantities, which you have to admit is pretty remarkable. Computer geeks prefer mathematical metaphors. It's a wonder we're not all "positing web aggregates." And these people aren't known for their poetic flair, so there's got to be something inherent to the process that lends itself to architectural terms.

If you're looking to this humble tome for an answer, I'm afraid you're in for a disappointment. I have no clue why web design seems to go with architecture, besides the extension-of-metaphor thing. And to tell you the truth, I hadn't thought much about it, until my editor lobbed me this book idea.

"Dreamweaver Design-Build," his email said. "Best design practices using Dreamweaver. Fast prototyping using Dreamweaver. Fast web development."

"Cool idea," I replied.

That's when he informed me, all coolness aside, that design-build is an actual architectural movement. It stresses fast-track, high-quality construction by consolidating the tasks of design and build. I wasn't surprised to learn that in this country, we typically have designers and builders. They're different contractors, each distrusting the other, sometimes trying to get away with as little as possible. Occasionally, they wind up in litigation, after busting the budget and blowing deadlines, and the resulting building is of poor quality and filled with defects.

The design-build philosophy seeks to change all that. In it, you have a single firm that takes ownership of a project from blueprint to ribbon-cutting. By necessity, design-builders are agile but muscular. They can't get away with knowing a lot about a little, nor can they succeed by knowing a little about a lot. They have to know a lot about a lot. In other words, they have to learn their trade. More than that, they strive to become master builders, like the kind who gave us the Parthenon and the pyramids, though without all the slaves and human sacrifices, one hopes. And with the master's skill comes the master's appreciation. When design-builders envision a structure, they don't see a price tag. They see vaults and arches. They're hopeless Romantics.

Sometimes established practices believe that profit, speed, and quantity trump quality, and that good design belongs in a museum. The failure of these ideas lies in the fact that design-build can be cheaper. And faster. And it can yield better, longer lasting, and more satisfying results.

If my editor was trying to appeal to my political sensibilities, he had certainly pushed the right buttons. One of the first things I did as a creative director was to build that bridge to the coding crew and concede to them whatever made development easier. In return, they stopped trying to design the front end. When we started acting like a single provider instead of two independent, competing departments, we got things done better. And faster. And cheaper.

I don't usually go in for marketing copy, but the tagline for the DBIA—the Design-Build Institute of America—really caught my eye: "Return to the time-honored approach of the master builder," it says, "where a single source has absolute accountability for both design and construction." When you're talking concepts for a Dreamweaver book, you can't get much better. Dreamweaver has always been an excellent fit for the single sources among us, the independent designer/developers for whom the Web is a passion, not just (or maybe not even) a paycheck, who build web sites to be used and enjoyed, not as an excuse to send out an invoice. It occurred to me then (and my editor long before me, I'm sure), that while there are millions of books about Dreamweaver on the market, several thousand of which I myself have contributed, there isn't one that specifically shows you how to use Dreamweaver to build great web sites that respect the user. Dreamweaver as a tool of Revolution. Now that *really* caught my interest.

By now I was basically sold, but I knew that, if I was going to write this, I'd have to tone down my rhetoric. It was no good delivering a rambling manifesto. I'd probably wind up in Guantanamo Bay. No, I'd have to play it subversively, couching the politics in the architecture metaphor, all of which begged one important question: If Web design was indeed like architecture, could you apply the principles of design-build to it? Could you become a Web design-builder? I was curious to see how far I could stretch it, so I delved deeper into the DBIA's brochure and turned up a list of design-build benefits. Entering comparative-mythology mode, I decided to check for correlations:

Single responsibility

Check. This book is especially for independent designer/developers, and you don't need to know anything about Dreamweaver or web production to read it. The design-build philosophy is about process and results, and you get plenty of both in these pages.

Quality

Check. This book puts at least as much emphasis on what you're building as it does on how you build it, and it shows you how your design choices can improve the quality of your production experience.

Cost savings

Check. This book saves you effort, and if that saves you capital, then all the better.

Time savings

Check. This book saves you time. The design and production phases come together, with the one always looking toward maximizing the other. It may feel like you're moving through molasses at first, but just wait until you start to generate the pages. It's like they're coming off a printing press. And when you get to Chapter 20, you won't believe how quickly you can redesign your site, having built it upon the principles from the previous chapters.

Potential for reduced administrative burden

Check. Because you're a single source, you aren't building your Web site by committee, nor do you have to, as this book shows.

Early knowledge of firm costs

Check. After you get a few projects under your belt, you'll have a very good idea about exactly what it takes to get a Dreamweaver site up and running. The accuracy of your bottom-line estimates goes up, and the hassles from your clients go way down.

Improved risk management

Check. This book discusses the strengths and limitations of various web-building techniques and puts the cardinal virtues of accessibility and standards compliance into the real-world context of the Dreamweaver environment. If you decide not to do something on your site, you'll know exactly why you're not doing it—and if you decide to break a rule, you'll know exactly why you're doing that, too.

A one-for-one match! Clearly my editor was on to something. The humble tome before you is the immediate result.

About This Book

This book serves as an introduction to creating web sites using Macromedia Dreamweaver 8. It also presents the basic principles of planning, designing, building, publishing, and maintaining a web site. The focus throughout is that sound design and usability are inextricably linked.

Who This Book Is For

This book is designed to appeal broadly to readers who are new to Dreamweaver 8, or who are new to creating their own web sites from the ground up and all that entails: planning, visualizing, and employing sound design principles are all illuminated.

How This Book Is Organized

The chapters are a bit like modules, particularly in Part 1 and Part 3, where you can take them in the order that makes sense for you, not necessarily in the sequence that I've given them. Part 2 and Part 4 are somewhat less flexible in this regard, so if you're new to web building or the Dreamweaver application, I'd say read the book from cover to cover. After you've achieved your comfort level, by all means, read the book as you see fit. For purposes of quick reference, I tried to make whatever utility this humble tome possesses as easy to access as may be.

It comes to you in four parts:

Part 1: Planning Your Site

> You don't construct a building without a blueprint, and you don't build a web site without a plan. These chapters take you through the planning process with an eye toward maximizing design and production.

Part 2: Designing Your Site

> With your plan in hand, you create a Dreamweaver template to control the layout of your pages, plus an external Cascading Style Sheet to control the look and feel of the content. By the end of this part, the pages of your site are rolling out your studio.

Part 3: Building Your Site

> Into the rough template-based pages go the navigation, the text, the images, the Flash movies, the links, and the forms that you've been planning since Part 1. By now, production is unstoppable. Each new addition to the template document fleshes out your site in a wonderful way.

Part 4: Publishing Your Site

> Before you realize it, your site is finished. Use Dreamweaver's site management features to check for broken links, orphaned files, and rogue

code. Then upload your site to the Web, and learn how the design-build approach by way of Dreamweaver translates into effortless site maintenance.

Conventions Used in This Book

The following typographical conventions are used in this book:

Plain text

> Indicates menu titles, menu options, menu buttons, and keyboard shortcuts.

Italic

> Indicates new terms, film titles, URLs, email addresses, filenames, file extensions, pathnames, and directories.

BEHIND THE SCENES

In the "Behind the Scenes" boxes, you'll find information about the deeper levels of Dreamweaver and web design.

TIP

Tips indicate ways to work around problems and streamline your workflow, and also warn you about potential problems that might arise.

BEST BET

In the "Best Bet" boxes, you'll find author recommendations and opinions to help you decide on the best choices for your web site.

TECHTALK

Definitions of technical terms and jargon that you will encounter frequently.

HOTKEY

Keyboard shortcuts that will help speed up your work.

We'd Like to Hear from You

Please address comments and questions concerning this book to the publisher:

> O'Reilly Media, Inc.
> 1005 Gravenstein Highway North
> Sebastopol, CA 95472
> (800) 998-9938 (in the United States or Canada)
> (707) 829-0515 (international or local)
> (707) 829-0104 (fax)

We have a web page for this book, where we list errata, examples, and any additional information. You can access this page at:

> *http://www.oreilly.com/catalog/dreamwvrmx*

To comment or ask technical questions about this book, send email to:

> *bookquestions@oreilly.com*

For more information about our books, conferences, Resource Centers, and the O'Reilly Network, see our web site at:

> *http://www.oreilly.com*

Safari Enabled

When you see a Safari® Enabled icon on the cover of your favorite technology book, that means it's available online through the O'Reilly Network Safari Bookshelf.

Safari offers a solution that's better than e-books: it's a virtual library that lets you easily search thousands of top tech books, cut and paste code samples, download chapters, and find quick answers when you need the most accurate, current information. Try it for free at *http://safari.oreilly.com*.

Acknowledgments

This book is for you, the single sources, but even autonomous bodies need a network behind them, and this one is mine. Thank you, John Neidhart, for sending this my way and creating favorable conditions for writer design-build. Thank you, Lynn Haller, Katrina Bevan, Renee Midrack, and the entire team at Studio B. Thank you, Rob Kamphausen and Michael O'Brien (design-builders both), for keeping me on the straight and narrow.

And a special thanks to those on the front lines of production who mixed their time and talent with this book. The philosopher David Hume is tempted to doubt your existence because he has no direct experience of you. I make no such claim. It is indeed a miracle that anything gets built at all, and you fine people are the miracle workers.

Planning Your Site

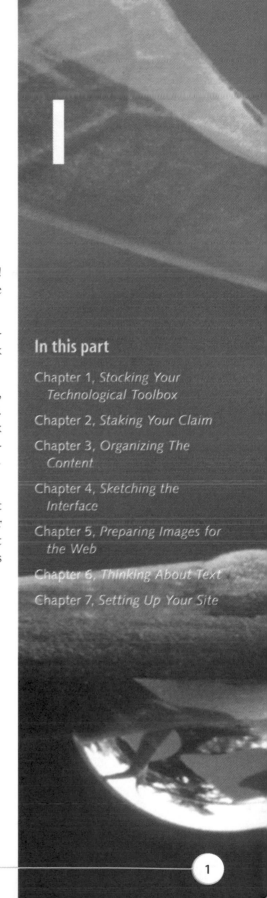

You bought this book because it promises speed. Fast design! Fast build! On with the show! You might also expect a book on Dreamweaver to have something to say about the Dreamweaver software.

So why, you may wonder, do the first seven chapters seem to have no purpose but to slow you down? Why does the entire first part of this book mention Dreamweaver only in passing?

The reasons are simple. If you want to build a web site at blinding speed, you need to have a solid plan in place, before you kick the engine in gear. Invest a little think-time at the top of your project, and you'll do less work and make fewer changes. When you build, you'll build quickly and accurately. Not only is this the secret of speed, it's also the secret of every successful web studio.

Dreamweaver, for all its strengths, doesn't build your web site for you. It can't tell you how to organize your site, how to design the look and feel, or what information to include. It's a software tool. It takes what you give it. It can't compensate for poor planning, but with the right plan in place, it helps you to produce more, produce better, and produce faster.

This part is all about devising your plan.

Stocking Your Technological Toolbox

1

Not to start this book on a philosophical note, but if you want to build something, you need tools. And because the quality of your tools helps to improve the quality of your creation, you want the best web design software that your budget can tolerate.

You're off to an excellent start by selecting Dreamweaver, by the way. It's the industry standard in web design for good reason, and it's particularly useful for building web sites quickly.

This chapter explains what else you'll need to weave the web site of your dreams.

Choosing Software

A web site is a patchwork of computer files of various types. Some are HTML documents. Others are image files. Yet others are multimedia files like Flash movies and Acrobat documents. To create and edit these files and organize them into a coherent, consistent whole—to turn them into a web site—you need several pieces of software.

Unfortunately, no single software package—not even Dreamweaver—gives you the tools to do everything from designing your pages to creating images and multimedia to previewing your site and sampling the user experience. With that in mind, here is a checklist for the well-rounded web designer's software library:

- Code editor
- Web browsers
- Image editor
- Multimedia design tools and plug-ins

In this chapter

Choosing Software

Comparing Static and Dynamic Sites

Choosing a Code Editor

A *code editor* is software that enables you to build web pages. Dreamweaver's got you covered here, so you can check the code editor off your list. In fact, Dreamweaver does you two better. It includes tools for organizing your pages into a site and then publishing your site on the World Wide Web.

As your code editor, Dreamweaver is the most essential piece of software in your studio, because it's the center of production from the beginning of your project to the very end. You use Dreamweaver to create the HTML files that become the foundation of your site. You build the layout of the pages, add the text, connect the links, and position the images and multimedia files. The site-management features help you to craft the flow of your site from page to page and section to section, and the publishing features help you to launch your site and keep it up to date with your latest changes and additions.

But the Dreamweaver feature that appeals the most to visually-oriented people like designers and graphic artists is that the code editing happens behind the scenes. You build your site in a WYSIWYG environment—that's What You See Is What You Get, meaning that you don't code your layouts into existence but draw them on the screen, much like you would on a piece of paper. Dreamweaver translates your design into code that's usable in any web browser.

> **BEHIND THE SCENES**
>
> Of course, you can also hand-code your web pages in Dreamweaver and switch between the visual environment and the coding environment with a mouse click. This book focuses on the visual aspects of Dreamweaver but sneaks in some coding every now and then to help you make the best site possible.

As you build your site, you'll use Dreamweaver to create three types of code: HTML, CSS, and JavaScript.

About HTML

HTML—HyperText Markup Language—is the language of the Web, and HTML files are its lifeblood. When you go to your favorite web site and choose a page, what you're actually seeing on screen is an HTML document that the browser has interpreted and displayed visually, in the form of a graphic design.

An HTML document is essentially a text file that has been marked up to indicate its *structure,* or the page elements that make it up. Take a web page that contains, among other things, the following paragraph:

```
The intelligence and facts were being fixed around the policy.
```

To indicate that this piece of text is a paragraph and not some other structural element, like a heading, for instance, or an item in a list, you drop special markers called *tags* around it. Most tags come in opening/closing pairs. The opening tag goes immediately before the element in the HTML code, while the closing tag comes immediately after it.

The correct pair of tags for a paragraph is `<p>…</p>`, so:

```
<p>The intelligence and facts were being fixed around the policy.</p>
```

You have now identified this piece of text as a paragraph. When a web browser comes to this line of code in the HTML file, it understands that this text is supposed to be a paragraph, which in turn determines how the browser displays the text on the screen.

Now say you have a list of items to present:

- Chemical
- Biological
- Nuclear

To mark these up as list items, you place the `<li>` (*list item*) tag around each one:

```
<li>Chemical</li>
<li>Biological</li>
<li>Nuclear</li>
```

As you'll see a bit later in this book, there are two kinds of lists in HTML: unordered (bulleted) and ordered (numbered). To display your items in the bulleted format, you mark up the entire list with the `<ul>` (*unordered list*) tag:

```
<ul>
  <li>Chemical</li>
  <li>Biological</li>
  <li>Nuclear</li>
</ul>
```

If you want a numbered list:

1. Chemical
2. Biological
3. Nuclear

you go with the `<ol>` (*ordered list*) tag:

```
<ol>
  <li>Chemical</li>
  <li>Biological</li>
  <li>Nuclear</li>
</ol>
```

Now, if you're starting to get that old clutch in your chest like the one from trigonometry class, worry not. When you work in Dreamweaver, it's more

---TECHTALK---

The elements that make up a web page are, collectively, its structure.

---TECHTALK---

Tags are the special markers in an HTML file that identify structural elements.

important to understand the *concept* of tagging, not the exact process behind it.

Figure 1-1 shows the three parts of building a page in Dreamweaver. As you build your page visually in Dreamweaver (A), it supplies the correct HTML tags on your behalf (B). When you're done and you save your work, it is written to the filesystem as an HTML document (B), which, when viewed in a web browser, is displayed as a graphic design again (C).

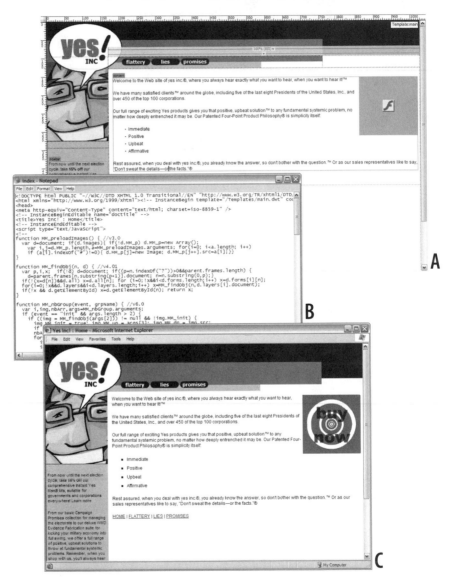

Figure 1-1. From design (A), to HTML (B), to graphic display (C)

About CSS

If an HTML document identifies the structure of a web page, a CSS file tells the browser how to display the structural elements that the web page contains. *CSS* stands for Cascading Style Sheets. CSS code, like HTML, is text-based. Instead of tags, though, CSS contains *style rules* or presentation instructions for the web browser.

Take the paragraph from the previous example:

```
<p>The intelligence and facts were being fixed around the policy.</p>
```

When the browser runs across this bit of structure, it normally displays the text in its default paragraph style, as Figure 1-2 shows.

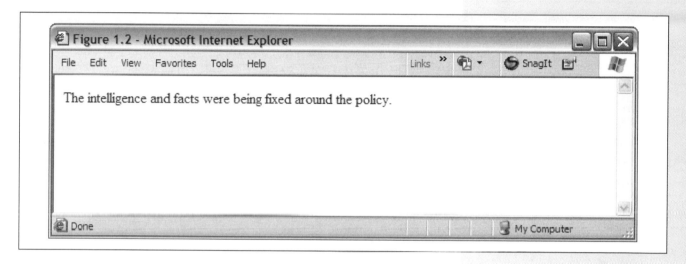

Figure 1-2. The default paragraph style in the browser lacks a certain gravity

With CSS, you replace the browser's built-in paragraph style with one of your own:

```
p {
    font-family: Arial, Helvetica, sans-serif;
    font-style: italic;
    font-weight: bold;
}
```

The p at the top of this style rule is called a *style selector*—it's the element to which the style rule applies, which in this case happens to be the paragraph tag, <p>. The lines between the curly braces are the *style definitions* that the browser applies whenever it comes across a paragraph in your HTML file. Attach this stylesheet to your HTML file, and you get something that looks like Figure 1-3 in a browser.

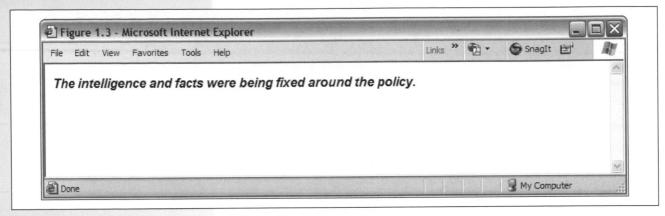

Figure 1-3. With CSS, you can give this paragraph the attention that it deserves

Again, in Dreamweaver, you don't have to write out the CSS code for your style rules manually unless you really want to. You simply choose the style definitions that you want to apply to any given structural element, and Dreamweaver writes the corresponding CSS code.

About JavaScript

JavaScript is a language for writing short computer programs called *scripts* that run in the visitor's web browser. In this sense, JavaScript is a different type of beast than markup languages like HTML and CSS. Markup languages are for telling the browser what's what—this is a paragraph, for instance, and it needs to look like this—but you'll never use a markup language to write useful functions, such as, "When the visitor clicks this button, I want you to check the order form for missing or incomplete fields." This is where scripting languages like JavaScript come in.

Scripts add a degree of interactivity to your pages that wouldn't ordinarily exist with HTML and CSS alone. They're perfect for clever features like order forms that tell you when you've forgotten to supply your email address or images that appear to change when you roll over them with the mouse pointer.

JavaScripts may be clever, but they can also be difficult and confusing to code. Thankfully, Dreamweaver takes away all the coding and subsequently all the hassle. Want button rollovers on your site? Done! No need wasting precious time making sure your detailed code is picture perfect. Dreamweaver comes with dozens of pre-built and completely customizable scripts called *JavaScript behaviors* that you may attach to your pages at will. You choose the behavior that you want, and Dreamweaver adds the necessary JavaScript to make the behavior work.

---TECHTALK---

A style selector is the structural element to which a style rule applies, while a style definition tells the browser how to display a particular feature or aspect of that element.

---TECHTALK---

JavaScript is a language for writing short computer programs, or scripts, that run in the visitor's web browser.

---TECHTALK---

JavaScript behaviors are prebuilt JavaScripts that Dreamweaver supplies for use on your site.

Stocking Up on Web Browsers

The visual representation of your web page in Dreamweaver is useful as a guide, but it isn't exact. It's an approximation of how your page actually looks in a web browser. And because different browsers tend to display the same web page differently, the only way to be sure about your pages is to test them—often—in a variety of browsers.

It isn't hard to assemble an arsenal of browsers for testing purposes, and you'll definitely like the price: it's free. Table 1-1 shows you which browsers to get and where to find a free download.

Table 1-1. Popular web browsers

Browser	Download
Microsoft Internet Explorer	*http://www.microsoft.com/*
Mozilla Firefox	*http://www.mozilla.org/*
Netscape Browser	*http://www.netscape.com/*
Opera	*http://www.opera.com/*
Safari	*http://www..apple.com/safari/*

Microsoft Internet Explorer (MSIE or IE for short) is by far the most popular web browser on the market today, mainly because it comes preinstalled on all Windows computers. Even if you don't personally use IE for your excursions on the web, most of your visitors do, so dust off your existing copy if you're a Windows user, or download your free copy if you're designing on a Mac.

The last couple of Mac OS X operating systems have come with a built-in browser called Safari. There isn't currently a version of Safari for Windows, but you don't need to run out and buy a Mac just so that you have Safari at your disposal. The percentage of Safari users is a very small fraction of all traffic on the Web, so if potentially alienating visitors who come to your site using Safari doesn't bother you, then you could just skip testing in this browser. However, if you would like to get a basic idea of how it looks on Safari, you could use Daniel Vine's excellent, free service at *http://www.danvine.com/icapture/* to see a screen capture of pages you've designed as they would be displayed in Safari.

Mac heads should also note that the Netscape Browser beginning with Version 8.0 is only available on Windows systems. However, the Netscape Browser is based on Mozilla Firefox, so testing in Firefox is fine if you can't have both browsers. Windows users should get and test in both, however, because Netscape Browser and Firefox are just different enough to cause mischief.

Choosing an Image Editor

An *image editor* is software for creating and editing computer graphics. Dreamweaver does not fall into this category. While you can use Dreamweaver to place image files on your web pages and make simple edits to the size and dimensions of these images, you can't actually edit the pictures themselves or generate image files from scratch.

When you add an image to a web page, it's important to note that the image remains as a separate file. You don't embed the image into the HTML document the way that you might add a picture to a word processor file. Instead, you add a pointer to the image in the HTML code. The pointer tells the browser where to find the image file online. The browser sees the pointer, follows it, grabs the image, and incorporates it into the page. This happens every time that the visitor requests the page. (Incidentally, when you load a web page that shows broken graphics, what's happening is that the browser can't find the image in the specified location.) When you publish your HTML documents on the Web, then, you must also be sure to publish all the image files for your site.

Image editors fall into two basic types: paint programs and draw programs. A *paint program* deals in *bitmap* or *raster graphics,* which are computer images made up of small colored boxes called *pixels.* Adobe Photoshop and Macromedia Fireworks are excellent paint programs.

A *draw program* is for *vector graphics,* which are computer images made up of *paths,* or outlines. Adobe Illustrator and Macromedia FreeHand are fine examples of draw programs.

For the Web, bitmap graphics are by far the most common, so you want to choose a paint program, not a draw program. Ideally, you should get yourself a copy of Photoshop or Fireworks for your image-editing needs. Fireworks in particular was made with the Web in mind, and it's well integrated with Dreamweaver. It comes with Macromedia Studio 8, so if you have Studio, you already have Fireworks. You can also buy it separately.

> **TECHTALK**
> *An image editor is software for creating and editing computer graphics.*

> **TECHTALK**
> *A paint program edits bitmap or raster graphics, which are computer images made up of pixels—very small, colored boxes.*

> **TECHTALK**
> *A draw program edits vector graphics, which are computer images made up of outlines or paths.*

BEST BET

Use a paint program as your image editor. Macromedia Fireworks works especially well with Dreamweaver.

Choosing Multimedia Software

Multimedia (or simply *media*) refer to a wide variety of digital data, including animations, audio, and video. To create multimedia for your site, you need dedicated authoring tools. You probably have a few of these already. Microsoft Windows Media Player springs to mind—you can use this application to capture audio from music CDs. To create different kinds of media formats, or for more robust editing capabilities, you'll need to invest in additional software.

Multimedia, like images, exist as separate computer files. You place them on your web pages in Dreamweaver. Dreamweaver adds the corresponding pointers to the HTML code, and, when you publish your pages, you upload the multimedia files so that the browser can find them.

However, unlike images, your visitors require additional pieces of software called *plug-ins* to open your multimedia files. Every multimedia format has its own browser plug-in. For Flash movies, it's the Flash Player. For QuickTime video, it's the QuickTime Plug-in. If your visitors don't have the necessary plug-ins installed on their computers, then your multimedia files won't work. It doesn't matter if you, the designer, have the correct plug-ins on your computer. Your visitors need to have the same plug-ins on their computers.

On the upside, the plug-ins for all the popular multimedia formats are free. Your visitors can download them, install them, and enjoy. On the downside, visitors generally dislike having to leave your site to download special software. Once they're gone, they might not come back. Plus, the vast majority of web users have no interest in knowing about plug-ins. When they go to a web site, they expect it to work. They don't want to understand why it doesn't work.

For this reason, it's the wise web designer who uses multimedia very judiciously. Your site doesn't need to be an extravaganza of animation, audio, and video. A few choice selections go a long way. Also, it behooves you to pick multimedia formats whose plug-ins the visitor is already likely to have. Table 1-2 lists many of these.

> **TIP**
>
> Use multimedia on your web site when it's impossible or impractical to present the information in any other way.

---TECHTALK---
Multimedia or media refer to special kinds of computer files like animations, audio, and video.

---TECHTALK---
Plug-ins are computer programs that add functionality to the Web browser. To open your multimedia files, your visitors require the appropriate plug-ins.

Table 1-2. Popular multimedia formats

Multimedia format	Type	Plug-in	Plug-in web site
Macromedia Flash	Animation	Flash Player (Shockwave Player also plays Flash movies)	*http://www.macromedia.com/*
Macromedia Shockwave	Animation	Shockwave Player	*http://www.macromedia.com/*
Apple QuickTime	Streaming audio and video	QuickTime Plug-in	*http://www.apple.com/*
Microsoft Windows Media	Streaming audio and video	Windows Media Player	*http://www.microsoft.com/*
RealMedia	Streaming audio and video	RealPlayer	*http://www.real.com/*
Adobe Acrobat	Rich text documents	Acrobat Reader	*http://www.adobe.com/*
Scalable Vector Graphics (SVG)	Vector graphics	Adobe SVG Viewer (among others)	*http://www.adobe.com/*

Virtually every computer on the Web today has the Flash Player plug-in, so if you want to include multimedia on your site, the Flash format is a very safe choice. Macromedia Flash Professional 8—the Flash authoring environment—comes with Studio 8, and it's available as a standalone product. Don't confuse the authoring tool with the free plug-in, though. The Flash Player plug-in allows you to view Flash movies, not create them.

Some multimedia formats, particularly for audio and video, open in a variety of plug-ins and applications. Table 1-3 shows the most common formats. The chances are good that your visitor has some means of viewing or hearing these types of files.

Table 1-3. Common audio and video formats

Format	Type	Stands for
AIF, AIFF	Audio	Apple Audio Interchange Format
AU	Audio	Sun Audio format
AVI	Audio/video	Microsoft Audio Video Interleave format
MIDI	Music notation data	Musical Instrument Digital Interface format
MPEG	Audio/video	Moving Picture Experts Group format
MP3	Audio	MPEG-1 Layer 3 format
WAV	Audio	Microsoft Wave format

Comparing Static and Dynamic Sites

Dreamweaver distinguishes between static and dynamic web sites. A *static site* relies solely on client-side technology, while a *dynamic site* mixes client-side with server-side technology. This explanation begs a glaring question, namely: what's the difference between client-side and server-side technology? The answer to this one gets a little hairy, so feel free to skip ahead to "Meeting the Demands of Dynamic Sites" if you have little desire for a technical discussion.

For those still with us, the client/server distinction has to do with the way that computer networks operate. In any network connection, you have two pieces of software that talk to each other. One of these is the *client*—that's the requesting software, the software that asks to see a particular file. The other is the *server*, the sending software, the software that pushes the file over the network in response to the client's request. In the case of the Web, the client software is the visitor's web browser, which runs on the visitor's personal computer. The server software runs on the computer that hosts the web site.

Client side technology, then, pertains to the client side—the requesting side—of the network connection. Everything that happens inside the web browser falls into this category. The browser requests HTML documents and displays them for you as visual web pages, presents page elements according to style rules, launches plug-ins, follows links, and executes scripts, so all of these are client-side functions. As long as it happens in the browser, it's on the client side.

By contrast, *server-side technology* pertains to the server side—the sending side—of the network connection. Server-side technologies come into play when you want to add information to an HTML document before it goes off to the client. Say that you're visiting an online bookstore, and you've packed your shopping cart full of this author's many excellent titles. You're getting ready to settle up, so you review the contents of your cart. Click goes your mouse pointer on the shopping-cart button, and your browser kindly requests the shopping-cart page from the web server. But before the server responds, the web site's ecommerce application intervenes, takes the basic shopping-cart page, and writes the particular items from your order into the HTML code. Upon completion, the ecommerce app hands your personalized shopping-cart page back to the web server. The web server then passes this page on to your browser, and you see your order in the cart, down to the last book, as Figure 1-4 shows.

— TECHTALK —

A static site relies solely on client-side technology, while a dynamic site mixes client-side with server-side technology.

— TECHTALK —

In a computer network, the client requests a file, and the server sends the file to the client in response.

— TECHTALK —

Client-side technology pertains to the requesting side of a network connection. If it happens in the browser, it's on the client side.

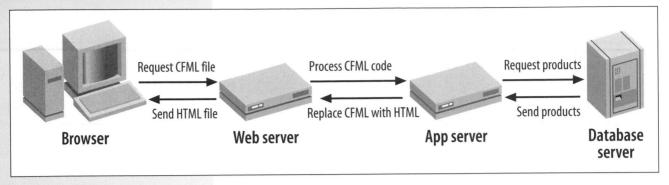

Figure 1-4. The logic of a dynamic Cold Fusion site reveals a lot going on behind the scenes

┌─ T E C H T A L K ─────

Server-side technology pertains to the sending side of a network connection. To write customized or visitor-specific information into a web page before the page goes to the client, you need server-side technology.

Now, getting back to static and dynamic web sites: a static web site relies solely upon client-side technologies, which means that the pages of the site don't require any special processing on the server side before they go to the browser, as shown in Figure 1-5. In other words, the pages are always the same for all visitors—hence, the term *static*. A dynamic web site, then, is dynamic precisely because the same basic page goes out with different information depending upon which client makes the request. If you have 100 different visitors with 100 different shopping carts, then the server sends out 100 different variations of the shopping-cart page, each customized to match the visitor's specific order.

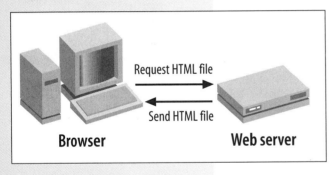

Figure 1-5. The logic of a static site is straightforward

Another common example of dynamic data in action is the ever-popular search feature. You know the drill: you type a few keywords into a text field, click a button, and get a page of results. If you're building this type of feature into your site, it isn't practical to create a separate results page for every possible combination of keywords you can think of, which would be the case with client-side technology alone. Depending upon the site, the results pages could easily number in the billions. But if you build the search feature by using server-side technology, you don't need a billion different results pages. One will suffice. The site compiles a list of results according to the visitor's specific keywords and then writes them dynamically into the page, which then goes off to the visitor's browser.

Meeting the Demands of Dynamic Sites

As you might expect, to build a dynamic site, you need a few additional pieces of software. All have the unfortunate name of *server,* which can very easily lead to confusion. To keep them straight, call them by their proper names: web server, application server, and database server.

A web server is software for responding to client requests over a network connection. Many times, the web server runs on a different computer than your personal machine, but this doesn't have to be the case. You can just as easily run a web server on the same computer as your web browser and Dreamweaver. Microsoft Internet Information Server (IIS) is one such personal web server that runs on Windows XP Professional. Apache is another very popular web server that runs on all operating systems, although the installation is on the technical side.

An *application server* or *app server* works in conjunction with the web server to process the server-side instructions on your pages. The files that make up a dynamic web site contain a mixture of straight HTML and server code. The server code explains what needs to be added to the page before it goes off to the client. When the browser requests a page, the application server checks to see if any customized content needs to be added. If so, the application server does its thing, replacing the server code (which the browser doesn't understand) with good old HTML (which the browser understands very well) and hands off the completed page to the web server for delivery to the browser.

There are many different kinds of application servers, and each requires its own specific type of server code. Dreamweaver supports five of the most common app servers. Table 1-4 lists them.

Table 1-4. Dreamweaver-compatible application servers

App server	Server code
Macromedia ColdFusion	CFML
PHP Hypertext Preprocessor (PHP)	PHP
Microsoft ASP.NET	ASP
Microsoft Active Server Pages (ASP)	ASP
Java Server Pages (JSP)	JSP

Finally, a *database server* works in conjunction with your application server, enabling the app server to connect with an online database; e.g., products, user accounts, sales information, inventories, or whatever else you might want to store in this fashion. If your site can make do without a database, then you don't need a database server, but most dynamic sites use databases extensively and wouldn't be very dynamic without them. The app server can write information from the database directly into the pages of the dynamic site, which is the main incentive here. MySQL (pronounced "My Ess Que Ell") is an excellent database server that offers support for many different operating systems, including Mac OS X.

---TECHTALK---
A web server is software for responding to client requests over a network connection.

---TECHTALK---
An application server or app server adds dynamic information to a web page before the web server sends the page to the client.

---TECHTALK---
A database server enables your app server to connect with an online database.

Respecting the Limits of Static Sites

Without server-side technology, the Web would be a very different place. There would be no search engines. No online shopping carts. No password-protected members-only areas. No customized front pages to match your preferences in news, sports, business, and weather. When many first-time web builders envision the site of their dreams, server-side technology figures largely in their thoughts.

While you can certainly build dynamic sites in Dreamweaver, this humble tome respectfully suggests that you make your first site a static one. Learning to build rock-solid, static pages without worrying about the subtleties of server-side code helps you to get a feel for the web-building process. You see exactly what the client side has to offer, which gives you a better understanding of the app server's role when you're finally ready to tackle dynamic pages.

Also, creating on the client side is easier. Because the HTML files of a static site are always the same, you don't have to do anything special in Dreamweaver to build them. You simply design them the way that you want them to look and then publish them to the Web. Even better, you don't need any special software to process your pages. Forget about the web server, the app server, and the database. To view your site, you need nothing more sophisticated than a web browser.

Unfortunately, this also means that you can't include any information on your pages that changes depending upon the visitor. If you need your site to take orders online, keep track of visitor preferences, create user accounts, and so on, you need the server-side support of a dynamic web site.

BEST BET

Make your first site a static one. Because so much happens behind the scenes on the server side, dynamic web sites can be challenging to build.

Remember, though, just because it's static doesn't mean that it isn't interactive. Dreamweaver's JavaScript behaviors give you plenty of interactivity—just not visitor-specific interactivity. As long as your interactive features don't need to keep track of somebody's username, provide a shopping cart, or build results pages from database queries, you can create your site on the client side and conveniently avoid the technical headaches that are part and parcel of dynamic sites.

Besides, static or dynamic, your site's going to be great. You're the designer, after all.

Staking Your Claim

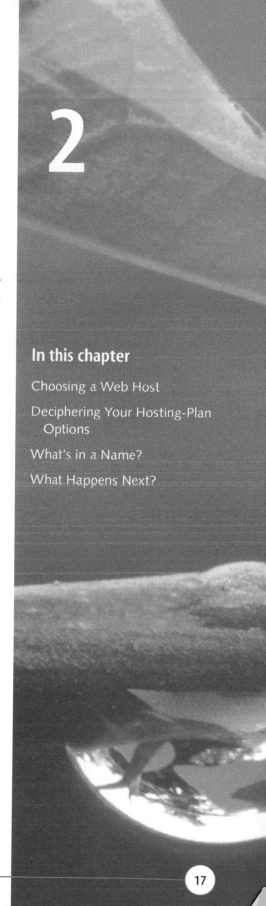

2

Dreamweaver provides the tools for designing, developing, and testing your web site. You can do it all from your computer. You don't even need to have an Internet connection—Dreamweaver stores the files for your site *locally,* on your personal machine, usually in a folder on your hard drive. This is fine for you, the author of the site. If you want to publish your site on the Web, you need some space on a host somewhere. Happily, web hosting is abundant and cheap. In fact, you might own some web space already.

This chapter guides you through the process of getting a web host and choosing an address for your site.

Choosing a Web Host

The first step in securing the publishing space for your site is choosing a web host. A *web host* owns or rents the computer that serves the files of your web site to your visitors when they come calling; and the first step in choosing a web host is checking with your Internet Service Provider (ISP). Many ISPs offer hosting space as part of their overall membership packages. If you're experimenting with web building for the first time, your personal ISP hosting is ideal, because you don't have to spend any more per month than you're already paying for your Internet connection. Even for more experienced web heads, ISP hosting is great for testing new ideas.

Having said that, ISP hosting is less than desirable in many circumstances. Your ISP doesn't usually let you choose your own *domain name,* or the web address of your site (*http://yoursite.com/*). Instead, it assigns you a generic domain name, usually something like *http://yourisp.com/your-email-name/* or *http://yourisp.com/your-account-login/*, and you either like it or you don't. While this may be fine for a personal home page or hobby site, it doesn't make sense for most businesses or organizations. The domain name is very important as a marketing tool, as you'll see in "What's in a Name?" later in this chapter.

Furthermore, your ISP's computers host the sites of tens of thousands or hundreds of thousands of customers like you. The more traffic a hosting computer receives, the slower it runs. Again, this may be fine for your home page, but it's the kiss of death for commercial sites. Customers shop the Web for convenience and speed. Make your visitors wait too long for pages to load, and they won't stick around.

It's also possible that your ISP will tack advertisements or their corporate branding onto the pages of your site without your permission. You might be able to live with this for your personal home page, but you definitely don't want it on any kind of site for your business or organization, where you need precise control over the advertising policy and your site's graphical look and feel.

Finally, your ISP usually gives you sufficient web space for a typical home page or modest web site. For larger sites, especially those that include multimedia files like MP3s, you can quickly exceed the amount of space that your ISP allots you.

Since you're just starting the process of building your site, you might not know how much web space you need, and it's not always easy to guess. At this stage, just find out how much space comes with your Internet account and refer to Table 2-1 for a rough guide. The important thing to remember is that your web host doesn't have to be your life partner. If at any point you discover that you need more room for your site, you can very easily hire a new web host. In the event of a host change, recalibrating Dreamweaver takes no more than a few simple clicks.

Table 2-1. Typical web site hosting requirements

Amount of server space	Typically hosts
5 MB	Small sites (10–50 pages) with light multimedia load (web-quality images, short Flash movies, short Shockwave movies, short Adobe Acrobat documents)
10 MB	Small sites (50–100 pages) with light multimedia load
100 MB	Medium-sized sites (100–500 pages) with typical multimedia load (print-quality images, audio clips, video clips, long Flash movies, long Shockwave movies, long Adobe Acrobat documents)
500 MB	Medium-sized sites (500–1,000 pages) with typical multimedia load
1 GB	Large sites (1,000–10,000 pages) with heavy multimedia load (audio files, video files)
10 GB	Large sites (10,000–100,000 pages) with heavy multimedia load

If your ISP doesn't offer hosting space or if you need to find a better web host for your commercial site, your next stop is your favorite search engine. Type in "web hosting," and watch the results pile up. Google gives you tens of millions! How do you sort through the static? A little research goes a long way. Check out the first few pages of results, and visit any web host that jumps out at you. Maybe you recognize the name, or maybe the service deal appeals to you, or the host's home page might strike you as particularly well done or professional—a good sign that the service shares similar standards of quality.

When you have maybe five to ten possibilities, type each host name into your search engine, and see what comes up. You're looking specifically for independent reviews. Quality web hosts often generate positive talk, but don't be discouraged if you come across negative reviews here and there. Nobody's perfect, after all, and negative press is a sign that the host has some experience in the business. Be more concerned if the Web is strangely silent about your host of choice. An experienced host who has weathered a few hits in the customer-service department is generally more desirable than a rookie host with little experience in handling the irate customer.

You can divide non-ISP web hosts into two categories: free and pay services. Free web hosts have an obvious advantage in that they're free—you don't have to pay an additional monthly charge to publish your site to the Web. However, the same provisos that apply to your ISP apply doubly or trebly so to free web hosts. Free services don't usually let you choose your own domain name. Their computers are crowded and therefore slow—much slower than your ISP's—and they almost always load your page with involuntary advertising. Choose a free web host for a personal page, but steer well clear of them for commercial sites.

BEST BET

For personal home pages, free web hosting is adequate. For commercial sites, find a pay service.

Pay services for web hosting may elicit a grumble from your wallet, because you're shelling out an additional monthly charge on top of what you already spend on your Internet connection. But for professional sites or serious personal pages and hobby sites, a pay service is the only way to go. At least you get a few nice premiums for your money: your choice of domain names, faster performance, larger amounts of hosting space, and control over advertising. If your pay service doesn't offer these benefits, find one that does.

Here are a few general criteria for choosing a good web host:

Reasonable monthly charge

Expect to pay about $10–$25 per month for a typical personal or small-business site. Pay less, and your web host is probably making up the difference with reduced features, spotty service, or advertising. Pay more, and you're probably buying more than you need. But definitely shop around and see what competitors are offering.

Reasonable (or no) setup charge

Some perfectly reputable web hosts charge a one-time setup fee when you first sign on. This isn't just soak money. The host does have to do a little extra labor to get a new account up and running. At the same time, many perfectly reputable web hosts don't charge a setup fee at all. The bottom line is, if you really like a particular web host, don't shy away from it just because of the setup fee. Some non-fee web hosts make up the difference at your expense. Your best bet is to catch a fee-charging host during one of its "fee waived" promotional periods. And don't pay more than $35 in any case.

Domain name registration (preferably free)

Some web hosts will register your site's domain name on your behalf, and some will even front you the standard annual $35 registration fee if you agree to stay with them for the entire year. As you will see in "Reserving Your Domain" later in this chapter, you don't have to use your web host's registration service if you don't want it or need it, but going with your web host helps to smooth over some of the technical minutiae.

Upgradeable service plans

A good web host offers several different plans at decent price points, maybe 10 MB of server space at the entry level to 10 GB or more for the premium package. While you can always switch web hosts at any time, why change when you can upgrade instead? Start with the cheapest plan, and as your site grows, you can simply graduate to the next rung of service.

Reliable customer support by phone

Round-the-clock support by email is fine, as are online knowledge bases and web pages for frequently asked questions, but you need phone support, period. You need to be able to call your web host and talk to a live human being. If you can't get 24-hour support by phone and a toll-free number at the price you're willing to pay, you can comfortably settle for a help line during normal business hours. You may only use that phone number once or twice in your entire relationship with the host, but you'll be glad you have the option of calling if something goes wrong.

Site reports

> You want a web host that provides you with detailed information about your visitors: where they're from, what browsers they're using, which pages they're visiting, and especially which pages they seem to be missing. These breakdowns are essential to helping you fine-tune your site. If everyone seems to be missing a key area, you can juggle the organization of your site in Dreamweaver and compare traffic levels in the next report.

Deciphering Your Hosting-Plan Options

Spend any time researching web hosts, and your head begins to spin with tech-sounding buzzwords like *bandwidth* and *MIME types*. Here is a quick tour through the most important options for your Dreamweaver site-to-be:

Hosting space

> This affects the total *weight* of your site, or the raw amount of disk space that your site can occupy. Refer to Table 2-1 for rough guidelines on how much web site you can expect to publish depending on the amount of space that your web host provides. In general, more is better, but make sure you're not getting too much, or you could be throwing money away. You don't need 10 GB of hosting space unless you're in a band with a full back catalog of original MP3s to share.

TIP

Some web hosts advertise that they are Dreamweaver-compatible. As it happens, *all* web hosts are Dreamweaver-compatible, so you don't have to choose a host based on whether this statement appears in the ad copy. By contrast, Microsoft FrontPage (a code editor similar to Dreamweaver) *does* require that the web host install special "FrontPage extensions" to enable certain visual effects. If you were working in FrontPage instead of Dreamweaver, you'd want to find a host that specifically mentions FrontPage compatibility.

Bandwidth

> Your web host measures the amount of activity on your site not in terms of "hits" but as data transfer of *bandwidth*, i.e., the amount of information that it pushes to your visitors over a given length of time, typically one month. You get a certain amount of bandwidth for free. If you exceed this limit, you have to pay extra. When you're first starting out, guessing at how much bandwidth you need is tricky business, because you don't know how much traffic your site is going to generate on average. One gigabyte of data transfer per month is a good place to start.

—TECHTALK—

Weight is the amount of disk space that a computer file requires. For example, a graphic file of 30 KB is lighter than a digital photo of 300 KB, which is lighter than an entire web site with a combined weight of 3 MB.

—TECHTALK—
Bandwidth or data transfer is the amount of information that your web host pushes to your visitors over a given length of time, typically one month.

A page view is one person viewing one page of your site one time.

That's roughly the equivalent of 20,000 *page views*, or a total of 20,000 pages served. This isn't the same as 20,000 "hits"; 20,000 page views is one person visiting 20,000 pages of your site or five people visiting 4,000 pages of your site or 20,000 people visiting one page of your site over the course of the month. This should be sufficient for most small businesses and more than enough for personal projects. Hopefully, your web host offers multiple service plans, so you can upgrade to more bandwidth (or downgrade to less) as your needs require.

BEHIND THE SCENES

When it comes to measuring your site's traffic, the page view is a much more useful statistic than the hit. A *hit* is nothing more than a request to the web server. If you have a web page that contains five images and a Flash movie, then viewing this one page creates *seven* separate hits or requests: one for the HTML file, five for the images, and one for the movie. By contrast, viewing that one page one time equals one page view, no matter how many requests go off to the server.

Marketing departments like to brag about "a million hits." You can have a million hits, too, if you really want them. Simply create a web page, add 999,999 image files, and view it once. View it twice, and that's two million hits. Web designers prefer page views, because they're more authentic and harder to fake. To get a million page views, you'd have to visit your web page a million times—a small matter of, oh, about two years, assuming you work 24 hours a day!

POP3 email accounts

—TECHTALK—
POP3 (Post Office Protocol 3) is a standard for Internet email delivery that allows users to download their email to their personal computers through client software like Microsoft Outlook and Mozilla Thunderbird.

You probably already have an email account, and you're likely to have several. Some web hosts offer additional email accounts to go with your web site and domain name, letting you be *bob@mysite.com* in addition to your usual *bob@yahoo.com*. For a personal home page, this is a luxury that you probably don't need. But for business or organizational purposes, you're likely to want those branded email accounts to reinforce a consistent image and keep your professional and personal lives separate. If additional emails are for you, make sure your host gives you POP3 email accounts in addition to or instead of web-based email. POP3 email accounts work with client software such as Microsoft Outlook and Mozilla Thunderbird, which means that you can jump online, download your email, and read and answer it offline at your leisure. With web-based email, the mail lives on the host's server and you browse your mail on their server just as you would a web page in your web browser, so you have to be online to read and respond.

Media types

If you plan on posting multimedia files such as Flash movies, Shockwave movies, Adobe Acrobat documents, MP3s, streaming audio, or streaming video, you need a web host that supports these media types.

Somewhere on your web host's site, you should find a list of supported file types or *MIME types*. Check the list for the types of multimedia files that you want to post, and if you don't see your particular multimedia type on the list, it's time to make one of those service calls to a live human being and get a definite yes or no. If your web host doesn't support the MIME type that you want to use, then your visitors won't be able to view or listen to those files. Not to worry, though—most hosts are set up for the full battery of the most popular MIME types on the Web, including Flash, Shockwave, Acrobat, RealMedia, and QuickTime. But if you tend to like obscure multimedia formats, make sure to check with your web host before you start posting.

—TECHTALK—
A MIME (Multipurpose Internet Mail Extension) type gives the format for a particular computer file. Some common MIME types are text/plain, audio/mp3, and video/quicktime.

> **TIP**
>
> If you're building a dynamic site, your web host needs to support your application server and database server of choice. ASP.NET sites connected to Oracle databases won't work if your web host supports PHP and MySQL only.

By contrast, because you're building your site in Dreamweaver, you don't need any of the following options, which, if you add them, can drive up your monthly cost:

- Web-based site-building tool
- Web site templates
- Web design services
- Web-based file manager
- Web-based FTP (File Transfer Protocol) client or uploading tool

Dreamweaver provides all of the above, including dozens of professionally designed pages.

What's in a Name?

You've found a plot of online real estate. You're ready to build your castle. Now: what to call the place? You need a catchy domain name, or web address, for your site.

> **TIP**
>
> Remember, if you're using your ISP or a free service as your web host, you'll probably get an assigned domain name—you won't be able to choose your own. Make a note of it, though, because you'll need it when you define your site in Dreamweaver.

The shorter the domain name, the better. Longer domain names are harder to spell, harder to type, and harder to remember. Anything over twenty characters is risky. Fifty-nine characters is the kiss of death.

As you begin thinking about your domain name, here are a few ground rules:

- A domain name can include alphanumeric characters and hyphens. Special characters like spaces, underscores, ampersands, money signs, punctuation marks, and asterisks are not permitted, and you shouldn't begin or end your domain name with a hyphen.

- Domain names aren't case-sensitive. *MYsITe.com*, *MYSITE.COM*, and *mysite.com* are all the same thing.

- For best results, a domain name should be no longer than 59 characters, not including the suffix, like *.com*, *.org*, or *.net* (which pushes the total length to 63 characters). Technically, your domain name can be longer, but some browsers have trouble resolving long names, so keep within the 59-character limit.

BEHIND THE SCENES

For the curious, a domain name actually consists of multiple levels that go from lower to higher as you read out the name (see Figure 2-1). The *third-level domain* is the prefix, the *www* part of the name for most sites on the Web, although, depending on your web host, you may assign as many third-level domains for your web site as you like—the *www* isn't written in stone. For instance, mammoth sites like yahoo.com often organize their many branches into separate third-level domains: *my.yahoo.com*, *mail.yahoo.com*, *weather.yahoo.com*, *movies.yahoo.com*, and so on.

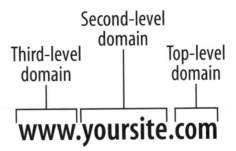

Figure 2-1. A domain name consists of multiple levels that go from lower to higher

The *second-level domain* is the "name" part, the part that most people mean when they talk about domains, such as Amazon or ebay. The *top-level domain* is the last part of the name, the suffix; e.g., *.com*, *.org*, and *.edu* are all top-level domains. So are international country codes such as *.uk* for Great Britain and *.ie* for Ireland.

Aside from those points, anything goes. If you're building a personal home page or hobby site, let your imagination run wild. Feel free to trend to the goofy or bizarre. A fun domain name entertains you and your visitors. Nothing is worse than a serious home page.

If you're building a site for your business or organization, you should take a more methodical approach. You don't choose the name of your business haphazardly, and your domain name is just as important. It goes on all your business cards. It goes in your letterhead. It appears in advertisements. Sales reps and consultants spout it out to potential clients.

With that in mind, here are some of the qualities of a smart domain name:

Brevity

Smart domains are short and sweet. This way, they're easier to remember, and they're easier to type into the address field of a web browser. Never underestimate the laziness potential of postindustrial Western society. We are the people of microwave dinners and remote controls. Also, most people are very poor typists. A short domain name equals less chance for a typo.

Ease of pronunciation

Smart domains roll off the tongue. Your sales reps can say them. Your clients can repeat them. This doesn't mean that your domain name has to be a word. It can be an abbreviation, like VHS or DVD, both of which have a nice rhythm and ring (and, yes, both are taken).

Ease of spelling

Your domain name has to be easy to pronounce. But when your sales rep says "beeconsultants.com," does she mean *be* as in "to be or not to be," or *bee* as in "bee in my bonnet," or the letter B, or B-hyphen? By the time she gets done explaining which it is, the client has moved on to the next booth at the trade show. For this reason, try to avoid homophones, or words that sound like other words, and stay away from cute phonetic spellings of common words, like *majyck* instead of *magic,* unless of course you want to direct traffic to someone else's site.

Consistent tone

Your domain name is like the title of a book or movie or the trade name of a store. It helps to set the stage for the contents of your site. You wouldn't walk into a place called Jari's Fresh Fish and expect to find a wide selection of aromatherapy candles. The same logic applies to your domain name. Try to choose a name that fits.

Whether you're building your site for personal pleasure or serious business, the challenge is coming up with a suitable domain name that hasn't already been registered by somebody else. Fortunately, you're the creative type. There are plenty of good names still available. You just have to be very clever about finding yours.

TIP

To see if a domain name is available, point your web browser to *http://www.internic.net/whois.html*, and fill in the online form to register it.

When you're busy at brainstorming, come up with a healthy list of possibilities, and include as many as you can. Fifteen or twenty is not too many. Depending upon your site, fifty might not be too many. A good place to start is the name of your business or organization. If this name is too long, of if it's already taken, think along the lines of an abbreviation or nickname. Chances are, if your business has existed in brick and mortar form for a while, you and your clients and partners have devised quick nicknames or shortened forms of your official trade name for ease of reference. These are ideal for the Web, not just because they're shorter, but also because they're more individualistic, and they convey more of your corporate culture or personality. You can't get enough of this kind of differentiation when you're in the marketplace with thousands of competitors worldwide.

Another strategy is to brand yourself to the type of business that you do. If you sell books, you might be extremely interested in acquiring a domain like *books.com* (which Barnes and Noble has already done). The only drawback here is that competition is even fiercer for these types of names. Who wouldn't want to be the spokesperson for books on the entire Web? Still, if you're in a fairly specialized business, you might have some luck securing this type of domain, or maybe you can diversify a bit. Pick two products that you sell, connect them with the word *and,* and try the combinations.

Reserving Your Domain

TECHTALK

A registrar is a service for reserving a domain name.

To check the availability of your domain name and then reserve it for your personal use, hop onto the Web and visit a *registrar,* of which there are many. Your web host might even be one of them. When you sign up for hosting service, see if you can reserve your domain name in the process. It's a convenience for you, and it might even save you the standard annual $35 registration fee. In addition, you won't have to point your domain name from your registrar's servers to your web host's servers when you publish your site. (See "What Happens Next?" later in this chapter for more information.)

If you'd prefer to shop around for the best deal, or if you'd like to get a specialty top-level domain (see "Comparing Top-Level Domains" later in this chapter), you're free to register with a service other than your web host. Some registrars charge substantially less than the typical $35 per year, but they may expect you to sign up with their preferred web-hosting partner or agree to a longer term than you might want, so be sure to read the fine print. On the other hand, don't pay more than $35 per year for registration, unless you have special requirements for your top-level domain.

TIP

Visit *http://www.internic.net/regist.html/* for an up-to-date listing of accredited registrars.

Domain ownership is something of a misnomer, in that you actually lease the use of a particular domain over a given period. The permanent transfer of a domain to your private ownership forever doesn't yet exist, much to the consternation of capitalists everywhere. Typically, your registration lasts for one year, after which you have the option of renewing. Also, you pay for the lease up front, not in weekly or monthly installments. If you choose not to renew the domain after your term expires, your name becomes available to anyone, so it's a good idea to stay on top of your registration. Most registrars send you an email reminder a couple months in advance of expiration, and some even automatically renew it for you unless you tell them otherwise. Still, if your term is a couple months from expiring and you haven't heard anything from your registrar, you might want to contact them and ask about their renewal options.

Different registrars offer different terms for their leases, up to ten years in some cases, and they usually give you a break in price for the longer terms, because, once again, you're paying up front. For most first-time web builders, a yearlong term is long enough to decide if you like being a web master. You can always get a longer lease when your renewal period comes around.

BEST BET

For first-time web builders, go with a yearlong lease on your domain name at first, but think about the longer lease options when it comes time to renew.

Comparing Top-Level Domains

The *top-level domain* or TLD comes at the end of a domain name. It's the suffix of the name, such as *.com*, *.org*, and *.net*. Depending upon your registrar, you will likely have several choices for your top-level domain. Which should you choose?

— **TECHTALK** —

A top-level domain (TLD) is the suffix of a domain name, such as .com, .org, and .net.

One consideration is applicability. Top-level domains were originally intended for web sites of a certain kind. For example, the famous and ubiquitous *.com* TLD was set aside for commercial purposes, but remember the old saying about how good intentions tend to pave a certain highway. When the Web exploded into popular consciousness in the late 1990s, competition for the best names became merciless, and the distinctions among the top-level domains began to blur. Anyone could (and can) register a *.com* domain, and nobody was checking to see that all *.com* owners were actually running commercial businesses.

Another consideration is availability. The same *second-level domain*, or the "name" part of the name as in amazon or ebay, when paired with a different TLD, gives you an entirely different domain. Therefore, *ebay.com* is *not*

— **TECHTALK** —

A second-level domain is the "name" part of a domain name, such as amazon and ebay.

the same domain name as *ebay.net* or *ebay.org*. If your second-level domain name of choice is already taken under your preferred TLD, you might think about registering under a different TLD, with one small proviso. While the distinctions among TLDs are blurry at best, you should at least try to keep their original intentions in mind, and be careful not to stray too far afield. For instance, if you're building a commercial web site, you should probably shy away from the *.org* TLD, which still has strong associations with the nonprofit sector.

On the other hand, if you're a nonprofit and you can get your hands on the *.com* version of the name, do it! The *.com* TLD is the one that everyone knows. It's synonymous with the Internet in Western culture. While *.org* is beginning to build up steam in this age of political blogs and grass-roots activism, the *.com* TLD is still the most desirable from a marketing standpoint, which is the third consideration as to which TLD you should choose.

> **BEST BET**
>
> Always try for the *.com* TLD, no matter the purpose of your site, because *.com* is synonymous with the Internet in Western culture.

BEHIND THE SCENES

The group responsible for creating top-level domains is a nonprofit organization called the Internet Corporation for Assigned Names and Numbers, or ICANN. Visit ICANN on the Web at *http://www.icann.org/*.

ICANN has no authority over country-specific top-level domains such as *.uk*, *.de*, and *.fr*.

The most common TLDs are unrestricted in the sense that anyone can register them for any purpose at a cost of no more than $35 per year. Table 2-2 lists them. Remember, not every registrar offers all TLDs, so if your TLD of choice isn't available at your registrar of choice, find a different registrar. A good place to start is the web site of the operator of your desired TLD.

Table 2-2. General purpose, unrestricted top-level domains

Top-level domain	Stands for	Originally intended for	Now used for	Operator
.biz	Business	Businesses	Businesses (mostly)	NeuLevel, Inc. (*http://www.neulevel.biz/*)
.com	Commercial	For-profit businesses	Anything	VeriSign Global Registry Services (*http://www.verisign.com/*)
.info	Information	Information	Informational sites, including advertising	Afilias Limited (*http://www.afilias.info/*)
.name	Name	Individuals	Individuals, businesses	Global Name Registry (*http://www.nic.name/*)

Table 2-2. *General purpose, unrestricted top-level domains (continued)*

Top-level domain	Stands for	Originally intended for	Now used for	Operator
.net	Network Service Provider	ISPs	Anything, especially service providers of any kind	VeriSign Global Registry Services (*http://www.verisign.com/*)
.org	Organization	Nonprofit groups	Nonprofits, political organizations, clubs	Public Interest Registry (*http://www.pir.org/*)

While general-purpose TLDs like *.com* and *.org* are open to anyone, you have to qualify for certain TLDs such as *.museum*, *.edu*, and *.pro* by providing credentials to the registrar and paying a premium above the standard $35 yearly fee. Table 2-3 lists some of these TLDs in case you're interested.

> **TIP**
>
> Some unrestricted TLDs like *.tv* come at a premium price. Be prepared to pay more than $35 per year—perhaps considerably more—for the privilege of attaching *.tv* to your second-level domain.

Table 2-3. *Specialized, restricted top-level domains*

Top-level domain	Stands for	Reserved for	Operator
.aero	Aeronautics	Any company, group, or individual in the aviation industry	SITA INC (*http://www.sita.aero/*)
.coop	Cooperative	Cooperatives and cooperative service organizations	DotCooperation LLC (*http://www.cooperative.org/*)
.edu	Education	Accredited postsecondary schools, colleges, and universities	EDUCAUSE (*http://www.educause.edu/*)
.museum	Museum	Museums	Museum Domain Management Association (*http://about.museum/*)
.pro	Professional	All certified professionals, but currently limited to medical, legal, accounting, and engineering fields	RegistryPro (*http://www.registrypro.com/*)

BEHIND THE SCENES

A *country-code top-level domain* (ccTLD) such as *.ie* for Ireland, *.us* for the United States, and *.ca* for Canada identifies the web site's country of origin—or at least it's supposed to. Many countries around the world make their ccTLDs available to virtually anyone. In general, some restrictions apply. Depending on the country, you may have to fill out some extra paperwork or supply a local address in your country of choice. Also, you may have to wait a few days before your registration is complete, unlike the instamatic, real-time registration of *.com* and its brood.

If you're interested in registering a ccTLD, begin your quest in your favorite search engine. Type *ccTLD registration* plus your preferred ccTLD, and see what comes up.

BEHIND THE SCENES

The story behind *.tv* is an interesting one. It's actually the country code for the island nation of Tivalu (population 10,000), somewhere in the Pacific between Hawaii and Australia. A few years back, the government of Tivalu licensed the rights to *.tv*, not because of the brisk tourist trade, but because TV means something entirely different to the pop-culture-obsessed Western world. Tivalu was hoping that we in the West would pay through our noses to associate ourselves with television, and we didn't disappoint. Tivalu's annual gross domestic product actually doubled as a result of the deal. Roads were paved and streetlights put up, but prosperity came at a price, as it so often does. Now the island nation has ongoing royalty disputes. Welcome to the global economy, Tivalu!

What Happens Next?

You have Dreamweaver and assorted other software tools. You have a domain name and a web host. You have everything you need to start building and publishing your site. You're not quite through with the preliminaries, though. Planning the scope and design of your site before you start building is the secret to smooth and lightning-fast production, as you'll learn in the next few chapters.

—TECHTALK—

A parked domain name has been reserved, but it doesn't yet point to an actual web site.

In the meantime, your domain and web host aren't going anywhere. Once you've reserved a domain name, it's yours for at least a year. In technical jargon, your domain name is *parked*. If you type your domain into the Address field of your browser, you'll likely get the generic "Under Construction" page that your web host or registrar supplies. When you publish your site, either you replace this default page with your actual home page (if your registrar and web host are the same), or you update your domain registration by supplying your registrar with the web address of your hosting server (if you used two separate services). Updating your registration isn't hard. You can usually do it yourself over the Web. Depending upon your registrar, though, you might not know where to find the update form, so, if all else fails, contact customer service.

The important thing is that your place is reserved. You have staked your claim on the World Wide Web. Now, on to your site!

Organizing the Content 3

What is a web site? What an odd question. If you're reading this book, you probably have a very good intuitive understanding of what a web site is. You've used the Web often enough. You may visit dozens of web sites every day. But when you cast your initial hunches into cold, hard words, you may find yourself on unsure footing. What *is* a web site, anyway? Is it a kind of high-tech book? Interactive TV? A repeated request for your credit card number?

Asking this question begs another: what exactly is the Web? The answer to this one is much more straightforward. The Web is an information medium. It's a vast network of data about every conceivable subject, from the latest scientific discoveries to financial records to unsolicited political opinions (lots of those) to shopping opportunities for just about anything to photos of you, your family, and your pets. When you hear Al Gore talk about the information superhighway, this is exactly what he means.

You might say, then, at its most basic level, a web site is a repository for information. In other words, it's a source of *content*. But information is only half of the answer, because information by itself is meaningless. As French philosophers like to remind us, all data require interpretation. An unformed, undigested lump of content is about as useful as an endless string of digits. If you look hard enough, there may be some underlying meaning or purpose, but who has the time or the patience for that? You're not a computer. You have better things to do.

Here is where web architecture comes in. A web site is no more a chunk of content than a building is an undifferentiated pile of bricks. The magic is in the organization, the architecture, if you will, of your virtual building. Without it, your site is an undecipherable jumble suitable only for wind talkers and tax attorneys.

You need to take the web site's raw material—the information that it contains—and organize or *structure* it in a way that makes sense to human beings. Instead of dumping a load of content on your visitors, you dole it out piece by piece. You break it into different categories and spread it out

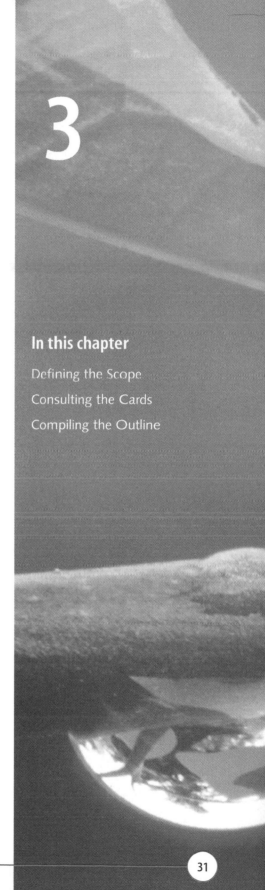

over a number of pages. You make it easy for people to find the specific bits that they want. More than that, with a sound structure in place, your web site is better able to withstand the never-ending ebb and flow of information. The top headlines of your favorite news site may change by the minute, but the location of this information is always right up front, just where you want it (and where you would expect to find it). The degree to which your web site's content is organized in an intelligible way is the degree to which your web site succeeds. This chapter gets you thinking about the structure of your site-to-be and leaves you with some practical tips for bringing order to the chaos.

Defining the Scope

The *scope* of a web site is the extent of its content, the range of ground that the web site covers. A web site's scope can be enormous. Amazon truly lives up to its name, with millions of items in its catalog. But most web sites aren't nearly this epic, nor does anyone expect them to be. Bigger isn't necessarily better. The secret is to choose the scope that fits, neither too big nor too small but just right for your content. You want to figure out what sort of ground you need to cover to present your content intelligibly.

A good way to start is to consider two questions: what are the goals of your site and who is the audience? The first question asks "why does this site exist?" The second question asks "who is likely to care?"

Stating the Goals

In the abstract, the goal of every web site builder is to organize the site's content in a useful and intelligible way. It's time to put this theory into practice. What are the specific goals of your particular site? What tasks does your web site need to accomplish? What, through it, do you want to say? You probably have several ideas about this already, so take out a fresh sheet of paper and jot down some notes.

> **TIP**
>
> As you begin to list the goals of your site, it's perfectly natural to repeat yourself. You're brainstorming, so let the words and ideas flow. After you finish, go back over your list, and look for items that are similar in intent or meaning. If you can, combine these into a single entry. If you can't, then the goals really are separate items, and leave them exactly as they are.

If you're building a site for your business or organization, your list of goals might look like this:

- To introduce potential clients to our business: who we are and what we do

- To tell potential clients how we can help them

- To provide a detailed list of our products and services

- To announce new products and initiatives (e.g., a press room)

- To give our contact information to potential clients

- To generate leads for our sales reps

The goals for a fan site about comic books aren't necessarily the same:

- To give monthly reviews of my favorite comic books

- To summarize the most recent storylines for people who may have missed an issue

- To post bits of news about comic books and upcoming comic book movies that I happen to pick up

- Tips from me and eventually other visitors about where to find rare comics at decent prices

- Gems from the bargain bin: recommendations for great older comics that have been overlooked by most collectors

Even at this early stage, you can tell that the tone of the sites is going to be different, just by comparing the list of goals. The first site means serious business—competitors beware. The second site exists solely for entertainment, both for the builder as well as the audience. Where the first is tactical, the second is relaxed, but not so relaxed that it lapses into disorganization.

All web sites, regardless of content, should include the following among their goals:

- To provide a way for visitors to contact the administrator of the site

This lifeline to your visitors is essential. First, you need to be on top of any miscellaneous bugs, glitches, and technical problems that might crop up. You'll test your web site thoroughly before you launch it, but no amount of testing can account for every possible combination of software and hardware that your visitors might use. If your site is performing poorly for some people, they'll let you know about it, and you can take measures to fix it. Second, direct visitor contact is the best way to judge the effectiveness of your site. Visitor comments help you to figure out what sections of your site are the most popular and which aren't making much of an impact. Based on this analysis, if your site isn't meeting one of its primary goals, you can see about improving matters.

> **TIP**
>
> A great way to encourage feedback is to set aside a special page of your site for visitor comments. Post the comments that you receive as well as your responses. If visitors feel like they're contributing to your site, they'll be more apt to participate.

Don't feel like you have to set up a toll-free number or hire a team of customer service reps in order to stay connected with your visitors. A simple email address is sufficient in most cases. Just make sure that you read the email that your web site generates and listen to what your visitors are saying. If you're able to send brief but personalized replies, that's all the better. It helps to foster the community spirit that enables your site to grow.

Identifying the Audience

All webmasters secretly dream that their web sites will appeal to everyone, but this isn't necessarily the best measure of success. The key to creating a successful web site is to find that percentage, however small, of those who are most receptive to your goals, and then do everything you can to cater to these people. The Web isn't a single, homogenous, monolithic market waiting for the right person to come along and exploit it. It's a tapestry of every conceivable niche. The site that identifies a clear, specific audience is in a better position for longevity than the site that attempts to dominate every niche on the Web.

Advertisers, marketers, and other money types spend considerable time, effort, and capital identifying their customers in microscopic detail. If you have access to this sort of information, by all means, use it. If you don't have these resources, don't worry about it. Most site builders identify their audiences without extensive market research and CIA-caliber customer profiling. You start out with some intelligent hunches. If you're building a web site for your business or organization, your audience includes your existing customers, along with the customers you'd like to attract. For a personal site, the perfect template for the typical audience member is you and others like you. Once your site begins to generate feedback, you may refine your assumptions about your audience and direct the growth of your site accordingly.

Defining the likely audience from the get-go helps you to figure out the most effective ways of achieving the goals of your site. It's Customer Service 101 in action: your particular audience comes to your site with a certain set of expectations, and you, the site builder, aim to please. Take the average businessperson. Businesspeople like charts and graphs. Your cubicle or office is probably surrounded by them. Why should this be? Charts and graphs are part of the language of business. If you can't get through to your boss in any other way, try plotting your point of view on some kind of curve, and watch the doors of perception swing open.

It stands to reason, then, that if your audience includes businesspeople, the content of your web site needs to resonate with those who speak the language of business. And if one of the goals of your web site happens to be, "To tell prospective clients how we can help them," see what you can do about getting some charts and graphs on your site. You don't want to be as flippant as that, though. Posting charts and graphs haphazardly, just for the sake of having them, is pandering, not catering, and your audience will see right through it. Always go back to your list of goals. Where would charts and graphs be most useful for your audience? Where would they make the most sense on your site?

> **TIP**
>
> Just as your audience helps you to determine the content of your site, the audience also helps you to figure out what not to include. Charts and graphs probably won't play as well to an audience of comic book collectors, unless you're posting them for laughs, in a tongue-in-cheek kind of way. Similarly, loud, flashy, video-game-style Flash animations may induct your comic book site to the ranks of coolness, but they will probably drive away business for insurance products.

As you think through the expectations of your audience, notice what begins to happen: the scope of your site comes more clearly into focus. You get a feel for the area that your web site needs to cover, which is precisely where you want to be.

Consulting the Cards

Now that you have a clearer idea about the overall direction of your site, it's time to start fleshing out the details and molding the underlying shape of your project. One particularly enjoyable way to do this is to shuffle some content cards, just like the oracles of old. The superstitious among us needn't worry—you aren't toying with dark forces beyond your control. It just appears that way to your client or employer, and anything that reinforces your mystique can only improve your job security.

Creating Content Cards

You don't need the Tarot for this procedure. A pack of ordinary index cards is more than sufficient. Here's how it works: with your list of goals in front of you, and keeping in mind your assumptions about your target audience, fill out the cards with ideas for content, one idea per card.

To get you moving in the right direction, start at the top of your list of goals. Read out the goal, and meditate upon this question: "O Content Cards, how can I achieve this goal on my web site?"

> **TIP**
>
> At this stage of the game, don't think in terms of the final product. Don't worry about how these pieces of content are going to link up or how you're going to collect them. Just get your ideas onto the cards.

For example, assume that you're building a web site for your business. The first goal might be to introduce potential clients to who you are and what you do, so you incant the mystical formula: how can I achieve this goal on my web site? Your content cards might look something like this:

- A brief history of our business

- Summary of our core competencies

- Brief profiles or biographies of our management team

- Chart that shows the growth of our stock over the last three years

- Chart that shows the rise in profits or sales over the last three years

- Downloadable brochure

- Downloadable business card

- A photo of our home office

- A photographic tour of our main facility

- Testimonials from current clients

- Statement of our underlying customer-service philosophy

- Statement of our 90-day guarantee

When you feel like you've adequately addressed this goal, move on to the next one, and repeat the process. At this point, keep all the content cards in the same pile. Don't try to organize them yet—that's coming soon.

As you work through your list, don't be surprised if you come up with ideas that fit better with one of your previous goals. This is perfectly normal. The human brain seems to delight in these kinds of tricks. If you find yourself backtracking, don't try to stop it. Just write out the content card and add it to the pile, and return to the current goal at your mind's leisure.

Depending upon the scope of your site, you may have dozens of content cards, maybe even a hundred or more, or you might be struggling to fill twenty. In general, the more ideas, the better, but don't try to push it. Let the site show you what it wants to be. (Try giving that explanation at the next staff meeting. Your reputation as a sorcerer is assured.) The only hard and fast rule is that you should have at least one content card for every goal in your list. If you don't, you aren't meeting all your goals.

> **BEST BET**
>
> In general, the more content cards, the better; make sure you have at least one card for every goal in your list.

Organizing Content into Categories

Here is where the fun begins, where the true magic of your content cards reveals itself in its fullness. You'll need some desk space for this one, so sweep away the clutter before you start.

> **TIP**
>
> You'll be astonished at how many ingenious ideas come about when fresh sets of eyes look for connections in the cards. If you aren't just a one-person operation, you might make copies of your content cards and have several people on your team divide them into categories individually. Then, compare their groupings with yours.

Collect your content cards into a single stack, and deal out the first card directly in front of you. Now read the second card, and compare it to the first. Do these pieces of content feel like they're related? In other words, do they belong to the same general category? If so, place the second card on top of the first one. If not, place the second card beside the first one. Move on to the next card. Does it belong to the same category as either of the first two? If so, discard to the appropriate pile. If not, create a new pile. You get the idea.

> **TIP**
>
> Don't use the original goal that inspired a content card as the sole criterion about whether it belongs to a particular category. Your categories may follow the goals of your site very closely, or they might not. For the purposes of this exercise, try to view your content cards as independent of their original goals, and see how else these pieces of content might link up.

After you deal the last card, count the number of piles on your desk. For most sites, anywhere from three to six piles is about right. If you have fewer than three, your categories are probably too general. Look over your cards again, and see if you can create another couple of piles. If you have more than six, which is highly common, your categories are probably too specific. Try to combine related piles into a single, larger pile. However, once again, don't force your site into an arbitrary structure. It's possible that very large sites might well cover more than six discrete content areas, while very small sites might fit into one or two areas. The three-to-six range is a guideline, not a rule. That said, most sites, even the very largest and the smallest, tend to work best within this range, so give a good-faith effort to trim your site down or bulk it up before you suspect that your site might be an exception.

> **TIP**
>
> Fewer content categories are better, so, when in doubt, go for the smaller number (as long as it isn't smaller than three). Once your site is up and running, breaking off new content categories when they warrant their independence is easier than collecting two or three separate strands and weaving them together again.

One common pattern to watch out for is to organize by type rather than by meaning. You might have grouped together all the image-type content cards, for instance, or, like in Figure 3-1, you may have placed all the download-type content cards in a single pile. This kind of thinking is perfectly logical. Even so, it isn't the most useful ordering scheme for a web site, because your visitors browse your site according to the content that they want to find, not necessarily the form that this content happens to take. Try putting yourself in your visitor's place. Where would you first look if you wanted to find a press release or a product brochure? You probably wouldn't go for the Downloads section. You'd search out the News or Products areas first. Redistributing type-only piles of content cards according to meaning, as in Figure 3-2, makes for a more web-friendly way of thinking.

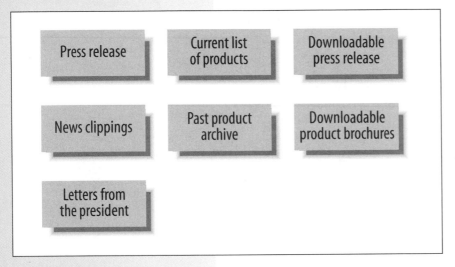

Figure 3-1. One pile of cards contains all the download-type content

When your piles are in suitable shape, take the first pile of cards, come up with a brief name that describes its category, and jot it down at the top of each card in the pile. Don't dwell on the names for hours on end. The obvious ones are usually the best: Products, Services, Sales, Contact Us, About Us, and so on. These category headings will eventually become the main sections of your site.

After you label the cards, consider each pile in turn. Gather up all the cards of a particular pile, and deal them into more specific groups—subcategories of the main category heading. Then label the cards according to their subcategory; Figure 3-3 shows the general Products category with two subcategories, Current and Past. If you don't find any obvious subcategories in any given pile, especially if the pile is rather small, that's fine, just as long as you're not being lazy about it. Your site will be better off in the end if you organize the content thoroughly and accurately.

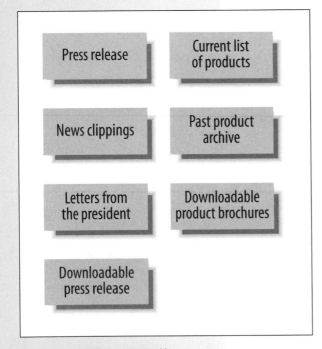

Figure 3-2. The piles reorganized by meaning rather than type

> **TIP**
>
> As before, fewer subcategories and sub-subcategories are better, especially when you're first starting out. Watch out for unnecessary depth!

Conversely, some of your subcategory piles, particularly the larger ones, may feel like they could use additional structure. If so, gather each subcategory pile in turn, deal them out into sub-subcategories, and tack the new designations onto the labels of the cards. You can repeat this process as often as your site requires, but be careful about going deeper than three levels of organization. Sub-subcategories like *products/current/American market* and *products/current/ European market* are fine if you need them, but *products/current/American market/Philadelphia* is probably pushing it. To organize at this precise level of detail, try removing one of the higher categories first before you resort to levels four and beyond. If you market products by city, then you probably don't need to divide the cities into American and European. The name of the city tells you everything that you need to know.

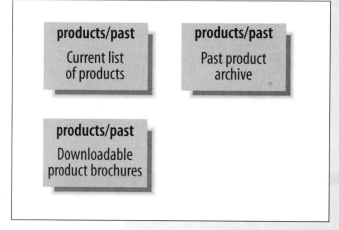

Figure 3-3. Current and Past subcategories in the Products category

> **BEST BET**
>
> Don't venture beyond sub-subcategories, or three levels of organization, unless you have a good reason.

Why keep within three levels of organization? It goes back to your visitors, as it always does, and something called the *three-click rule:* your visitors should be able to find the content that they want within three clicks from anywhere on your site. If you think of each level of structure as a click— home page to reviews section, reviews section to rock section, rock section to Pink Floyd page—then those are your three clicks. Remember, your visitors are impatient people. That's why they're on the Web and not in a library somewhere or wandering through a shopping mall. Their attention spans are short. They want your content now, not five seconds from now or however long it takes for the additional clicks. Also, a simple, straightforward web site is easier to navigate than a large, complex one. The fewer levels there are in your site structure, the less likely you'll lose your visitors.

Now, whenever somebody mentions the three-click rule in a room full of web designers, all conversation about everything else immediately stops, and the great unresolved debate about whether the three-click rule actually works picks up where it left off last week or last month or four years ago. Far be it from this humble tome to resolve the matter once and for all. Suffice it to say that the three-click rule works at least for some designers, and everyone agrees that fewer clicks are better, so the three-click rule can't be too far from the truth.

> **TECHTALK**
>
> *The three-click rule states that your visitors should be able to find the content that they want within three clicks from anywhere on your site.*

Compiling the Outline

Your content cards have one last rabbit for you to pull from their hat. Using nothing more than the labels of your cards, you can cause a surprisingly accurate, working outline of your web site to appear.

Start with your first top-level category—Comic Book Reviews, for example. On a blank sheet of paper, write *Comic book reviews*. Directly underneath the top category, list all the subcategories in the Reviews group, along with their respective sub-subcategories, if there are any. For instance, if your Reviews subgroups are Current and Past, with Superhero and Fantasy/horror/sci-fi divisions under the Current heading, then your outline looks like this so far:

- Comic book reviews
- Comic book reviews/Current
- Comic book reviews/Current/Superhero comics
- Comic book reviews/Current/Fantasy comics
- Comic book reviews/Past

Repeat this procedure for every category in your cards, and you have an outline for the structure of your site. Your outline is the blueprint for production, so keep it in a safe but convenient place, and be prepared to refer to it often.

> **TIP**
>
> Your outline isn't set in stone. As you build your site in Dreamweaver, you can add to the structure, delete from it, or move pages and even entire sections to different locations in the hierarchy with ease. This initial outline simply gives you a place to start.

Each item in the outline represents a single web page. By looking at your outline, you know that the main Reviews page will have links to the Current and Past pages. The Current page, in turn, has links to reviews about superhero comic books as well as fantasy/horror/sci-fi comics.

But what content appears on the Superhero, Fantasy, and Past pages, the ones at the bottom of the organizational hierarchy? To answer this question, simply return to your cards, some of which appear in Table 3-1. According to your content cards, the reviews themselves appear on your bottom-level pages, along with cover images and selected panels from the comics.

Table 3-1. *Sample content cards and their category labels*

Content description	Card label
Current superhero comic reviews	Reviews/current/superhero
Cover images of currently reviewed superhero comics	Reviews/current/superhero
Selected panels from currently reviewed superhero comics	Reviews/current/superhero
Current fantasy comic reviews	Reviews/current/fantasy
Cover images of currently reviewed fantasy comics	Reviews/current/fantasy
Selected panels from currently reviewed fantasy comics	Reviews/current/fantasy
Previous comic book reviews, both superhero and fantasy	Reviews/past
Cover images of previously reviewed comics, both superhero and fantasy	Reviews/past
Selected panels from previously reviewed comics, both superhero and fantasy	Reviews/past

If, however, you plan to write a large number of reviews, you might bog down these pages with too much content, especially the Past page, which combines reviews of both kinds of comics. You may decide to fill your bottom-level pages with links instead, links that go to individual review pages, one for each particular comic book that you review. All it takes is a minor revision to your outline:

- Comic book reviews
- Comic book reviews/Current
- Comic book reviews/Current/Superhero comics
- Comic book reviews/Current/Superhero comics/Individual review pages
- Comic book reviews/Current/Fantasy comics
- Comic book reviews/Current/Fantasy comics/Individual review pages
- Comic book reviews/Past
- Comic book reviews/Past/Individual review pages

Notice, though, that you're now four levels of organization deep under *Current/Superhero* and *Current/Fantasy*. After careful consideration, you decide that you can't justify going beyond the three-level limit in this case, because you don't really need to create separate pages. You can link to reviews of both kinds of comics from the Current page, maybe by dividing the page into Superhero and Fantasy sections. In fact, you like this idea so much that you borrow the same logic for the Past page, and your outline takes the following form:

- Comic book reviews

- Comic book reviews/Current (Superhero section, Fantasy section)

- Comic book reviews/Current (Superhero section, Fantasy section)/ Individual review pages

- Comic book reviews/Past (Superhero section, Fantasy section)

- Comic book reviews/Past (Superhero section, Fantasy section)/ Individual review pages

Now your outline abides by the three-click rule, and the Current and Past pages are more closely parallel, both of which are excellent organizational attributes for any web site, regardless of content. Apply the same kind of thinking to the remaining content categories, and you can't help but build an effective site structure.

Sketching the Interface

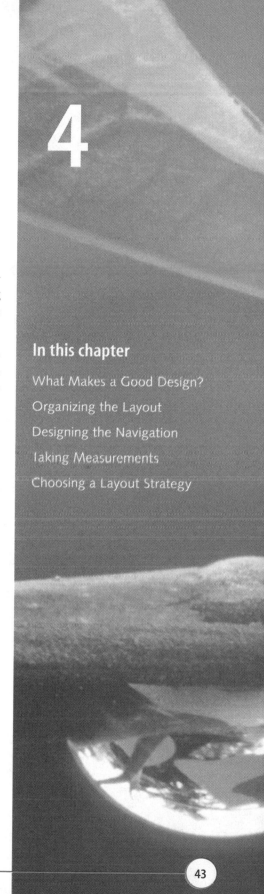

4

The logic of your site is in decent shape. You've divided the content into categories and subcategories. Now you want to think about how you're going to present your content. What's your web site going to look like? And does it really matter?

Uh, oh, you've done it now. You just posed one of the Big Ones—the existential questions of web design. Every web builder has to ask them eventually. There's no going back, and you're on a tight schedule, so this chapter directs you to some practical answers.

What Makes a Good Design?

Does web design matter? The answer to this one is a resounding *yes*. The way that you present your content is as important as the content itself. Imagine that you've written the greatest novel of all time, but your publisher puts it out on plastic sandwich wrap instead of paper, or uses pages three feet wide with miniscule type, or prints the text in reverse so that you need a mirror to read it. After your first few royalty statements, you may come to realize that appearances count.

At the same time, the content has to be the star of the show. People visit your site for the information that it provides, not for the artistic innovation of your graphic design. Web design is more like architecture than painting, in that the end result has to be functional. Doorways have to be tall enough so that humans can walk through them. Floors have to support a certain minimum load, or furniture will fall through them. You, the architect, have to account for certain physical realities in your design. If this limits your creativity, then so be it. Web design, like architecture, isn't hardcore outside-the-box thinking. The box can only change so much before it loses its function. Therefore, the creative aspect of web design isn't about exploding the box, inverting it, or rendering all its perspectives simultaneously. Rather, given a box, how cleverly do you arrange its contents?

Going back to your problems with your publisher, you might be inclined to put the art department on a leash. Nobody is clambering for a new book format. The one that we've had for the last couple centuries works just fine. Your publisher's creativity would be better spent looking for ways to heighten the effect of your prose—to complement and support it—while maintaining the reader's ease of use.

You can boil down good web design to a single word: *usability*. The degree to which your design makes your web site easy to use is the degree to which your design succeeds. It's a very simple formula:

Navigation
  Your visitors have to be able to get to the content that they want.

Accessibility
  Once there, they have to be able to pull the content off the page in a form that makes sense to them.

If your site is a breeze to navigate, and if its content is always at the ready, then you've done your job as a designer admirably.

One of the best methods for making a usable web site is to divide the layout into specific areas according to their purpose or function. Believe it or not, this trick works because of human psychology. It's based on the principle of *grouping,* by which the human brain expects to find similarities in things that happen to be in close proximity. Grouping is the reason that all the number buttons on your TV remote control are collected together, while all the picture buttons are in another group and the DVD buttons that never seem to work are in yet another.

So how does grouping work in a web layout? At the simplest level, you have navigation and content. Grouping suggests that you divide the page into two distinct groups or areas: one for navigation and one for content. As long as you place your navigation in the navigation area and your content in the content area, you're well on your way to having a usable design before you've sketched a single layout. Your visitors, being humans, will notice the physical distinction between the two areas and infer from this two different purposes. If your content looks like it ought to be read while your navigation looks like it ought to be clicked, then all the better—this simply reinforces the underlying logic of the groups.

── TECHTALK ──
Accessibility is the degree to which the content of your site is available to your visitors. Sometimes this term applies specifically to content that is unavailable to people with certain disabilities. For example, those without sight can't perceive a Flash movie, so the movie by itself isn't accessible. But accessibility in the broader sense applies to those without disabilities, too. Dark gray type against a black background isn't particularly accessible for the sighted.

── TECHTALK ──
Grouping is the psychological tendency for humans to find similarity in things that happen to be in close proximity.

BEHIND THE SCENES

Grouping isn't just a visual phenomenon. If you hear two things in close temporal proximity, your brain tends to associate them. This is why grouping is an effective design strategy, even for visitors who can't see your web site with their eyes. When a screen reader or text-to-speech converter reads out the content of your site, your visitor, hearing the navigation choices one after the other, associates them as a group with an underlying meaning or function.

The layout you envision is probably more sophisticated than a simple navigation/content split. Maybe you want a banner or header across the top of the page for your logo, the date, breaking news, or other masthead-type content. You might want a footer across the bottom of the page for a copyright notice. Depending on your site, you may need a special sidebar for links or a prominent place for advertisements. If so, simply add additional areas to your layout. Do you need a banner? Add a banner area. Do you need a sidebar for links? Add a sidebar area.

Before you start sketching, then, come up with a short list of the areas that you need to include in your layout. Don't go much beyond six or seven. Screen real estate is at a premium, and having too many divisions crammed into too small a space runs interference with the grouping principle.

BEST BET

Don't try to incorporate more than six or seven distinct areas into your design, and if you can do it in fewer, do it in fewer.

Organizing the Layout

Assume that you come up with a list of five areas for your layout: navigation, content, header, footer, and sidebar. Get out a piece of scratch paper, and let the doodling commence. Here are the rules:

Think in rectangles

Not to jump ahead too much here, but both of the major methods for web layout—tables and layers—are based on rectangular areas, so don't think in terms of circles or triangles. Rectangles and squares are the shapes for you. All the elements of your design—blocks of text, image files, Flash movies—are rectangular also, so they'll fit perfectly into the corners and along the sides of your layout.

TIP

Because of the rectangular nature of HTML elements, you might use graph paper to sketch your design.

Don't superimpose areas

Your areas shouldn't overlap, and you shouldn't put one area inside another. In the case of tables, overlapping areas are technically impossible. In the case of layers, overlapping areas are possible but not desirable, because you can easily obscure valuable content.

The areas should butt against each other

Don't leave any alleys or corridors of whitespace between the areas. You'll add the breathing room later.

Use all available space

Don't leave any holes in the layout. Your areas should cover the entire web page.

Place the most important areas toward the top of the layout

A web page reads like a newspaper: you always lead with the most important stuff. The logo for your business falls into this category, as do advertisements and especially your navigation.

> **TIP**
>
> To help you make the best use of space, start by drawing a large rectangle to represent the browser window. Then, divide it into smaller rectangles to represent your areas.

Keeping these suggestions in mind, you may come up with a layout for your site that looks something like Figure 4-1. It's equally possible that what you draw is closer in spirit to Figure 4-2.

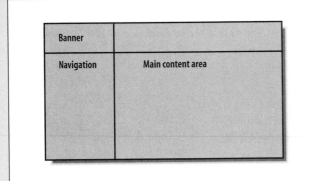

Figure 4-1. This is a classic side-nav layout

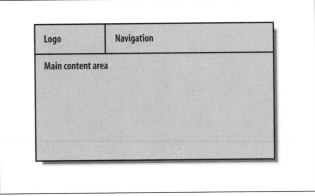

Figure 4-2. This is a classic top-nav layout

—TECHTALK—

In a side-nav layout, the navigation area runs down the side of the page. In a top-nav layout, the navigation area stretches across the top of the page.

The sketch in Figure 4-1 is a *side-navigation* or *side-nav layout*, because the navigation area runs down the side of the page. By comparison, in Figure 4-2, the navigation area runs across the top of the page, so you have a *top-nav layout*. Side-nav and top-nav are the two most common layouts on the Web, and for good reason. Whether by instinct or repetition of experience, your visitors tend to look for the navigation along the side or at the top of the page. Whatever the cause, it makes good sense. The steering is always easy to find in a very convenient place on the screen. Better still, when your visitors want to focus on the content, their eyes can scan the middle of the page and ignore the navigation entirely.

Looking at Side-Nav Layouts

In a side-nav layout, the navigation choices sit one below the other, usually at the top of the navigation area. This stack of five or six items doesn't usually add up to too much height, so side-nav layouts tend to offer a healthy amount of built-in whitespace. The extra visual buffer helps to distinguish the navigation area from the others in the layout, which makes your design more usable.

> **TIP**
>
> Another consideration for side-nav layouts is that the side of the page that feels more natural for navigation depends upon cultural and biological factors. Right-handed people, and people who come from cultures where written language is read from left to right, prefer navigation down the left side of the page. Left-handed people, and people who read from right to left, like their navigation on the right. If you expect to have visitors from both groups in large numbers, then a side-nav layout might not be the best choice.

At the same time, you can see by comparing Figure 4-1 and Figure 4-2 that the content area in a side-nav layout isn't as wide as the content area in a top-nav layout, because the navigation area sits beside it and therefore accounts for a certain portion of the width of the page. A narrower content area means that less content fits inside it before the visitor has to scroll. Especially in the case of Figure 4-1, where the links area takes away additional width from the content, you have to be careful about what kind of content you plan to add to your pages. Text and typical images should fit without incident. Your visitors will probably get vertical scrollbars, but that's all right. Scrolling vertically, up and down the page, is fine. There's really no avoiding it. But if the content—an image, for example—is wider than the available space, the visitor gets horizontal scrollbars in the browser window, which you should avoid at all costs. You may consider switching to a top-nav layout, or maybe you can do without the sidebar area in your current layout.

> **BEST BET**
>
> The navigation area in side-nav layouts is often easier to use, but be careful about the kinds of content that you add to your pages. Wide images and the like may generate horizontal scrollbars.

Looking at Top-Nav Layouts

When the navigation area runs across the top of the screen, it doesn't compete with the content area for page width, which means that your content is less likely to generate horizontal scrollbars in the browser windows—a definite advantage.

The main drawback of top-nav layouts is that the navigation choices run horizontally, one beside the other instead of one below the other, which isn't particularly efficient. If you string together too many navigation choices, you can push up against the width of the page, and you risk getting horizontal scrollbars anyway.

To reduce the likelihood of horizontal scrollbars, you have two remedies:

Shorten the names of the navigation choices

Go for quick, few-syllable names like *Store* instead of *Browse Our Catalog.*

Design the navigation to be small

Build small graphical buttons or use small text hyperlinks in your navigation area. Be careful, though! If your navigation becomes too small, you risk overwhelming it with the rest of the layout, and your visitors might lose their bearings.

> **BEST BET**
>
> Top-nav layouts leave more page width for the content area, but the navigation choices can't take up much room, or you increase the likelihood of horizontal scrollbars.

If neither of these options seems to work for your site, then you might reconsider a side-nav layout.

Designing the Navigation

You set aside an area in your layout for the navigation. Now, what specifically are you going to put in that area? Graphical buttons? Text hyperlinks? Something else? This section gives you a brief tour of your options.

Tackling the Main Navigation

Strictly speaking, the main navigation is what appears in your navigation area. The *main navigation* is the primary method for getting around your site. As such, it's important for you to get this navigation right.

You won't go wrong if you pull the navigation choices directly from your outline. Grab your sheet from Chapter 3, and read off the top-level content categories. Maybe yours are Products, Services, Pressroom, About Us, and Contact Us. These are the items that should go into your main navigation. Now, what form should these items take?

TECHTALK

The main navigation is the primary method for getting around your site.

Using text hyperlinks

Regular old text works fine as your main navigation, as long as you clearly separate it from the text in the content area (see Figure 4-3).

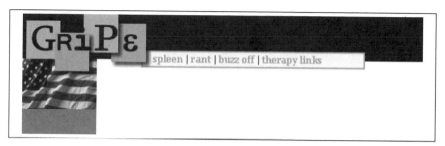

Figure 4-3. Text hyperlinks work fine in your main navigation

One advantage to plain text is that it downloads almost instantly to the visitor's browser, so your web site loads quickly. Also, plain text is immediately accessible to people who rely upon screen readers or text-to-speech converters to browse your site, and it's worth noting that you can create any kind of text hyperlink in any imaginable visual style within Dreamweaver itself—you don't need any outside authoring tools.

The main disadvantage to text navigation is that it isn't terribly interesting to look at. Then again, maybe your site doesn't need the extra dazzle. Remember, the content should be the star of the show. Just make sure to separate your plain-text navigation from the running text of your page. You don't want the visitor confusing the two.

Using static images

In lieu of ordinary text hyperlinks, you can place images in your navigation area and make them clickable (see Figure 4-4). These are commonly called *buttons*, even if they don't necessarily look like buttons.

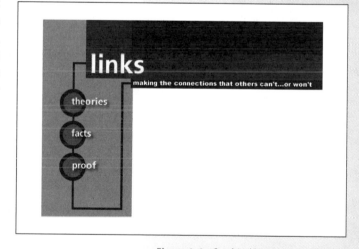

Figure 4-4. Graphical buttons are an old standby for the main navigation

Unlike plain text, you can design graphical buttons to look like anything. You can give them an overtly button-like appearance, or you can remove any trace of the button metaphor. You can place icons next to them or inside them. You can label them with wacky or obscure fonts (see Chapter 6 for more information about typefaces on the Web). Your good taste and what your audience finds useful are the only limitations on your creativity.

At the same time, images come with some drawbacks. They don't download as quickly as plain text, so your web site may take a performance hit, although the delay usually isn't too noticeable in these days of high-speed and broadband Internet access. Further, web images aren't immediately

—**TECHTALK**—
Buttons are clickable images on a web page.

accessible to screen readers and text-to-speech converters. Current technologies can't examine the content of an image and render in spoken language what it's an image of, so you have to attach a short *text equivalent*—a literal description—to each button in your navigation. This procedure isn't hard, but it is something to take into account. However, the main drawback to graphical buttons for many first-timers is that you can't create the images in the Dreamweaver software. You need a dedicated graphics tool, preferably something high-end like Adobe Photoshop or Macromedia Fireworks, to design images for your site.

Using rollover images

A *rollover image* appears to change when the visitor hovers over it with the mouse pointer (see Figure 4-5). What actually happens is that the Web browser pulls a magic trick called a *swap*. When the visitor hovers over the image, the browser replaces it with a second image file. The swap happens so quickly that it's like an animation effect—the eye perceives that the original image has transformed itself into something else. When the visitor moves the mouse pointer away, the browser swaps back the original image, and the rollover seems to revert to normal.

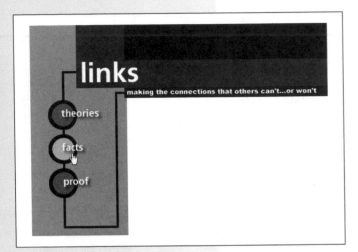

Figure 4-5. **A rollover image in action**

You can use rollover images instead of static, everyday web graphics in your navigation area, and in fact this makes good sense. Nothing says "Click me" like the intuitive prompting of a rollover effect. An image seemingly springing to life is hard to resist. While Dreamweaver adds the necessary JavaScript code to enable the swap, it's up to you to supply the images, and because each rollover requires two image files (or more, depending on the level of interactivity), the visitor has extra content to download. All the other limitations of standard images apply to rollovers as well.

> **TIP**
>
> In a simple rollover, you have two states: the default state, which is how the image appears normally, and the rollover state, which is how the image appears when the visitor hovers over it with the mouse pointer. A good strategy for designing rollovers is to make the rollover state appear to be more dynamic than the default state. In other words, rolling over the image should make the image appear to be turning on or powering up. If you do it the other way around—making the rollover state look less dynamic than the default state—you run the risk of confusing your visitors, because the button appears to be shutting off.
>
> High contrast between the button states is another good trick. Don't try for too much subtlety in their designs. One should be obviously different from the other.

Using flash buttons

A *Flash button* is a short, interactive Flash animation that works exactly like a rollover graphic: when the visitor hovers over the Flash button, the image changes. The dazzle factor on these things is high. The usability factor is, eh, so-so.

Unlike standard rollovers, you can create Flash buttons within Dreamweaver. You don't need any outside authoring tools, so that's a definite plus. The minuses, unfortunately, tend to rule out this option as a serious contender for your main navigation. It's not that Flash buttons aren't interactive enough. In fact, they tend to be more interactive than regular rollovers. The problem is that each Flash button resides in a separate instance of the Flash Player plug-in. As you may recall from Chapter 1, the Flash Player is standard equipment on the vast majority of computers, so compatibility isn't an issue here. However, the Flash Player takes time to load, and having five or six Flash Players on a page, each running its own movie file, can slow down performance considerably. Furthermore, Flash buttons by themselves aren't accessible to screen readers and text-to-speech converters, and, unlike images, there isn't a quick and easy way to provide text equivalents. The bottom line is this: if you use Flash buttons as your main navigation, know what you're getting into and proceed with caution.

> **TIP**
>
> Navigation buttons of all stripes, be they static images, rollover images, or Flash buttons, should always have text labels. Don't rely on icons or some other purely graphical method of conveying the button's purpose, as these are easy to misinterpret.

For your reference, Table 4-1 summarizes the four choices for your main navigation.

Table 4-1. Design choices for main navigation

Element	Speed of download	Accessibility	Rollover effect?	Additional software to create?
Text hyperlinks	Nearly instantaneous	Fully accessible	Yes	No
Static images	Nearly instantaneous to a few seconds	Accessible with text equivalents	No	Yes
Rollover images	A few seconds to several seconds	Accessible with text equivalents	Yes	Yes
Flash buttons	Several seconds too long	Accessible if you edit your buttons in Flash 8	Yes	No

TECHTALK

A Flash button is a short, interactive Flash movie that works just like a rollover graphic.

TECHTALK

The secondary navigation is an alternate navigation scheme that reinforces the main navigation of the site.

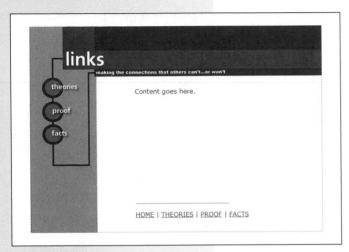

links

making the connections that others can't...or won't

theories

proof

facts

Content goes here.

HOME | THEORIES | PROOF | FACTS

Figure 4-6. Secondary navigation beneath the main content area

Adding Secondary Navigation

All good web sites provide an alternate to the main navigation as a convenience to the visitor and as a kind of failsafe. Call this the *secondary navigation*. The secondary navigation reinforces the main navigation, but it doesn't appear in the navigation area. Instead, you place it somewhere else in the layout, usually at the very bottom of the content area.

After that long-winded speech about grouping, you might think it a heresy to add navigation-type content to the content area, but it really isn't as bad as that. As long as you clearly separate the main content from the secondary navigation (see Figure 4-6), you maintain the integrity of your groups.

The secondary navigation should be text-based—don't use images, rollovers, Flash buttons, or any other type of interactive goody. This speaks to the failsafe nature of the secondary nav. If your visitor has trouble accessing your main navigation for whatever reason, as long as the secondary navigation is in text form, it is as accessible as it can possibly be.

> **TIP**
>
> The customary format for secondary navigation is a horizontal listing of your main content categories with pipes (|) separating the navigation choices.

Dealing with Multiple Levels of Structure

When you created your outline, you may have organized some of the content for your site into multiple levels. The top-level Products category, for instance, might lead to second-level categories like CDs and DVDs, and each of these might lead to further division according to genre or artist. If the top-level categories are the ones that go into the main navigation, how do you present the second-level and third-level categories? Where do you put them in your layout?

One solution is to open up additional navigation areas in the general page layout. This way, you always know where the levels of navigation go, and the navigation choices are always at the ready for the visitor. Even better, the navigation for the various levels always appears in the same place on the page, which improves the consistency and therefore the usability of your design.

Just because you set aside areas for second-level and third-level navigation doesn't mean that you have to fill them if you don't need them. In fact, you probably have very good reasons not to fill them. If your visitor is on a top-level-content page—Products, for example—then what do you put in the third-level navigation area? If the visitor happens to follow the CDs branch of from the Products page, then the third-level navigation choices might be Rock, Pop, Jazz, and Classical. But if the visitor follows the DVDs branch, then the third-level navigation becomes Horror, Science Fiction, Comedy, and Romance.

A good rule of thumb for fine-tuning your navigational flow is this: "Link one level down and all levels up." That is to say, on the home page of your site, direct your visitors to the top-level content. The links in the main navigation area do just that, so you don't need to add anything to your second-level and third-level navigation areas in this case—simply leave them empty. On a top-level content page, you want to get your visitors to the second-level pages ("Link one level down..."), so make use of your second-level navigation area but keep the third-level area clear. The main navigation stays the same. The only other item that you need is a link back to the home page ("...and all levels up"). On a second-level content page, get your visitors to the third level of content with links in the third-level navigation area ("Link one level down...") while keeping the same choices in the second-level and main navigation areas, plus the link to the home page ("...and all levels up").

> **BEST BET**
>
> Your plan for navigation: link one level down and all levels up.

Another solution is to create pop-up menus (see Figure 4-7). A pop-up menu appears when the visitor hovers over a link in the main navigation area. The pop-up provides links to the second-level content pages in that particular main-nav category. When the visitor hovers over a link in the pop-up menu, another pop-up menu appears with links to the third-level content pages.

Figure 4-7. Pop-up menus present multiple levels of structure at once

Pop-up menus are nice, because they don't clutter up your layout. You don't have to find room for second-level and third-level navigation areas. Instead, these areas pop up as the visitor needs them. The effect is very sophisticated, so it's not surprising that pop-up menus are a popular choice among web builders today.

Creating pop-up menus in Dreamweaver is easy enough. You fill out a dialog box, and you're good to go. However, the underlying code that makes Dreamweaver's pop-up menus work is quite complex and it has been known to cause compatibility problems. For best results, your visitors must use Internet Explorer. All other browsers tend to choke, as do non-traditional browsing devices like cell phones, PDAs, and MSNTV. You also lose a degree of control over how the pop-up menus look. Different browsers interpret Dreamweaver's pop-up menus differently, so your menus might not appear exactly where you want them, or other odd formatting bugs may crop up.

If you decide to use pop-up menus, test your site thoroughly in a variety of browsers, and be prepared to compromise on appearance in some cases. Above all, remember that your navigation is mission-critical. It's not the best place to push the technological boundaries. Depending upon the goals and the likely audience of your site, you might want to forego pop-up menus entirely and add a couple new nav areas to your layout instead.

BEHIND THE SCENES

Because pop-up menus are going to slow you down too much with compatibility headaches, this book doesn't go into specifics about how to add them to your site. If you're really interested, check out Help→Dreamweaver Help, and search for *pop-up menus*.

TIP

Another solution to the pop-up menu problem is to implement pop-ups with somebody else's code. There are hundreds of free pop-up menu scripts available, many of which are superior to Dreamweaver's.

Getting the code into your pages isn't hard—you basically just copy and paste—but you really ought to have some experience with web building from the coding side to make sure everything goes smoothly. You have to insert the code at the correct place in the HTML document with all the correct formatting, right down to the last semicolon and curly brace, which is beyond the scope of this book.

If you're comfortable bluffing your way through an HTML listing, then you might launch your favorite browser, call up your favorite search engine, and search for "pop-up menu script" or something to that effect to see what's available online. You might also have a look at *Web Design Garage* (Prentice Hall PTR) by this humble author for a pop-up menu script and specific instructions about how to add it to the pages of your site.

BEST BET

Pop-up menus are elegant and sophisticated, but they raise compatibility issues for some of your visitors, and the pop-up scripts that Dreamweaver supplies don't work well (if at all) in any browser but IE.

Taking Measurements

The width of the visitor's monitor screen is a key consideration, because it directly affects the width of your layout. Unfortunately, this measurement is completely out of your control. Your visitors decide what size monitors they buy, what screen settings they pick, and whether they prefer to browse the Web with a fully maximized browser window. If your layout is too wide for the visitor's screen, then your site generates horizontal scrollbars, which are never good.

The best way to proceed is to make an educated guess. Table 4-2 lists common monitor settings and the corresponding widths for your layout. In each case, the layout width is less than the screen width to account for browser features like vertical scrollbars, which eat up some of the available screen real estate.

Table 4-2. *Common screen widths*

Screen width (in pixels)	Layout width (in pixels)	Comments
640	600	Safe for virtually any layout
800	760	The current standard width
1024	955	The new, emerging standard width

According to Table 4-2, if you want to be absolutely safe, you should design your layout to be 600 pixels wide. Nearly every device on the Web today can handle 640-pixel displays (with the notable exception of MSNTV, formerly WebTV, which holds firm at 544 pixels). However, most visitors have enough computing power to go beyond 640-pixel screens, and 600 pixels across doesn't leave you much room for design, so the 760-pixel layout has become the standard width. It accommodates the vast majority of people browsing the Web.

Computers manufactured within the last four years tend to display at 1024 pixels (or higher), so as long as your audience isn't using antique hardware, 955-pixel layouts are generally fine. Don't push past 955 pixels, though. While many of your visitors wouldn't have a problem with higher screen widths courtesy of their brand new or high-end computers, those who have older or less prime equipment probably make up the greater part of your audience.

> **TIP**
>
> Even if your visitors can handle layout widths of 955 pixels, you might want to consider 780 pixels anyway as a courtesy for those who prefer to surf the Web in unmaximized browser windows.

TECHTALK

A pixel is a very small, colored box. It is the smallest component of a bitmap graphic—the name is a contraction of picture element. It is also the standard way to measure lengths and widths in web design. On a typical Windows monitor screen, there are 96 pixels for every inch. On Macintosh monitors, there are 72 pixels per inch.

Looking at Fixed-Width Layouts

A *fixed-width layout* always keeps the same width, no matter the width of the browser window (see Figure 4-8). If you design your layout to a width of 760 pixels, then the width remains 760 pixels wide. Visitors with 640-pixel screens get horizontal scrollbars when they visit your site, while visitors with 1024-pixel screens or higher get fields of whitespace around your layout.

The advantage to building fixed-width layouts is that the measurements of your areas are always pixel-perfect. You can calculate exactly where a specific element appears, which makes it easier for you to achieve more ambitious designs. It's also easier to create fixed-width layouts in Dreamweaver, because it takes fewer steps, and you have less to edit and troubleshoot.

The main disadvantage to fixed-width layouts is that they don't take full advantage of screen real estate for those visitors who happen to have wider displays. On the widest displays, your site can look cramped, which doesn't help in the usability department. As a workaround to this, many designers center their fixed-width layouts on the screen so that all the extra whitespace doesn't appear to one side. Instead, you get smaller fields of empty space on either side of the layout.

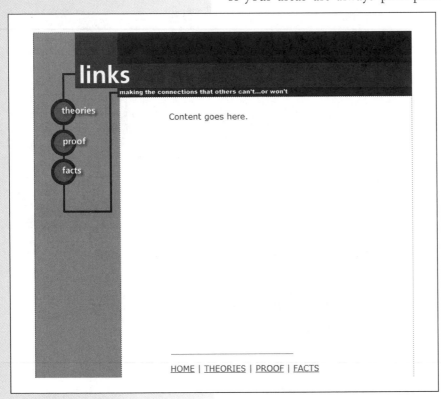

Figure 4-8. A fixed-width layout always retains its width

> **TIP**
>
> Another way to handle the abundance of whitespace in a fixed-width layout is to place a pattern image on the background of the page. The browser treats the background image like desktop wallpaper, automatically *tiling* or repeating it to fill up all available space. This way, the whitespace isn't completely empty, and if you choose a pattern that ties in with the graphical theme of your site, you can very easily approximate the look of a liquid layout.

Looking at Liquid Layouts

In a *liquid layout,* the width of the layout changes to match the width of the browser window (see Figure 4-9). As the width of the browser window expands, the width of your site expands in step. This solves the problem of cramped layouts handily, because you never get whitespace around your design. A visitor could come along with a 1,600 pixel-wide screen, and your layout would dutifully fill up the space.

Liquid layouts begin as fixed-width layouts, in that you design your layout to fit within a certain size screen. Then, to enable the liquid effect, you specify that certain areas of your site—the content area, for instance—shouldn't have a fixed size; they can expand as needed. The initial fixed width of your layout then becomes your minimum width. Go below this threshold, and you can anticipate horizontal scrollbars, because there might not be enough room in the browser window to accommodate all your content. But keep to the minimum width or exceed it, and the liquid effect works as advertised. You won't get horizontal scrollbars, and you won't leave fields of empty space.

Liquid layouts in general are easier for the visitor to use, but they can be difficult for you to implement properly, especially when the layout is design-intensive. Straightforward designs work best in liquid form.

---TECHTALK---

A liquid layout changes size to match the width of the browser window.

Figure 4-9. A liquid layout expands to fill the width of the browser

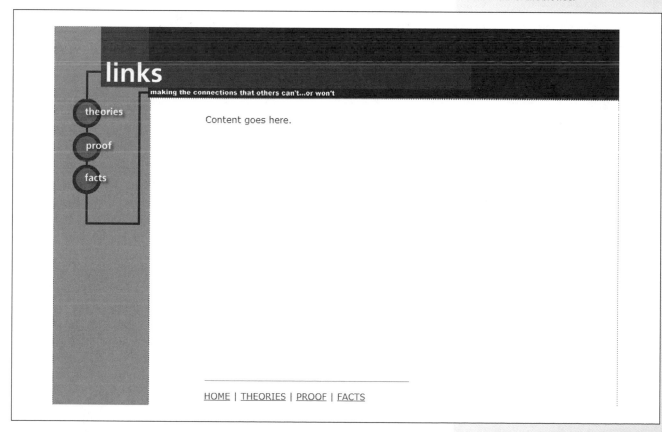

Filling in the Details

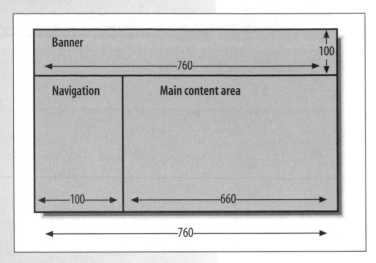

Figure 4-10. Use pixel measurements to express widths and heights

After you've decided upon a width for layout, you can begin to assign pixel measurements to the individual areas, as Figure 4-10 shows. When in doubt, eyeball it. Your measurements don't have to be precise, your sketch doesn't have to be to scale, and you can always modify your numbers later. The purpose here is to give yourself a starting point for when you construct your layout in Dreamweaver. A few things to keep in mind:

Keep the most important content above the fold

The phrase *above the fold* refers to everything that appears in the browser window when the visitor first lands on the page. (The content that the visitor has to scroll down to see is *below the fold*.) Table 4-3 gives the above-the-fold height for your page width of choice. In a 760-pixel layout, for instance, you have a maximum height of 420 pixels before content starts disappearing off the screen. Make sure that you have plenty of room above the fold for your main navigation and your best pieces of content. You may want to limit the height of your banner area, for instance, to make more room for the content area.

Table 4-3. Above-the-fold heights

Screen width (in pixels)	Above-the-fold height (in pixels)
640	300
800	420
1024	600

Make the content area as large as possible

The content area delivers the goods, so it should be the keystone of your layout. Feel free to trim down your navigation area or any other area that competes for screen real estate.

> **TIP**
>
> If you're planning a top-nav layout, pay special attention to the height of your nav area. Because the monitor screen is wider than it is tall, it's very easy for the navigation area to push the main content area below the fold. A height of 100 pixels is more than enough, and it might even be excessive, depending upon how you plan to present the main content.

Don't assign widths to liquid areas

If you're building a liquid layout, choose the areas of your layout that should expand with the browser. Typically, these are the content area, the header, and the footer. Don't assign fixed-width values to these areas. Label them with the asterisk (*) instead, which is web shorthand for *whatever* (see Figure 4-11). But definitely assign fixed widths to the non-liquid areas in your design, such as the navigation or sidebar areas.

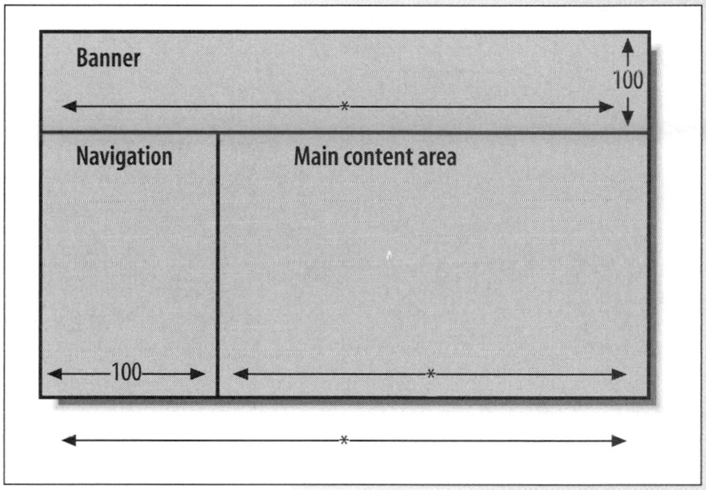

Figure 4-11. Asterisk characters indicate variable width areas

Assign heights only to areas with fixed heights

The navigation area in a top-nav layout and the banner area are likely to remain fixed at a given height, so supply rough height measurements for these. On the other hand, the main content area of your design needs to expand vertically to accommodate the amount of content that you place inside it, so it doesn't have a fixed height value. The browser will automatically determine the correct height when it renders your page. Feel free to mark unfixed heights with the asterisk character, or simply ignore them.

Choosing a Layout Strategy

When you construct your layout in Dreamweaver, you have your choice of two strategies: building with tables or building with layers. In both cases, you break the web page into rectangular sections, just like the areas in your sketch, and fill them with the corresponding content. More often than not, the results are indistinguishable. So which method should you use? This section helps you to make the right choice for your particular site.

────TECHTALK────

A table is an HTML structure for organizing rows and columns of data. You can also use it to build the layout of a web page.

Building with Tables

A *table* is an HTML structure for organizing rows and columns of data. In the early days of the Web, when scientists and mathematicians were the only people building web sites, the table was a convenient method for displaying the results of some experiment or other. But in what was perhaps the greatest act of subversion since postmodern literary theory, visually oriented people realized that the table could be "borrowed" to mark off the areas of a graphic design, resulting in far more sophisticated page layouts on the Web than Al Gore had ever dreamed possible. As a direct result, the Web became interesting to people who had never heard of hypotenuses, stock prices soared, and art majors found their degrees in welcome demand.

The problem was—and still is—that the specifications of HTML are very clear: you identify elements according to what they are, not according to what you want them to look like. Standards organizations like the World Wide Web Consortium (W3C) argue with great conviction that the table element, regardless of how it looks in the browser, is specifically for marking up rows and columns of data. It has no business defining the layout of a web page, because that isn't its purpose. This may seem like a trivial point, but the technology of the Web turns on this principle.

When the browser sees a table in an HTML document, it assumes rows and columns of data, not a page layout. To most visitors, this doesn't matter. They don't care if they're looking at what the browser thinks is a table. They're more interested in the content inside it. But what about those visitors who can't see your layout? When a non-visual browsing device like a screen reader comes along, it also assumes rows and columns of data, and it reads them out as such. While your web page may make good visual sense, it might not translate logically in table form, and the screen reader can very easily take the areas of your design out of order. The navigation area might come after the content area, and who wants to sit through paragraph after paragraph of unwanted content just to get to the links?

Despite the accessibility drawbacks and the continued protests of the W3C, tables have one major advantage in that they are completely and utterly stable. Tables-based designs look much the same in IE as they do in Firefox or Opera or any other browser, so your visitors receive the same experience, no matter which browser they prefer. Tables are also hard to break, in that you can push their limits without your layout coming apart at the seams, especially when you nest tables and add spacer images (more on that in Chapter 9).

If stability is your overriding concern, as it is if you're designing a site for your business, then building with tables is the better option. You won't win many friends in the W3C, but at least you'll be in good company, as most of the Web comes courtesy of tables.

Building with Layers

You know that a table is rows and columns of data, which many designers just happen to use for divisions of page content instead. But a *layer* or *div* is precisely that. It's a division of content—a section of the page—just like the areas in your design sketch.

No strict rows-and-columns-of-data formulation here. When you mark up a section of your page as a layer, you're telling the browser that this group of content belongs together. The browser doesn't have to perceive the layer in the context of the graphic design to understand this, either, because you've translated the purely visual divisions in your design into logical, structural divisions in the HTML code. What the human brain does for visual groups, the layer does for logical groups. Not even the W3C can object to that.

In fact, layers are so logical that you can arrange them in any order in the HTML code—the order in which a screen reader should read them out, for instance—without affecting their visual placement in your design. But layers aren't all about the code. They come with a wide variety of formatting options and effects. Tables are locked into a grid of rows and columns, but layers know no such limitations. You can position them anywhere on the page. You can animate them or make them draggable with the mouse. They can overlap. You can even make them invisible.

TECHTALK

A layer or div is a logical division of a web page.

> **TIP**
>
> Because of the way that Dreamweaver adds layers to your page, it's beastly hard to center a fixed-width, layers-based layout in the browser window. To pull it off, you have to get into the code and rewrite just about all the layout formatting by hand, which defeats the purpose of using a WYSIWYG editor in the first place.
>
> If your inner artiste is leading you toward a fixed-width, centered layout, then go with tables as your design strategy. It is incredibly easy to center a fixed-width, tables-based layout in Dreamweaver, as you'll see in Chapter 9.
>
> If you can live with a fixed-width, layers-based design that sits flush left against the browser window, then Dreamweaver's implementation of layers is more than up to the task.

At least that's how it works in theory. In practice, browsers don't support layers as well as they should. Layers-based designs tend to vary from browser to browser in odd ways, so that when you get the layout looking the way you want it in IE, you find annoying inconsistencies in Firefox, or the other way around. Sometimes the browser completely misinterprets your intentions, and the layout breaks down.

Nevertheless, layers are very much on the cutting edge for all the right reasons. A layers-based design is forward-thinking, standards-compliant, and more accessible. Layers are the future of web design. If you can afford to lose a little in the way of stability, and if you can live with a lean and straightforward visual style, then a layers-based design is an astute choice.

> **BEST BET**
>
> If you can't decide, choose tables. CSS gives you more in terms of layout and accessibility, but it's fussier, and it isn't as stable across browsers and platforms.

For your consideration, Table 4-4 summarizes the pros and cons of tables and layers. If, after carefully reviewing the arguments, you're still not sure which to use for your site, tables is the safer bet—a crime, perhaps, but a crime of convenience.

Table 4-4. Comparison of tables and layers

Considerations	Tables	Layers
Standards compliance	Tables are for rows and columns of data, not page layouts.	Layers are for divisions of content on a page, so they're perfect for page layouts.
Stability	Tables look and behave in much the same way across different browsers, devices, and platforms.	Layers look and behave differently and unpredictably across different browsers, devices, and platforms.
Accessibility	Screen readers can easily misinterpret the logical order of the layout.	Screen readers are less likely to be confused with a layers-based layout.
Flexibility	Tables are more reliable than layers for adventurous designs, and they work well with simple designs, too.	In spite of impressive formatting options, layers do better with straightforward designs because of uneven browser support. Avoid graphical complexity when you design with layers.
Dreamweaver compatibility	Tables are easy to build in Dreamweaver and extremely stable. What you see is what you get.	Layers are extremely easy to build in Dreamweaver but not always stable. The document window sometimes does strange things with them.

Preparing Images for the Web

5

The images on a web site have a dual role to play. On the one hand, they're one of the most effective forms of content that you can choose to include. We in the West are the people of the picture. It's part of our language and our culture, going all the way back to those philosophical Greeks. Even Plato knew that nothing gets your point across like a well-placed image. On the other hand, images adversely affect the performance of your site. They take time to download, even in this broadband age, and your visitors are nothing if not in a hurry. That's why they're on the Web. Your site has to be fast and nimble, or your visitors won't stick around.

So on the one hand, you should definitely include images on your site. On the other, you should think twice before you do.

This chapter helps you to resolve a schizophrenic dichotomy or two (as far as your site is concerned) and reap the benefits of our cultural inheritance.

Comparing Image File Types

Image files come in dozens of formats, but for the Web, you work with just three of them, all from the raster or pixel-based category. These are the GIF, JPEG, and PNG formats (see Table 5-1). All the major browsers support them, so you don't have to worry about compatibility. Some browsers support other image types as well. Internet Explorer displays Windows bitmaps (BMP), for instance, while the other browsers don't, so it's a good idea to stick with the big three.

Table 5-1. Web image types

File type	Pronounced	Stands for	Palette?	Transparency?	Animation?
GIF	*jiff* or *giff*	Graphical Interchange Format	Yes, up to 256 colors	Yes, one level of transparency	Yes
JPEG	*jaypeg*	Joint Photography Experts Group	No	No	No
PNG	*ping*	Portable Network Graphics	Yes, up to 256 colors	Yes, multiple levels of trans-parency	No

Oftentimes, an image that you want to use for your web site exists in some other format. You might have a piece of Windows clip art (Windows Metafile Format or WMF), some corporate branding from your friends in the marketing department (Electronic PostScript or EPS format), or high-quality images for print publishing (Tagged Image File Format or TIFF). If so, you should open the original images in your graphics software and save copies as GIFs, JPEGs, or PNGs. Don't post the images in their original format, or your visitors won't be able to see them.

To determine which format to use, it's helpful to consider the content of the image. In general, images with a lot of color information work better as JPEGs, while images with just a few colors work well as GIFs or PNGs.

About GIF

Graphical Interchange Format (GIF) images tend to work best with line art, cartoons, charts, graphs, logos, and other images that have large areas of flat color. Images like photographs, which often have subtle gradations in tone and shading, don't usually work well in the GIF type.

The reason? GIF images come with a built-in *palette* or color chart of up to 256 colors. The computer uses these colors to display the image file. It doesn't matter which 256—they can be 256 shades of red. You just can't have more than 256 colors total in the image.

This might seem like a lot of colors, yet it's next to nothing when you con-sider that most computers are capable of displaying some 16 million colors, more than the human eye can distinguish accurately. Photographs and the like burn through those 256 color slots in a hurry. To keep within the limits of the palette, your graphics software converts similar colors to the same basic shade, and you lose the subtle tonal shifts. As a result, photos take on a blocky or grainy aspect in GIF format.

Still, a 256-color palette is often more than sufficient for non-photographic images. As long as you stay away from shadow effects and gradient fills, your navigation buttons and other interface elements work well as GIFs.

— T E C H T A L K —

The Graphical Interchange Format (GIF) image type works well with images that have large areas of flat color.

— T E C H T A L K —

The palette in a GIF or PNG image is a built-in color chart of up to 256 colors. The computer uses these colors to display that particular GIF or PNG image file.

When you create a GIF in your graphics software, you can select one of the color slots in the palette to be a transparent color, which gives you a *transparent GIF* (see Figure 5-1). In a transparent GIF, all the pixels of this particular color become see-through. Place a transparent GIF on your web page, and the background color of the page shows through the transparent pixels. Web designers often use transparent GIFs for button images that need to appear against various backgrounds. Instead of creating separate image files with the same button on several different background colors, you make one button with a transparent background color. In Figure 5-1, because the background color of the GIF image was marked transparent in the graphics software, you can place it against any background.

— TECHTALK —

In a transparent GIF, all the pixels of a particular color in the palette become transparent or see-through.

Figure 5-1. Transparent GIFs can be placed against any background

TIP

The see-through region in a transparent GIF works best when it's square or rectangular in shape. The computer can't blend the edges of curved shapes with varying degrees of transparency, which often leaves you with visibly jagged edges.

The GIF format also supports animation. *Animated GIFs* are like those flipbook animations you used to draw on the corners of the pages in your high school math text, in that they contain several separate images or *frames* (see Figure 5-2). The computer displays each frame in turn, which creates the illusion of motion. The great thing about animated GIFs is that they're viewable in the browser without any kind of plug-in. Post them on your page, and your visitors don't require any special software to see the animation. The GIF image in Figure 5-2 contains four separate frames, which are played in sequence to get animation.

Figure 5-2. The individual frames of a single animated GIF image

To create animated GIFs, you need the right software. Not every image editor provides tools for assembling them, but the better packages like Macromedia Fireworks do.

About JPEG

The Joint Photography Experts Group (JPEG) format does especially well with photographs, movie stills, and all other images with a wide range of color or shading. Unlike GIFs and PNGs, JPEG images don't have a built-in color palette. Instead, these images pull from the same set of colors that the visitor's computer is capable of displaying, so you get the full crayon box of 16 million options.

Because JPEGs don't have a color palette, you can't specify a transparent color. Also, unlike GIF, the JPEG format doesn't have frames, so you don't get animation.

About PNG

The Portable Network Graphics (PNG) format originated as a non-proprietary alternative to GIF, which CompuServe used to own. The patent on GIF has since expired, and with it went much of the incentive to convert the Web from GIF to PNG.

PNG images are very much like GIFs (although they tend to weigh less than GIFs, which is a definite advantage). They have a built-in palette of 256 colors, so they work well for images with large areas of flat color. Use them for the same types of images that make sense as GIFs, with the exception of animations, which PNG doesn't offer.

On the other hand, PNG does give you transparency, and it's a great improvement over the GIF version. In a transparent GIF, you get one level of transparency for one color, so pixels are either completely transparent or completely opaque. With a transparent PNG, in addition to GIF-style, single-color transparency, you also get *alpha channel transparency*, which comes by degrees, and it applies to all the colors in your image, not just one. Your entire image can be 50% opaque, for example, which means that the image is only 50% transparent and therefore still partially visible on screen (see Figure 5-3). In Macromedia Fireworks and other image editors, you can set the alpha channel of a transparent PNG from 0% (completely transparent) to 100% (completely opaque).

Unfortunately, PNG images with alpha channel transparency appear as regular, non-transparent images in Internet Explorer, which is another major strike against the PNG format. If you want to use transparent PNGs, go with the single-color variety, which IE displays correctly.

Figure 5-3. This transparent PNG image is 50% transparent

TECHTALK

Alpha channel transparency gives a transparent PNG its range of opacity.

Optimizing Images for the Web

TECHTALK

Web optimization is getting the lightest possible image file while maintaining overall image quality.

On the Web, lighter image files—files that consume relatively smaller amounts of disk space—download faster than heavier files. It's one of the few absolutes in this game. A light image load improves the performance of your site. At the same time, lighter image files contain less visual information than heavier image files, so they're more likely to look cheap and cheesy, which doesn't help anyone. Your images have to look good. But they also have to download quickly. This is the balancing act called *web optimization*. For every image that you plan to use, your goal is to achieve the lightest possible image file while maintaining the overall image quality.

BEHIND THE SCENES

It's not just the weight of your images that slows down a web page. It's also the number of unique images appearing on the page. A page with one 100K image file, for instance, tends to download faster than the same page with ten different 10K image files. Why? Because more image files means more requests to the server, and more requests to the server means time, plain and simple.

Granted, for most sites, the difference is negligible. It might not even be practically measurable, unless you have a very busy site. Also, your visitors like the pretty pictures. They expect something to look at, so casting off the graphics load entirely isn't usually the wisest course of action. You might consider making every image earn its keep, though, and if you can do without a particular image because it isn't really adding anything, then why not get rid of it?

Optimizing Resolution

TECHTALK

Resolution is the pixel density of an image. In web graphics, the common measurement for resolution is pixels per inch (ppi).

Resolution is the pixel density of an image—the amount of pixels that appear in any given area, usually expressed as pixels per inch (ppi). As resolution increases, more pixels are packed into the same amount of space, which allows for finer detail and increases the overall clarity of the image. The pixel density is what makes high-resolution images sharper than their lower-res counterparts.

More pixels per inch means more visual information, but it also means a heavier image file. As it happens, the weight of a raster graphic is directly related to the number of pixels that it contains. Add more pixels, and you increase the weight. Take pixels out, and you decrease the weight.

Happily, the images that you plan to use on your site don't require very much in the way of resolution. Web images are supposed to be viewed on screen, and even the best monitors are relatively low-res output devices. Windows monitors typically display at 96 ppi. Macintosh monitors are lower still, at 72 ppi. By way of comparison, an image needs to have a resolution of 300 to 600 ppi to look good on the printed page. If you have a digital camera, your photos probably come out somewhere in this range.

The first, best thing that you can do to optimize your images for the Web is to reduce the image resolution to 72 ppi. Web designers have adopted this number as the universal standard for all web graphics, and that number has stuck. It's one of the few things that most of us agree on. The reason why it's 72 instead of 96 isn't because most of us are on Macs. An image at 72 ppi looks fine on Windows screens, despite the slightly better Microsoft pixel density. More importantly, 72 ppi means fewer pixels, so the 72-ppi image weighs less.

The best part is that a high-res image looks exactly the same on screen as a 72-ppi web-optimized image. You get no (or negligible) loss of image quality by reducing resolution, yet you reduce the weight of the file dramatically. Talk about a win-win. A 1 MB digital photo suddenly weighs in at 40 or 50 KB while looking just as crisp and clear, as Figure 5-4 shows. The photo on the left has a resolution of 300 ppi, while the photo on the right has a much lower resolution of 72 ppi, yet they look exactly the same on the monitor.

Figure 5-4. Comparing low- and high-res versions of an image

TIP

To optimize the resolution of an image for the Web in Macromedia Fireworks, choose Modify→Canvas→Image Size from the main menu, or click the Image Size button on the Property Inspector. Then, in the Image Size dialog box, type 72 in the Resolution field, choose Pixels/Inch from the menu next door, and click OK.

Keep in mind that, when you reduce the resolution of the photo, say from 300 ppi to the web standard 72 ppi, you're losing more than three quarters of the visual information. On your monitor, you can't tell the difference, because all that extra resolution in the 300-ppi version goes to waste. Remember, the monitor tops out at 72 or 96 ppi. Print out the 72-ppi version, though, and you notice the difference immediately. This is why images that you print from the Web look razor-sharp on screen but grainy or blurry on paper.

This is also why, when you decrease the resolution of an image for the Web, you should always save the Web version under a different filename (see "Naming Images for the Web" later in this chapter), and keep the original in a safe place. You never know when you might want that higher-res version.

> **TIP**
>
> If you want your visitors to be able to download a higher-res image for the purposes of printing—maybe it's a protest sign; maybe it's a T-shirt decal—don't use the high-res version on your site. Use a web-optimized version instead, and add a link to the high-res version. This way, your page loads faster for those who are just browsing, and only those visitors who really want the high-res image get access to it.

TECHTALK

When you resample an image in Dreamweaver, you automatically fine-tune the resolution and size of the image for your site.

If you don't have image-editing software, you're not out of luck. Dreamweaver comes with image *resampling,* a tool for fine-tuning resolution and size, as you'll see in Chapter 13.

Optimizing Image Size

Reducing the physical dimensions of an image to the precise size that you need for your page is another sure remedy for excess weight on the Web. If an image is physically smaller than another image, and both have the same resolution, then the smaller image contains fewer pixels, and fewer pixels equals less weight.

When you place an image on a web page, you specify, among other things, the image's width and height—but nothing prevents you from making up your own numbers. You can scale down a 1600-by-800-pixel image very easily in this way by reporting the width as 400 pixels and the height as 200 pixels instead of their true 1600 and 800 values. This gives you, in essence, a 75% reduction in size. The problem with this approach is that, while the images on your page *appear* to be smaller, they really aren't. The image files themselves still retain their full width and height; the browser simply makes them *look* smaller. And of course, they remain as heavy as before the browser scaled them.

Your best bet is to figure out the exact width and height that you need for each image and then physically change the images to this size. If you know this information ahead of time, that's great. Fire up your image editor and shrink those images. Don't forget to save the smaller versions under different filenames than the originals. It's always good to be able to go back to the large version and make a new smaller version if your size requirements change.

> **TIP**
>
> To resize an image in Macromedia Fireworks, choose Modify→Canvas→ Image Size, or click the Image Size button on the Property Inspector. In the Image Size dialog box, enter new width and height values. If you check the Constrain Proportions option, you don't have to give both width and height. Supplying either one automatically adjusts the other in a proportionate amount. Click OK to finish.

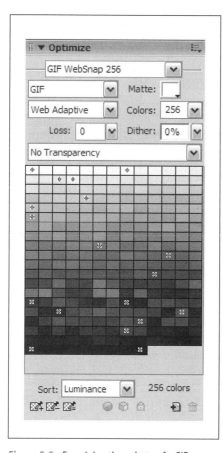

Figure 5-5. Examining the palette of a GIF

If you don't know the correct size because you haven't built your site yet, that's fine, too. Do nothing for now, and fiddle with the dimensions once you place them on your pages. But when you *do* know the correct dimensions, you want to make sure that you resample your images at their modified size— more on that in Chapter 13.

Reducing the Number of Colors

In GIF and PNG images, each color in the palette contributes a little extra weight to the image file. So, if your image is in the GIF or PNG format, you can modestly decrease the weight of the file by reducing the number of colors in the palette. You'll need to use your image editor for this operation, as shown in Figure 5-5. Dreamweaver's built-in graphics tools don't get into this much detail.

> **TIP**
>
> In Macromedia Fireworks, you can inspect and edit the color palette of a GIF or PNG in the Optimize panel.

Keep in mind that removing colors affects the image quality of your GIF or PNG. However, you can generally afford to lose a good many of them before you notice a visible change.

Increasing Compression

JPEG images don't have a built-in palette, but you can adjust their level of compression.

Compression is a method for reducing the weight of a computer file. There are two types: *lossless compression,* which retains all the information in the file and simply organizes it more efficiently; and *lossy compression,* which organizes the data in addition to throwing some of it out, but hopefully not so much of it that the human on the other side of the screen notices.

Compression doesn't just apply to computer graphics. Popular audio formats like MP3 are compressed as well. Their lighter weight makes them convenient to download, but the discerning audiophile can hear a difference in the fidelity of an MP3 when compared to the uncompressed original.

The JPEG format is lossy by nature, which means that, when you save an image as a JPEG, you automatically lose a little image quality. In graphics software like Fireworks and Photoshop, you can manually adjust the level of compression to jettison more and more of the visual data. As compression goes up, file weight goes down.

Most JPEGs can withstand a serious crushing before they noticeably degrade. The trick is to find the level of compression at which the quality deteriorates too significantly and then back off ever so slightly. As you can see in Figure 5-6, Fireworks has crushed this JPEG image fairly well (image quality 33/100), but it is just beginning to show signs of pressure.

TECHTALK

Compression is a method for reducing the weight of an image file. Lossless compression retains all the visual information in the image, while lossy compression doesn't.

Figure 5-6. Visible degradation occurs at high compression levels

> **TIP**
>
> When you work with JPEGs, look for a quality slider in your image editor. This affects the level of compression of the image. In Macromedia Fireworks, the quality slider appears in the Optimize panel.

Naming Images for the Web

When you store images on your computer, you probably prefer long, descriptive names like "Lloyd and Deborah investigate the meteor, May 2013." For personal use, these kinds of names are fine, but for the Web, you want something a bit more compact. Here are some suggestions:

Always include a standard extension

An extension is a short label that you attach to the end of a filename with a dot (.). In the case of image files, the extension tells the browser what type of file the image happens to be. For JPEGs, it's *.jpg* or *.jpeg*; for GIFs, it's *.gif*; for PNGs, it's *.png*. Good graphics programs automatically append the correct extensions to your files.

Stick to alphanumeric characters

Don't use punctuation or other typographical marks in your filenames. Use letters and numbers only. Instead of spaces, use the underscore character (_) or hyphen (-).

Try for eight characters maximum (not counting the extension)

If you really want to act like an old-school web designer, try keeping your filenames to eight characters maximum, not counting the extension. Vintage software and hardware insist upon the eight-character cap. The newer stuff isn't so picky, so if you find yourself going beyond eight characters, you should be all right.

Use plain language whenever possible

Why choose *flwr.jpg* when you can have *flower.jpg* instead? Plain-language names are easier and clearer.

> **TIP**
>
> There are at least two side benefits to using plain-language names for your images. First, your images appear in search-engine results. Second, your images have built-in text equivalents (but don't forget the actual alternate text—see Chapter 15).

Use prefixes for images that belong to a group or set

When you build your site, you'll store all the images for all the pages in a single folder. As you might imagine, your image folder fills up quickly, and it's no joke trying to find a particular image when you have five or six hundred items to weed through. To save yourself some hassle, try attaching prefixes to images that belong together. For instance, you might decide that the filenames for all product images should begin with *prod_* or simply *p_*. This way, when you view the contents of your image folder in Dreamweaver, all the *p_* images appear together in the alphabetical listing of files.

Use suffixes for different versions of the same image.

When you have two different versions of the same image—a small thumbnail version for one page and a full-sized version for another page, or a default button state and a rollover button state for your main navigation—use the same general filename for both images, but attach a short suffix to one or both that explains the difference. The filenames *flower_sm.jpg* and *flower_lg.jpg* tell you exactly what you need to know when you're scanning the contents of your image folder. For rollovers, you might use the *_ro* suffix. Save your default-state image as *button.gif* and your rollover-state image as *button_ro.gif.*

Creating a Tracing Image

A *tracing image* is a to-scale mockup of your layout. You draw the tracing image in your graphics software, save it, and file it away. When design time rolls around, you attach your tracing image to the document window in Dreamweaver and literally draw your layout on top of the mockup.

This isn't a mandatory step. If you don't have graphics software, or if you'd rather not bother with a tracing image, then you may certainly proceed in Dreamweaver without one. Still, having the tracing image almost always works to your advantage.

Toward the end of Chapter 4, you assigned pixel measurements to the widths and heights of the areas in your layout sketch. Most of these measurements were probably estimates, not that anyone can blame you for guessing. You were working in the abstract, with empty rectangles standing in for the sections of your design. Making the tracing image is your first step toward finalizing those measurements. You see firsthand what a 100-pixel-wide navigation area looks like in relation to the rest of your design, and if the area seems too narrow, you can widen it.

You might also take the opportunity to start filling the areas of your tracing image with sample content. You can design the banner of your page and connect it to the navigation bar that you envision running down the left side of the screen. You can type some sample text in the main content area. You can try out different color schemes. Experiment as much as you like, and save when you're happy with the results. As long as you build your layout in Dreamweaver to match the size of the areas in your tracing image—which is extremely easy, since you're tracing over them—there's no reason why your design can't look exactly like your mockup. You don't even need to recreate the art. Simply export the graphics from the tracing image.

To create a tracing image, here's what you do:

1. Get out the sketch of your design from Chapter 4, and open a new document window in your graphics software.

TECHTALK

A tracing image is a to-scale mockup of your layout for use in Dreamweaver.

2. Start by setting the canvas size of your document to match the dimensions of the browser window. Your tracing image should be to scale, so make sure the width of the canvas is exact. Refer back to the page width that you chose for your layout sketch in Chapter 4. (If you're planning to build a liquid layout, use the page width on which you initially based your design.) The height doesn't matter so much in this case, because the height of your main content area is variable—it changes from page to page depending upon the content. Make the height of the canvas a hundred pixels or so longer than the above-the-fold cutoff. You may want to draw a line to mark the above-the-fold threshold. Also, for your convenience later, you can label the areas and give their dimensions.

> **TIP**
>
> To resize the canvas in Macromedia Fireworks, choose Modify→Canvas→ Canvas Size, or click the Canvas Size button on the Property Inspector. Type the width and height values for your page in the appropriate fields of the Canvas Size dialog box, and click OK.

3. Now, simply draw rectangles for each of the areas in your design, following the width and height guidelines that you established in your sketch. If your guesses were off, feel free to adjust them as needed.

When you finish, your document window looks something like Figure 5-7. This is all you need for a tracing image, so feel free to stop here. Save your file in GIF, JPEG, or PNG format, and you're done. But if you're feeling inspired, by all means, flesh out your tracing image with sample graphics, as shown in Figure 5-8. The more you do now, the less you have to do later.

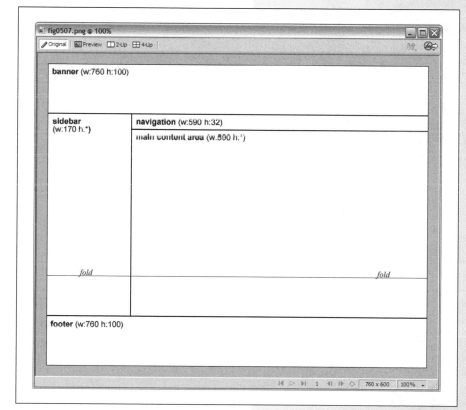

Figure 5-7. An example of a tracing image

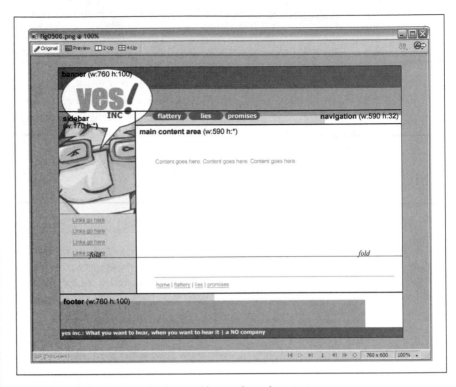

Figure 5-8. Flesh out your tracing image with art and sample content

---

TIP

The art that you mock up in your tracing image doesn't have to go to waste. You can use the very same art on your site. To do this, export the desired areas as separate image files. Eventually, you'll place these image files into your Dreamweaver document.

If you're using Macromedia Fireworks, select the rectangle from Step 4 that you want to export. Right-click the mouse button, and choose Insert Slice from the context menu. Fireworks adds an identical, rectangular slice to the web layer. Right-click again, and choose Export Selected Slice. You now have a web-ready image, tailored exactly to size, for your layout.

Thinking About Text

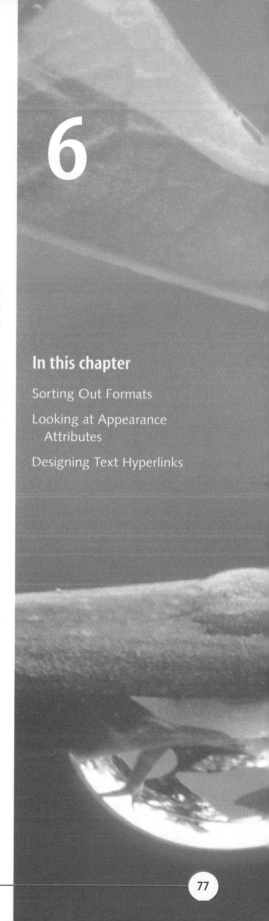

6

Most of the content on your site will probably take the form of text. Just like you took some time at the beginning of the project to plan the structure and the layout of your site, it's worth thinking about the form that your text will take.

You want text that is easy to read on screen. More than that, you want text that is easy to skim, because most of your visitors don't have the patience to sift through your copy word for word, no matter how crisp, no matter how scintillating. Your visitors want you to get to the point. They want main ideas. They want results. Also, reading on screen is a chore. Headaches and eyestrain are par for the course. You want to do what you can to minimize the burden.

This chapter gets you thinking in the right direction. By planning through how to present text on your site, you increase the accessibility of your content for everyone, not just those with disabilities.

Sorting Out Formats

Here's the best piece of advice that you're going to get in this entire chapter: when you're building a web page, you should always classify every block of text on the page according to its category or *format,* to use the Dreamweaver jargon. The reason is simple. The format identifies the text as a certain kind of thing—i.e., a paragraph or a heading—which in turn tells the browser how to display the text in question. As you saw in Chapter 1, when you apply a Dreamweaver format to a block of text, Dreamweaver marks it up with the corresponding HTML tags on your behalf.

It's entirely possible to leave unformatted text on your page. That is to say, you don't have to mark it up with any HTML tag whatsoever, and the browser still displays it as text.

While leaving text in the raw might sound like a tempting time-saver, this humble tome advises you in the strongest possible terms not to succumb. *Always* classify every piece of text according to its proper format. If you don't, you don't get the full benefit of applying CSS styles, because the browser isn't sure what the text is supposed to be: a paragraph, a heading, a table caption, or what have you. So when it comes time to design the default look of your paragraphs, only those paragraphs that you have expressly formatted as such receive your custom style, and your raw, unformatted text remains its boring old self in the browser window.

The browser comes with built-in style rules for the various text formats, so if you give the browser a paragraph, it displays the text in a certain way. In most browsers, paragraphs appear in relatively small type, much like the running text in this book. If you like the way that the browser displays a particular format, then your job is done. But if you take exception to the generally poor aesthetic quality of built-in browser styles, as most designers do, then you have an excellent remedy at your disposal: you simply redefine its appearance to suit your needs.

You do this by way of a Cascading Style Sheet (CSS), which, as you'll recall from Chapter 1, is a set of style rules that govern the appearance of the elements that make up your site. In essence, a Cascading Style Sheet says something like this to the visitor's web browser: "When you see a block of text in the paragraph format, please display it in the Arial typeface with a type size of 10 points. But when you see a first-level heading, I want it in 16-point Verdana, and make it boldface."

Better still, you can define special styles to distinguish among several different appearances for the same format. Using these styles, you can create a general paragraph style for the content area of your layout, a separate paragraph style for the items in your sidebar, another paragraph style for the secondary navigation, and yet another paragraph style for the copyright notice in the footer, all in the same stylesheet.

You'll begin to construct your stylesheet in Chapter 12, after you've built the layout for your pages. For now, it's worth looking at the most common text formats and figuring out how best to use them.

About Headings

Use headings to mark off sections of content in the running text of your page.

Web browsers recognize six levels of headings. Level-one headings are the most important, like the front page headline in a newspaper. Level-six headings are the least important, like the headline of a classified ad. Figure 6-1 shows the standard appearance of the six levels of headings in a browser. Whatever custom designs you conceive for the headings in your stylesheet should follow the same basic idea of decreasing visual importance. At level one, your headings should scream. At level six, they should squeak.

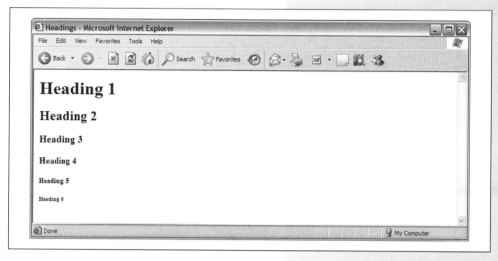

Figure 6-1. The default appearance of the six levels of headings

> **TIP**
>
> It's very unlikely that the content on any given page of your site requires six levels of organization, so don't feel compelled to think of designs for six levels of headings. Three is usually more than enough.

The trick to using headings correctly on a web page is to start at level one and work your way down. The main content divisions in your page begin with first-level headings. If you require subdivision within each section, go to second-level headings, and then third-level headings, and so on, but don't skip from a first-level heading directly to a third-level heading. Always move down in incremental steps. This helps browsing devices to ascertain the underlying structure of your content.

> **TIP**
>
> Be careful about using headings for the page title, the links in your navigation area, and so on. Many designers reach for the heading format whenever they want to make a certain piece of text stand out. But remember, with Cascading Style Sheets, you don't need headings for their appearance. You can make a special paragraph class style that's just as big and bold as a level-one heading. You should identify a piece of text as a heading only when it actually functions as a heading in the running text by separating sections of content.

About Paragraphs

It should come as no surprise that the paragraph format is for paragraphs of running text, much like the paragraph that you're currently reading. Figure 6-2 shows the default appearance of paragraphs in a browser. Notice that paragraphs aren't indented. Instead, the browser adds a line of whitespace to separate them. When you create a stylesheet for your site, you're not locked into this kind of formatting. Your paragraphs can be indented, and they don't need to have whitespace between them.

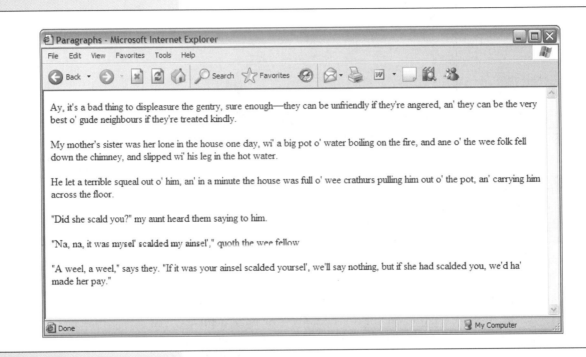

Figure 6-2. HTML paragraphs look like this by default

What may not be obvious is that the paragraph style is also the catchall for any block of text that isn't a heading or a list. The title of the web page, the items in the main navigation, and the copyright notice in the footer all fall into this category, so you mark them up as paragraphs in Dreamweaver. To distinguish the various types of paragraphs that you use, you create CSS class styles. This prevents the paragraphs in the running text from looking like the paragraphs in other areas, such as the navigation area.

About Lists

In web publishing, there are two types of lists: ordered lists and unordered lists. What distinguishes them is their *leading character*, or the typographical mark that precedes each list item. In an *ordered list*, the leading character is sequential—either numerically (1, 2, 3) or alphabetically (a, b, c). By default, the browser gives you numerically sequenced ordered lists, as shown in Figure 6-3. With Cascading Style Sheets you can easily change the leading character to letters or Roman numerals. One nice feature of ordered lists is that that you don't have to number (or letter) the list items by hand. The browser automatically numbers them on your behalf. Remove an item from the middle of the list, and the browser renumbers your list.

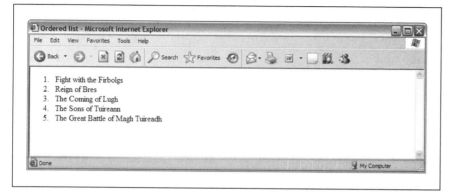

Figure 6-3. Ordered lists are numbered by default

In an *unordered list*, the leading character is a bullet, as Figure 6-4 shows. Again, with Cascading Style Sheets, you can change the default bullet to something other than a solid circle. You can even supply an image file of your own design.

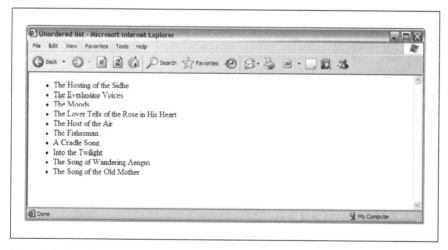

Figure 6-4. Unordered lists are bulleted by default

Lists are most effective inside the running text of your page, although some designers choose to format their main navigation as a list. There are no special merits to marking up your navigation in this way as opposed to using paragraphs, although if you want to offset your navigation choices with bullets, then using an unordered list is smart thinking. As always, you can create a special class style for your navigation list to distinguish it visually from the lists that appear in your running text.

Looking at Appearance Attributes

With CSS, and by extension with Dreamweaver, you get a host of styling options or *appearance attributes* for the text on your site. You get so many, in fact, that this humble tome can't possibly explore them all. What it can do is to present the most important of these to give you a feel for the possibilities and leave the excitement of exploration to you.

Considering Fonts

The typefaces or *fonts* that you choose for your web site make an important contribution to the overall look and feel of your design as well as the readability of your pages.

Before diving into this discussion, it's worth pointing out that the fonts that the browser displays on your site come from the visitor's computer, not your computer, which tends to limit your typographical choices. If you're a graphic designer, no doubt you have accumulated an impressive collection of obscure fonts over the years, but sadly you must overlook them for your web project, simply because your visitors aren't likely to have these fonts on their computers. You want to go for the obvious picks instead, the fonts that everyone has. Some designers refer to these as *web-safe fonts,* although perhaps *safe* isn't the best word for them. You won't crash the Internet if you happen to use a non-web-safe font on your site. Your pages just won't look the way that you want them to look for the majority of your audience.

With that in mind, you can divide web fonts into three types: serif, sans-serif, and monospaced, as shown in Figure 6-5. *Serif* fonts have little decorations on the ends of the characters, while *sans-serif* fonts don't. In monospaced fonts, all the characters in the set have the same width, much like the text from a typewriter. Aside from this, monospaced fonts can be either serif or sans-serif, although they are more commonly serif fonts.

TECHTALK

Appearance attributes are the styling options for a page element such as a block of text.

TECHTALK

The font is the typeface of the text.

TECHTALK

A web-safe font is a font that most computer users have on their machines.

Figure 6-5. Here are the three types of web fonts

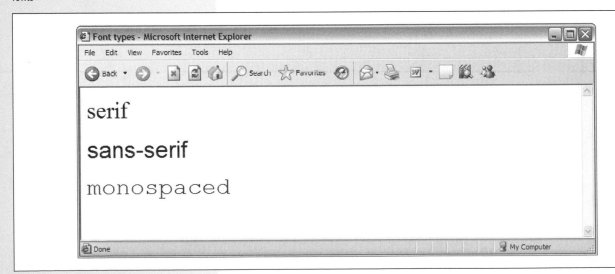

Table 6-1 lists the most common fonts of all three types. You should strongly consider using these fonts in your site rather than chancing it with less web-safe candidates.

Table 6-1. The most common fonts on Windows and MacOS systems

Font type	Windows fonts	Macintosh fonts
Serif	Times New Roman, Georgia	Times
Sans-serif	Arial, Verdana	Helvetica, Geneva
Monospaced	Courier New	Courier

> **TIP**
>
> The proviso about web-safe fonts applies only to the text that appears as text on your page. Text that you include inside images, like the label on a button, is part of the image file—the letters in their particular typeface are built into the image. Therefore, the visitor doesn't need to have the same fonts to see the image exactly as you designed it.

To compensate for the visitor-centric model of font selection, the browser allows you to supply a list of acceptable fonts instead of locking you into a single pick. For instance, you might decide that your general paragraph style looks best in Geneva but that Times for your Mac users and Times New Roman for your Windows users who don't have Geneva are all suitable substitutes. You'll get into the concept of font lists more thoroughly when you actually build your stylesheet in Chapter 12. For now, just keep in mind that you can give a range of fonts for each of your text elements.

> **BEST BET**
>
> At most, define one serif font list, one sans-serif font list, and one monospaced font list for your site.

In theory, you can specify a different font list for every style rule in your Cascading Style Sheet, but in practice you pick one or two lists and use them for all the text formats and class styles that you define. At most, you want one font list of each type: one serif list, one sans-serif list, and one monospaced list. Use more font lists than this, and your site takes on something of the ransom-note aesthetic, with too many competing typefaces.

Here are a few general guidelines for font selection:

Serif fonts work well as running text

The little decorations on the ends of the characters create a kind of horizontal channel at relatively small sizes, helping the reader to follow the lines of text. This is especially helpful on the Web, where your visitors absolutely will not read your text word for word. They skim the page instead and only slow down when they come to the exact piece of information that they want. For the typical paragraph or list style, the serifs are a good choice.

Sans-serif fonts work well as headings

Sans-serif fonts, with their unadorned style, tend to look bold and commanding in larger type sizes. This helps to draw attention to your headings. Furthermore, if you choose a serif font for your paragraphs, the sans-serif font in your headings makes a nice visual distinction to reinforce the conceptual one between the formats.

Serif fonts tend to be more serious

If you want to lend an informed, authoritative air to your text, consider casting it in a serif font. The more formal style of the serifs helps to reinforce the idea that your words are sober, reliable, reasonable, and correct, don't you know.

Sans-serif fonts tend to be less serious

Informal, jovial, friendly, or welcoming text works better in a sans-serif cast. The characters in a sans-serif font are straightforward and unpretentious, so the reader tends to associate these attributes to your words.

Reserve monospaced fonts for display text

Monospaced fonts work exceptionally well on the Web in small quantities. They're particularly effective for offset blocks of text such as lines of computer code, instructions about what to type next, or quoted passages from books or movies. You can also use monospaced fonts to highlight the names of keyboard keys or buttons inside standard running text, but avoid them for the standard running text itself, as it tends to be hard to read in large chunks.

Considering Type Size

Type size measures the length or height of the characters in a block of text. The higher the type size, the larger your text appears on screen. You may specify a different type size for every style rule in your stylesheet.

CSS gives you a number of ways to measure type size, including traditional typographic measurements like points, picas, and ems, but for the Web it's usually best to think in terms of pixels. The page width, the width of your layout, and the dimensions of many of your design elements are expressed in pixels, so it's convenient for you to measure the size of the text in the same way. Also, pixel-based text tends to be more consistent across browsers, so you have a higher degree of confidence that your visitors see your text as you designed it.

——TECHTALK——

Type size measures the length of the characters in a block of text.

BEHIND THE SCENES

The pixel is a relative measure of length. You may recall from the discussion in Chapter 5 that, by increasing the resolution, you pack more pixels into the same physical area, thereby giving you smaller pixels.

By contrast, points, picas, inches, and millimeters are absolute measures of length. A point is always a certain fixed length. While this might sound advantageous for type sizing, browsers aren't especially good at these types of measures. What IE says is a point isn't necessarily what Firefox says on the subject. But browsers are very good at measuring pixels. They do it often enough.

Also, because points are absolute, what happens if your type size is absolutely too small for some of your visitors? They have no easy way of adjusting the size of your text, because a point is always a point. Not so with pixels. Your visitors can increase the text-size setting in their browser or decrease their screen size if all else fails. Either way, the text gets bigger and easier to read. Besides, most computer monitors display at 96 or 72 ppi, so pixels are more or less the same size for all your visitors anyway. When you express type size in pixels, you get "virtual" absolute sizing without the drawbacks.

As a point of reference, the average type size for running text on the Web is about 12 pixels, but depending upon your design, 12 pixels can easily feel too large. Screen real estate is always a precious resource in web design, so it behooves you to think small. You don't want to think so small, though, that your text becomes illegible. Reading on a computer screen is hard on the eyes as it is. Add to this the fact that your visitors are skimmers, and legibility becomes the driving goal of your online typography.

TIP

At smaller type sizes, relatively wide fonts like Georgia and Verdana work best.

The best approach to sizing your text is to experiment with different length values during the building of your site. Many variables affect the overall legibility of your text, including the background color of the page and your selection of font. However, even in the best case, the smallest useful type size is about 8 pixels. Set this as your lower boundary, and work your way up.

BEST BET

Don't go smaller than a type size of 8 pixels.

Considering Spacing

You want spacing? You got spacing. CSS gives you spacing in every conceivable sense of the term, as this section illustrates.

To begin, let it be known that a block of web text, whether it's a single line or an entire paragraph, sits inside a rectangle or *box*. By default, the box is completely transparent, but its rectangular shape becomes apparent when you give it a border or background color (see "Considering Colors and Borders" later in this chapter). It's good to bring this up now, as visualizing your text as sitting in a box helps you to make sense of some of the spacing options available to you.

Looking at line spacing

Normally, lines of text on the page are roughly as tall as the type size. Therefore, if you're displaying 16-pixel text, your lines are about 16 pixels tall. But with CSS, you can change the *line height*, as Figure 6-6 shows.

Because your lines are normally as tall as your type, you can very easily compute the line height for different kinds of spacing. Assuming that you have 16-pixel text, a line height of 16 pixels is the equivalent of normal, single-spaced text. A line height of 24 pixels gives you line-and-a-half spacing (16 times 1.5). For double spacing, increase the line height to 32 (16 times 2).

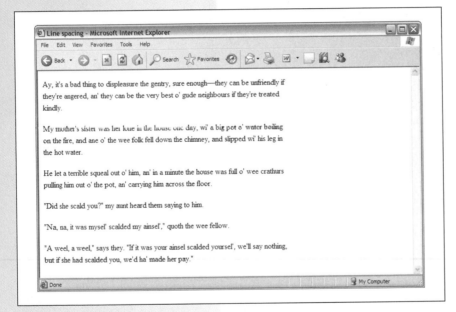

Figure 6-6. These paragraphs in 16-pixel type have a line height of 24 pixels

> **TIP**
>
> To improve the legibility (and skimmability) of your running text, particularly when you have multiple paragraphs one after the other, you might try line-and-a-half-style spacing. To do this, set the line height to 1.5 times the type size.

Looking at word and character spacing

You can control the amount of spacing between the words in a line of type. In Figure 6-7, the second paragraph has three extra pixels of word space, which makes it easier to read at this small type size.

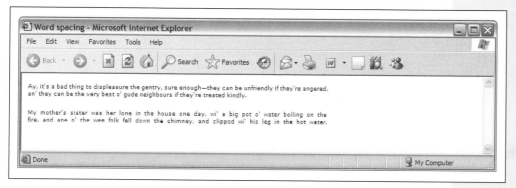

Figure 6-7. Increasing the word space improves readability

Generally speaking, the larger the type size, the less word space you need. It's smart to decrease the word spacing for headings and the like, so you can fit more words onto a single line. Conversely, if your running text is 8 or 9 pixels long, you could probably stand to increase the word spacing to improve legibility.

> **TIP**
>
> Wide fonts like Verdana often look better with extra word and character space. Condensed fonts often look better with less of both.

Similarly, you can control the amount of spacing between characters in a line of type, as Figure 6-8 shows. Character spacing follows the same general guidelines as word spacing in terms of when to increase and decrease it. For large type sizes, less character space works well. In Figure 6-8, the words in the second heading have two fewer pixels of character space, giving it a more compact look and making it easier to read.

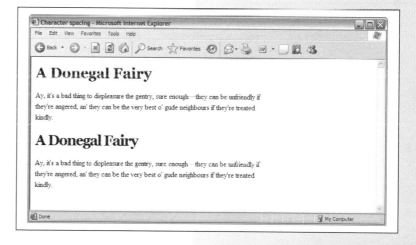

Figure 6-8. The second heading has two fewer pixels of letter space

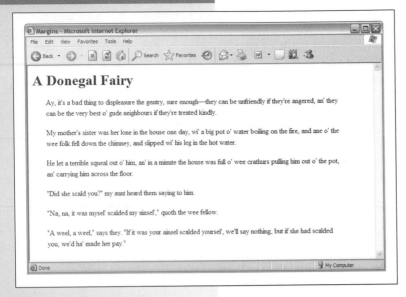

Figure 6-9. Offsetting text by adjusting the left and right margins

Looking at margins

Normally, the box of a text element is as large as it needs to be to accommodate the text inside it. The four margin attributes—top, bottom, left, and right—determine the size of a box above and beyond its normal size. Most often, you use margins to set the "printable" area of the entire page, but individual text elements like paragraphs can also have margins. For example, you can design your paragraphs to have shorter margins than those of the page, which gives your text an offset appearance. In Figure 6-9, the paragraphs on the page have a left margin of 30 pixels more than the page's left margin and a right margin of 60 pixels less than the page's right margin.

Looking at padding

The *padding* attribute controls the amount of whitespace between the margin of the box and the edge of the content inside it. Like margins, padding also comes in four flavors: top, bottom, left, and right. In Figure 6-10, the top paragraph has no padding, while the bottom paragraph has 10 pixels of padding on all four sides.

Use padding to position content inside its box. Because the areas of your design sit tightly against each other, padding is an essential attribute for helping your design to breathe. For example, if you have a side-nav design with a banner across the top of your page, your main content area probably sits in the lower right of the layout. Some tasteful padding along the top and down the left side of the main content area gives you a nice cushion of space, which helps to separate the content from the interface-type elements in your design.

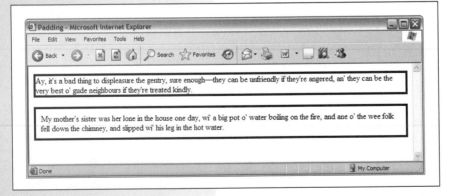

Figure 6-10. The effect of padding on paragraphs

Considering Colors and Borders

To give your text that extra graphical appeal, you can apply color to both it and its box, and you can set its box in various types of borders.

Looking at text color

Use any one of your computer's 16 million distinct shades to color your text. Applying color to the text element's box creates an opaque rectangle on the page with the text inside it, as shown in Figure 6-11. You can also color the text itself independently of the box's color (or lack of one).

But just because you *can* do something doesn't mean that you should. While coloring the box of a text element is appropriate whenever you need this effect, coloring the text itself can cause problems, particularly if you single out individual words here or there for the color treatment. Text of one color in the middle of text of another color looks suspiciously like a hyperlink to your visitors, who will no doubt try to click it. When nothing happens, they become frustrated—not a good thing.

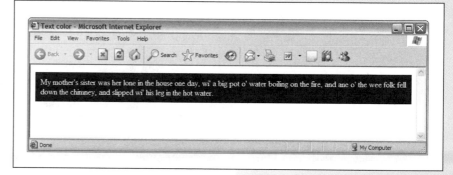

Figure 6-11. This paragraph has white text against a black background

That said, you can often get away with colored text if you use it consistently. For instance, setting all your headings in a different color than your running text doesn't normally lead to confusion, because the headings serve a different purpose than the paragraphs on your page. They're designed to separate sections of content, so your visitors are expecting them to contrast with the running text and therefore won't necessarily conclude that they are hyperlinks.

> **BEST BET**
>
> Avoid using two or more different colors inside the same text element.

—TECHTALK—
The weight of a border is its thickness.

Looking at borders

When you add a border to a text element, you outline its box, as Figure 6-12 shows. The border can be of any color and *weight* or thickness, and you may choose from several styles, including solid, dashed, and dotted.

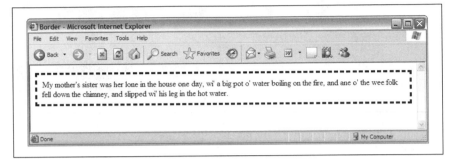

Figure 6-12. This paragraph has a dashed border

Borders around text elements work especially well when you also color the element's box. The effect is perfect for sidebars, special-attention-type announcements, and the like.

> **TIP**
>
> You can set each side of the border independently. So the top and left borders can be one color, weight, and style, for example, while the right and bottom borders can be another color, weight, and style.
>
> You can also leave off any of the four sides of the border while keeping the others.

Designing Text Hyperlinks

The best hyperlinks are like bad ties in that they leap off the background and burn themselves assiduously into the foreground. Therefore, the design of your hyperlinks isn't the place to demonstrate your subtlety and sensitive artistic nature. Your links have to catch the roving eyes of your visitor and entice the mouse to the all-important ritual of the click. They do this by standing out in sharp contrast from their surroundings. An old web designer trick is to stand about five feet from the monitor and squint hard. If all you see is the vague shape of your layout, the blur of your main navigation, and the hyperlinks buried in the running text of the main content area, then consider your job done.

Looking at Link States

Hyperlinks have three different appearances or *states*: the unvisited state, the visited state, and the active state. The *unvisited state* is the appearance of the link when the visitor hasn't yet been to the destination of the link, at least as far back as the browser remembers. Not surprisingly, the *visited state* is the appearance of the link when the visitor has already been to its destination. Finally, the *active state* is the appearance of the link when the visitor is actually clicking the link or, in the case of Internet Explorer, when the visitor passes focus to the link by pressing the Tab key.

Traditionally, web designers have used different colors to distinguish the three link states. Blue is the standard color for unvisited links, while purple or magenta is standard for visited links, and red is standard for active links. While you can easily set the colors of the three states to be anything that you want, you should go out of your way to use the standard colors in your design. Most of your visitors already know what these colors mean, which makes your site that much easier to use. If you do deviate from the standards, make sure that you apply your color choices consistently, across all the pages of your site. It's no good using green for unvisited links on one page and yellow for unvisited links on another page. Make them all green or all yellow. Your visitors will thank you.

> **BEST BET**
>
> Stick to the standard colors for link states. Barring that, use custom link colors consistently.

Getting Rid of the Underline

Most links come with underlines. The underline, along with the link-state color, helps to call attention to the link when it sits in the middle of running text.

It used to be that the underline of a link was unchangeable. The browser automatically added the underline to all links, and that was that. But with the advent of Cascading Style Sheets, the omnipresent underline became fair game. You can now remove the underline with a simple instruction in your stylesheet.

The wisdom of this practice is debatable, though. The underline is synonymous with the hyperlink in the conceptual vocabulary of the Web, to the extent that visitors click on anything with an underline, even if it isn't a link. When you remove the underline from your links, your design can't benefit from this powerful, universal *affordance*, or visual cue.

TECHTALK

Text hyperlinks have three different appearances or states: the unvisited state, where the visitor hasn't yet been to the link's destination; the visited state, where the visitor has been to the link's destination; and the active state, where the visitor is actually clicking the link.

TECHTALK

An affordance is a visual cue that suggests the purpose or function of an element.

If you insist upon removing the underline anyway, make sure that you replace it with something, and not just a different color. One of the guidelines of usability is that you don't identify something by color alone. When you remove the underline of your hyperlinks, your links might become invisible to people with color blindness and the users of the two or three black and white monitors still in service somewhere. Your links will certainly become less useful to the visitor who prints out your page on something other than a color printer. So if the underline has to go, replace it with boldface or italics or something that translates into a color-free medium, and use your new link affordance consistently so that the visitor gets the gist of it.

Adding Rollover Effects

Cascading Style Sheets provide for a fourth link state: the *hover state*, or the appearance of the link when the visitor rolls over it with the mouse pointer. When you add hover states to your stylesheet, your links can't get much more clickable. A link that changes appearance in response to the mouse reinforces the idea that it does something.

How exactly the link changes is entirely up to you, but here are a few tips for your consideration:

Don't lose the underline

When the visitor rolls over an underlined link and the underline disappears, you send a mixed message. The link should look like it's powering up, not shutting off. If anything, *add* the underline when the visitor rolls over the link—but make sure that something else besides color calls attention to the non-underlined version. (See "Getting Rid of the Underline" previously in this chapter.)

Changes in color are fine

For best results, choose a rollover color that looks like it's ready for action. Something bright and high-energy should do nicely.

Applying boldface and italics are generally all right

Rollover links can turn bold or italic if you'd like, but be careful about where and how you use this effect. Boldface and italic type styles usually take up a little extra space on the screen than the normal font. To make room, the browser redraws the line of type on which the link occurs, which may force a reflow of the surrounding lines. If this happens, the visitor might suddenly lose the link.

Avoid changes in type size

Small changes in size, like within a pixel or two, might be all right, depending upon your site. Anything larger than that forces reflow, and you get a lurching page. Talk about movable type.

—TECHTALK—

The hover state is the appearance of a link when the visitor rolls over it with the mouse pointer.

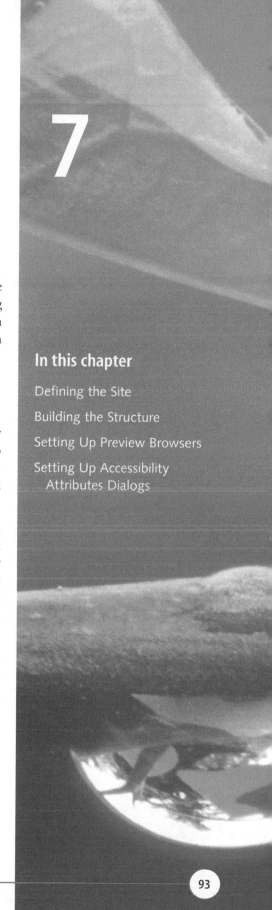

Setting Up Your Site

7

All right, you've thought through things enough. You've reserved your place on the World Wide Web. You know what the structure of your site is going to be. You've sketched the general layout of the pages. You've sorted through your options for images and text. Now it's time to get down to business. In this chapter, you set up your site in Dreamweaver.

Defining the Site

The first step in creating a new site in Dreamweaver is to provide a few key details about your project, such as where to save your files and how to connect to your web host. In Dreamweaver lingo, this is *defining* your site. When you define a new site, you calibrate Dreamweaver, so to speak—you set up Dreamweaver to work with the site.

While you don't have to define a site to start building and editing web pages, you should never skip this important step. Many of Dreamweaver's most useful features, such as checking for broken links and keeping track of your images, won't work unless you've defined your site. Also, if you manage more than one site at a time, your site definitions become all the more essential. Dreamweaver can handle multiple sites simultaneously, but it needs to know which site is which.

Defining a site isn't hard. As a matter of fact, you did the hard work already when you planned your site in the first part of this book. What you want to do now is describe your plan to Dreamweaver. This chapter takes you through the process.

Starting with the Basics

To begin your site definition, choose Site→Manage Sites from the main menu. The Manage Sites dialog box appears, as Figure 7-1 shows. Click New, and from the drop-down menu, choose Site. This gives you the Site Definition dialog box shown in Figure 7-2.

> **TIP**
>
> To bypass the Manage Sites dialog box and jump right into the Site Definition dialog box, choose Site→New Site. But see "Backing Up Your Definition" later in this chapter for a good reason why you might want to keep the Manage Sites dialog box handy.

Figure 7-1. From the Manage Sites dialog, click New to define a site

Notice the two tabs at the top of the Site Definition dialog box: Basic and Advanced. Basic mode works very much like a wizard, in that Dreamweaver takes you through the most important parts of the site definition step by step. This is an excellent way for beginners to start, so click the Basic tab if it isn't already selected.

First, type a name for your site in the specified field. This can be the domain name of your site, but it doesn't have to be. Choose whatever name you like, and feel free to use spaces to separate the words. You don't have to give something that looks like a filename. Also, the site name isn't written in stone. You can edit or change it at any time, even after your site is complete.

The next field asks for the site's *URL*—the Universal Resource Locator, which is just another name for the web address, which is the same as your domain name. You reserved your domain name in Chapter 2, so you know your URL. Type it here, including the *http://* part, and click Next.

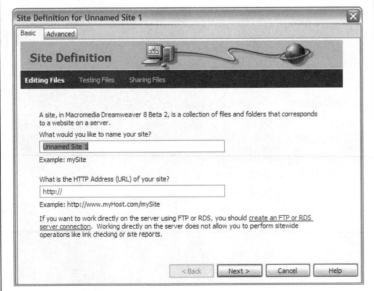

Figure 7-2. Use the Site Definition dialog box to define a new site

The next screen in the Site Definition dialog box asks if you're building a site with server technology such as ColdFusion or PHP, as shown in Figure 7-3. You know from Chapter 1 that server-side technology is essential for building dynamic, database-driven sites, but with that extra power comes a host of extra responsibilities and new technical challenges. For your first Dreamweaver site, client-side-only is the preferable option, so choose No if it isn't already selected, and click Next.

TIP

If you say yes to server-side technology, the Site Definition dialog box asks you to choose your server software before you click Next.

Now Dreamweaver asks about your production setup, as in Figure 7-4. The exact text of this screen changes depending upon your previous selection, but unless you're sharing site files over a local area network or working with a remote testing server, you want to select the option for editing locally. Local editing means that you store your site files on your personal computer. You make changes to your web site offline, and then, to publish your changes, you upload the revised pages to your web host.

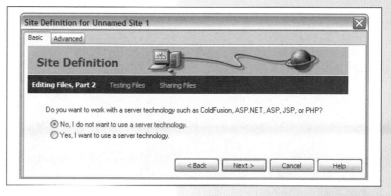

Figure 7-3. Specify whether your site uses server-side technology

The second part of this screen asks you about the *local root folder*, or the folder on your personal machine in which you store the files for your site. Dreamweaver supplies a default location and automatically creates the folder for you. On Windows computers, Dreamweaver creates the local root folder in *My Document*, an eminently convenient place. If you want to choose something else, click the folder icon, and navigate to your preferred location. Otherwise, go with the Dreamweaver default, and click Next.

The next screen in the site definition asks about your connection to the remote server. Remember that a remote computer is a computer other than your local, personal machine. In this context, the remote server is your web host. Unless you own a web server and host your site yourself, choose FTP from the drop-down menu. The appropriate fields appear in the Site Definition dialog box, as Figure 7-5 shows.

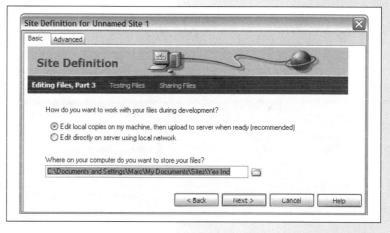

Figure 7-4. Choose your production setup

To fill out this screen, refer to the "Important Account Information" email that you received from your web host when you first signed up. If you can't find this email or never received one, visit your host's web site and look for the information there. If you still can't find it, get on the phone with customer service.

TECHTALK

The local root folder is the folder on your personal machine in which you store the files for your site.

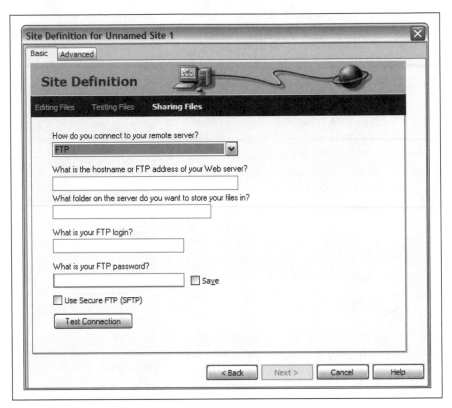

Figure 7-5. Supply information about your web host

BEHIND THE SCENES

You may have noticed that the Site Definition dialog box went from the Editing Files screens directly to Sharing Files, skipping over Testing Files entirely. The Testing Files portion of the site definition is for setting up a testing server—the computer that runs the server-side software in a dynamic site—which you don't need when you're building a web site with only client-side technologies.

—TECHTALK—

The remote root folder is the folder on your web host in which you store your live site files.

TIP

If you check the Save checkbox next to the field for your FTP password, you won't have to retype your password every time you upload changes to your site. Keep in mind, though, that by saving your password, you make it easier for mischief-makers in your household to get into Dreamweaver and make unauthorized changes to your site.

Pay special attention to the field labeled, "What folder on the server do you want to store your files in?" Here, Dreamweaver is asking for the remote root folder. Just as the local root folder is the folder on your personal machine in which you store your private site files, the *remote root folder* is the folder on your web host in which you store your live site files—the ones that your visitors actually browse when they come to your site. Your web host may require you to store your remote files in a particular location. If so, give that location here. Otherwise, leave this field blank. Don't automatically type the name of your local root folder! The folder names don't necessarily (and probably won't) match.

When you're done, click Test Connection. If Dreamweaver can't connect, double-check the information from your web host, and make sure that you've entered it exactly as your host recommends, down to the last dot and slash.

TIP

Windows Firewall may send you a security alert the first time that you test your connection, informing you that it has blocked "some of the features" of Dreamweaver "for your protection." The features that Windows has blocked are the ones that allow you to connect to your web host and publish your site. Dreamweaver isn't malicious software, so click Unblock.

Click Next to go to the next screen, where Dreamweaver asks you about Check In/Check Out, as in Figure 7-6. This feature is handy if you're working as part of a design team and you need to prevent multiple team members from editing the same web page at the same time. If you're a one-person production house, then Check In/Check Out doesn't make much sense, so choose No.

When next you click Next, you get a summary of your site definition, as Figure 7-7 shows. Review this information for accuracy. If you need to make any changes, click the Back button to step through the various screens in reverse order. Before you click Done, though, continue to the next section of this book, because you're not quite finished with the site definition.

BEHIND THE SCENES

On the summary screen, Dreamweaver reports that you'll set up access to your testing server later. Don't believe it. If you're building a client-side-only web site, you don't need a testing server, so you can ignore this cryptic remark.

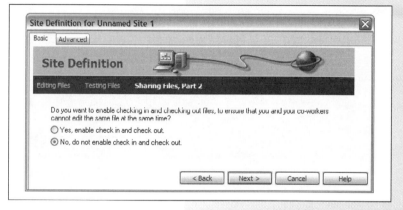

Figure 7-6. Specify your preference for the Check In/Check Out feature

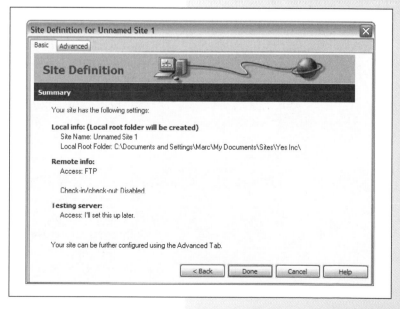

Figure 7-7. Review your site definition so far

Filling in the Gaps

While the Basic method of defining a site hits all the mission-critical categories, it doesn't ask you about every Dreamweaver feature that you might want to enable or disable. Therefore, after you arrive at the summary screen but before you click Done, switch to the Advanced view of the Site Definition dialog box by clicking the Advanced tab, as shown in Figure 7-8.

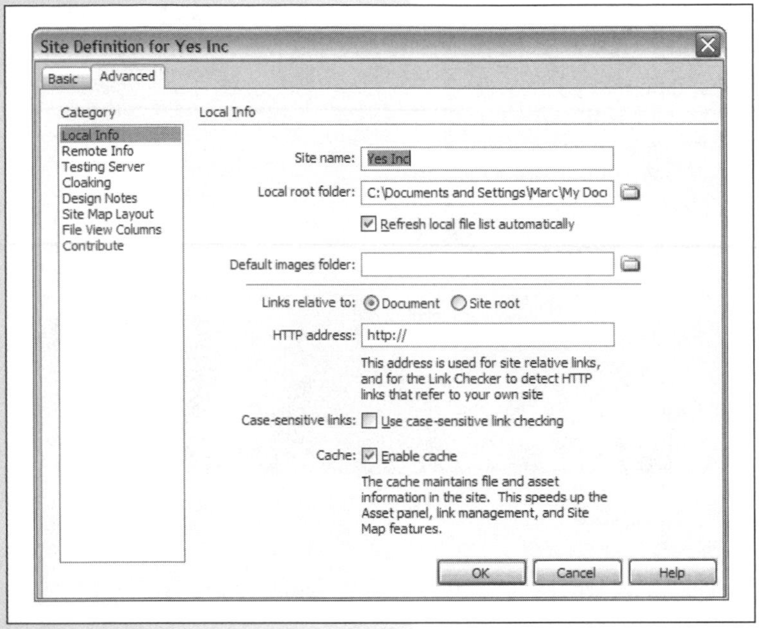

As you can see, Advanced view isn't a step-by-step wizard. Instead, you pick categories from a list, and the appropriate fields appear in the dialog box. By working through the Basic method, you've already supplied a lot of this information, so there's no need to revisit each category. You'll jump around a bit here.

Start by selecting the Local Info category. Then, toward the bottom of the dialog box, look for the Use Case-Sensitive Link Checking checkbox. Enabling this feature looks for discrepancies in the casing of your links (like *products.html* in the code when the actual filename is *Products.html*). Mismatched cases may cause problems with some web servers.

Figure 7-8. Fine-tune your site definition from Advanced view

---

TIP

After you've done a few site definitions, the Basic method might begin to feel like it's slowing you down. If so, you can always forego the wizard and jump directly into Advanced view.

Directly below this option, find the Cache checkbox, which should also be checked. The cache is Dreamweaver's internal record of your site's assets—links, images, multimedia files, scripts, templates, and so on. Enabling the cache speeds up site management operations.

Now switch to the Cloaking category, and the Site Definition dialog box changes to the screen in Figure 7-9. Under Options, make sure that the Enable checkbox is checked. Cloaking, in essence, hides certain file types from Dreamweaver. If you store these files in your local root folder, Dreamweaver ignores them, which is very convenient for files that you don't want to upload to your web host but that belong in your local root folder anyway.

Click the Cloak checkbox, and you see that
Dreamweaver is preset to ignore FLA and PNG
files—Flash and Fireworks documents, respectively. (Remember that Fireworks uses the PNG
image-file format for its production files.) You
may edit this list as your needs require. Just
remember to separate file types with a single
space, and don't forget the dot at the beginning
of each file type. Table 7-1 lists some of the most
common file types to cloak.

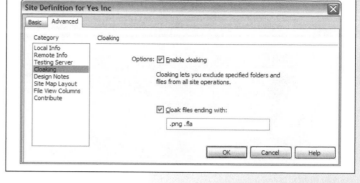

Figure 7-9. Cloaking hides certain types of
files in your local root folder

Table 7-1. File types to cloak

Files to cloak	File type
Director	.dir
Electronic PostScript (EPS) format	.eps
Fireworks	.png
Flash	.fla
FreeHand MX	.fh11
Illustrator	.ai
Photoshop	.psd

> **TIP**
>
> If you use PNG images on
> the pages of your site instead
> of or in addition to GIFs, be
> sure not to cloak PNG files!

Finally, select the Design Notes category, and the Site Definition dialog box
changes to the screen in Figure 7-10. Design Notes is a system for attaching comments to the pages that you build. This feature is helpful if you're
working on a production team. You can share
ideas, make constructive criticism, and submit
pages for approval through Design Notes. In addition, Dreamweaver uses Design Notes inter-
nally to improve the level of integration with two
other pieces of web design software, Fireworks
and Flash. If you don't have Fireworks or Flash,
and if you work alone, you should uncheck the
Maintain Design Notes checkbox.

After you've reviewed the status of these features,
you're finished with your site definition, so click
OK. The Site Definition dialog box closes, and
Dreamweaver adds your new site to the Manage
Sites dialog box.

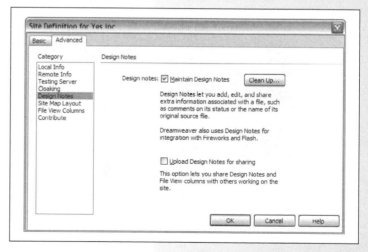

Figure 7-10. Enabling Design Notes

Backing Up Your Definition

Your data are valuable, and storage is cheap, so get into the habit of making
backup copies of everything, including your site definition. To do this, click
Export on the Manage Sites dialog box. (If the Manage Sites dialog box

isn't already open, choose Site→Manage Sites from the main menu.) The Exporting Site dialog box appears, as Figure 7-11 shows. Choose the option for backing up your settings, and click OK. The Exporting Site dialog box closes, and the Export Site dialog box opens.

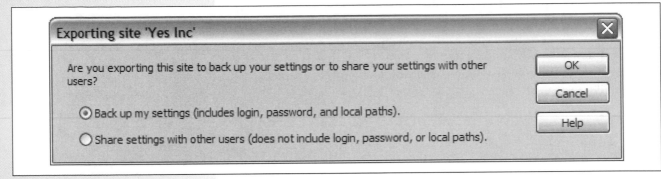

Figure 7-11. Back up your site definition with the Exporting Sites dialog box

Dreamweaver stores your site definition in a special file of the STE type. Browse to a convenient location on your computer, and click Save in the Export Site dialog box to make your backup.

If you ever need to recover a lost site definition, choose Site→Manage Sites from the main menu, click Import in the Manage Sites dialog box, use the Import Site dialog box to navigate to the STE file that you exported, and click Open.

Now that you've backed up your definition, click Done in the Manage Sites dialog box.

> **TIP**
>
> Remember to keep your backups up to date! Whenever you edit your site definition, export a fresh copy of your STE file.

Building the Structure

Remember in Chapter 3 when you created an outline for your site? At the time, it was a way to focus your thoughts about how best to organize your content. That outline is the gift that keeps giving, as you'll soon see.

During the process of defining your site, Dreamweaver created a local root folder, which is where you store your site files. You might be wondering how to go about organizing these files. To keep your web site tidy, it's common practice to create a set of subfolders inside the local root folder: one subfolder for each of the main sections of your site. The main sections come straight from your outline. All you have to do is create the subfolders.

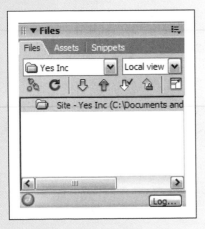

Figure 7-12. The Files panel lists the contents of your local root folder

Use Dreamweaver's Files panel for the job, as shown in Figure 7-12. The Files panel lists the contents of your local root folder (or remote root folder, depending upon your selection from the drop-down menu on the right). If you don't see the Files panel in the Dreamweaver workspace, choose Window→Files from the main menu.

First things first: make sure that the Files panel is set to Local View of your newly defined site. If not, change the drop-down menus at the top of the panel.

Now, pull out your site outline, and review the main content categories. Yours might be Products, Pressroom, About Us, and Contact Us. Four top-level categories equal four folders inside the local root folder.

To create the subfolders, click the local root folder in the Files panel so that this folder is selected. Then, right-click for the context menu, and choose New Folder. Dreamweaver adds a subfolder called *untitled* to the local root folder. Now, simply give the new folder a more descriptive name. Here are the rules:

- Try to keep the name to no more than eight alphanumeric characters—no punctuation marks or typographical symbols.

- Don't use spaces. Use underscores (_) or hyphens (-) instead.

- Stick with lowercase letters. Avoid capitals.

If your first content category is Products, then a logical folder name is *products*. Type this name, and press Enter or Return.

Notice that your new folder is selected in the Files panel. This is very important: make sure that you reselect the local root folder before you create a new subfolder. Why? Because Dreamweaver adds subfolders to whatever folder is selected. You don't want your second content-category folder to go inside the first one. Rather, you want both content-category folders to sit inside the local root folder at the same level.

> **TIP**
>
> Some of your main content categories may have subcategories. For instance, your Products section might be divided into Products/Current and Products/Archive. While you can certainly create subfolders called *current* and *archive* inside the products subfolder, this level of organization usually isn't necessary unless you're building a massive site.

After you have selected the local root folder again, right-click and choose New Folder. Dreamweaver creates a new, untitled folder. Give this folder a descriptive name, and repeat the process until you have subfolders for all your top-level categories.

You need one more subfolder to seal the deal. Go back and reselect the local root folder, right-click, choose New Folder, and call this one *images* or *img*. This subfolder will store all the images and multimedia files for your site.

This might seem counterintuitive at first. It may seem more logical to store product images in your *products* subfolder and digital snapshots of the home

— HOTKEY —
Press F8 to toggle the Files panel.

Figure 7-13. Add subfolders for main content categories and images

office in *aboutus*. Logic aside, it's more practical to have a single subfolder for all site images for two reasons. First, you don't have to remember which subfolder contains a particular image file. If all images go in a single folder, you always know where to look. Second, you don't have to move an image file to a different folder if you decide to place it in a different section of your site—a convenience that you'll appreciate if you ever need to do a major structural overhaul. Third, you improve the performance of your site. If two or more pages use the same image file, the visitor downloads it one time only.

When you're finished, your Files panel looks something like the one in Figure 7-13.

> **TIP**
>
> Want to make your first edit to your site definition? Set up a default images folder. Choose Site→Manage Sites from the main menu, select your site from the Manage Sites dialog box, and click Edit. Switch to Advanced view if it isn't already selected, and choose the Local Info category. Click the folder icon next to the Default images folder field, and another dialog box appears. Navigate to your *images* subfolder, double-click to open it, and click Select. Don't forget to export a new backup of your site definition before clicking Done in the Manage Sites dialog box.
>
> Now, when you add images to your web pages, Dreamweaver automatically saves copies of the image files in your default images folder.

Setting Up Preview Browsers

In Chapter 1, you assembled a small arsenal of web browsers for testing purposes. It makes sense now, here at the top of the production process, to configure Dreamweaver to work with these browsers.

From the main menu, choose Edit→Preferences, and the Preferences dialog box opens. The Preferences dialog box works just like the Advanced view of the Site Definition dialog box, in that you get a list of categories in the list on the left. Select a category, and the appropriate fields and options appear. To set up preview browsers, you want the Preview in Browser category, so click Preview in Browser.

Dreamweaver automatically detects your computer's default web browser and sets it as your primary preview browser. On Windows machines, the default is Microsoft Internet Explorer, so don't be surprised to see IE pre-configured in the preview-browser list. The *primary* designation means that this browser is associated with the hotkey F12. That is to say, when you're building a web page in Dreamweaver, you can press F12 at any time to view the page in your primary preview browser.

— **HOTKEY** —

Press Ctrl-U or Command-U to open the Preferences dialog box.

— **TECHTALK** —

Your primary preview browser opens and loads the current page when you press F12 in Dreamweaver.

No matter your personal browser preference, Microsoft Internet Explorer should *always* be your primary preview browser. The vast majority of people on the Web use IE. Most of the visitors to your site will use IE. If your site doesn't look right or work correctly in IE, then your site doesn't look right or work correctly, period.

To add a preview browser—Mozilla Firefox, for example—click the plus button. The Add Browser dialog box appears, as Figure 7-14 shows. Click Browse, and navigate to the location of your preview browser's EXE file. (For Firefox, on Windows machines, this is usually *C:\Program Files\Mozilla Firefox\firefox.exe*.) Double-click the EXE file, and Dreamweaver fills in the Name

Figure 7-14. Add a preview browser with the Add Browser dialog box

and Application fields in the Add Browser dialog box. If you prefer a less tech-sounding label, feel free to edit the value of the Name field to *Mozilla Firefox, Firefox browser, FF*, or whatever, but don't change anything in the Application field.

Under Defaults, you might consider making Firefox your *secondary preview browser*, which opens when you press Ctrl-F12 or Command-F12 and loads whatever web page you're building at the time. Check the Secondary checkbox to make it so.

When you click OK, the Add Browser dialog box closes, and Dreamweaver appends your new preview browser to the list in the Preferences dialog box.

> **HOTKEY**
>
> *Your secondary preview browser opens and loads the current page when you press Ctrl-F12 or Command-F12 in Dreamweaver.*

Repeat this procedure for Netscape and Opera, so that you have four preview browsers set up, as shown in Figure 7-15. With IE as your primary preview browser and Firefox as your secondary, Netscape and Opera don't have associated hotkeys, but you can still launch them from Dreamweaver with a few quick clicks, as you'll see in Chapter 8.

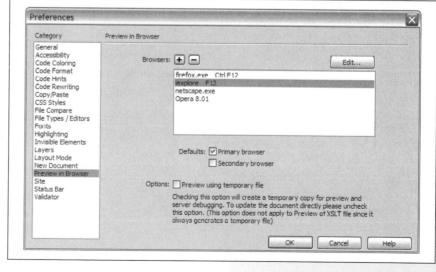

Figure 7-15. Your preview browsers are ready for action

Setting Up Accessibility Attributes Dialogs

Before you close the Preferences dialog box, you have one more quick trip to make. Click the Accessibility category on the left, and the Preferences dialog box presents a few handy options, which are shown in Figure 7-16.

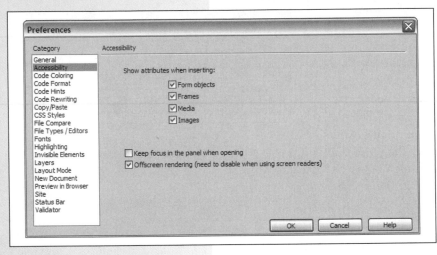

Figure 7-16. Review the accessibility options

TECHTALK

The long description attribute of a clickable image gives the complete URL of the page that loads when the visitor clicks the image.

The content that you add to your site should be as accessible as possible to people with disabilities. You may recall from Chapter 4 that the best way to make purely visual content more accessible is to provide text equivalents, or literal textual descriptions of the visuals. Standards organizations like the World Wide Web Consortium (W3C) recommend that you take additional measures in the HTML code to spell out exactly what's happening on the visual side of things. For instance, when you insert an image that also serves as a hyperlink, the W3C likes it when you supply a *long description*, or the complete URL of the page that appears when the visitor clicks the image.

To help you to remember these small details, Dreamweaver gives you four Accessibility Attributes dialog boxes. These dialogs pop up when you place a particular type of content on your page. To fill them out, you supply the relevant accessibility information. For example, when you place an image, the Image Tag Accessibility Attributes dialog box appears and asks you for the text equivalent of the image as well as its long description. You fill in this information and click OK, and Dreamweaver adds the correct markup to the HTML code.

Definitely make use of these dialogs. Check all four of them under Show Attributes When Inserting, and click OK to close the Preferences dialog box.

Designing Your Site

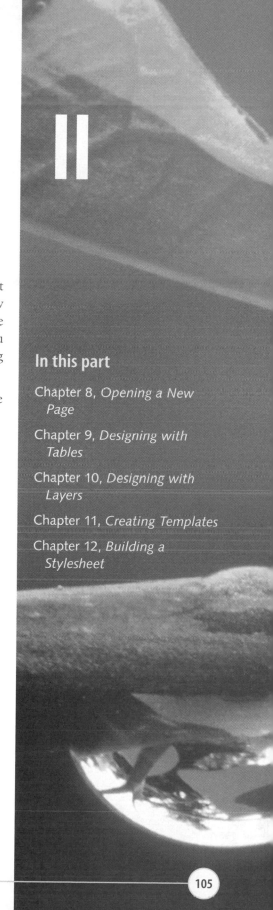

In Part I of this book, you developed a blueprint for your site. In this part of the book, you put your blueprint into action. You start by opening a new document window. Then you turn your layout sketch into a working page design, which then becomes the basis for all the pages in your site, and you transform your ideas for text presentation into a full-fledged Cascading Style Sheet.

Dreamweaver's ready to go, and so are you. Turn the page, and let the dreamweaving commence.

Opening a New Page

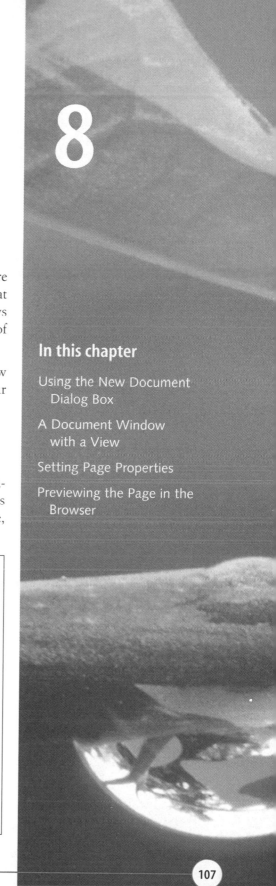

8

In most applications, to open a new document, you click an icon. There isn't much to think about. In Dreamweaver, it isn't quite as simple as that because of the sheer number of document types that the software allows you to create. The last thing you want to do is wade through dozens of options when you're eager to open up a new web page and start building.

This chapter gives you a straight course through the wilds of the New Document dialog box and shows you how to set the basic properties of your newly minted web page.

Using the New Document Dialog Box

Choose File→New from the main menu, and you get the New Document dialog box, as Figure 8-1 shows. This dialog box is a bit of a beast. The various categories of Dreamweaver documents appear in a list to the left. Select one, and the specific document types with their icons fill the list to the right.

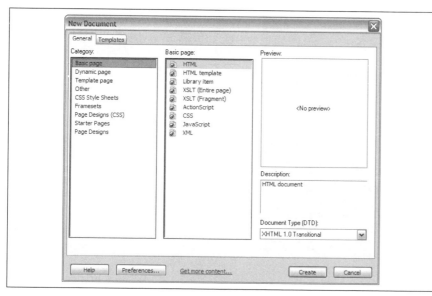

Figure 8-1. Exploring the New Document dialog box

Table 8-1 offers a peek inside the categories to give you an idea of what you can build in Dreamweaver.

— HOTKEY —

Press Ctrl-N or Command-N to open the New Document dialog box.

Table 8-1. Dreamweaver document categories

Document category	Includes
Basic page	Standard client-side document types, such as HTML, ActionScript, CSS, JavaScript, and XML
Dynamic page	Standard server-side document types, such as ASP, ASP. NET, ColdFusion, JSP, and PHP
Template page	Blank Dreamweaver document templates for static and dynamic sites
Other	Specialized client-side document types, such as Java, WML, C#, VB, VBScript, and plain text
CSS Style Sheets	Predesigned stylesheets
Framesets	Predesigned framesets
Page Designs (CSS)	Predesigned layouts using CSS layers
Starter Pages	Predesigned layouts with images
Page Designs	Predesigned layouts using tables

— TECHTALK —

The home page of your site is the page that loads when your visitor types your URL into the Address field of the browser.

For the time being, stick with the basics. You want to create a standard, client-side-only web page, so what you need is an HTML document. From the Category list, choose Basic page. Then, from the Basic page list, select HTML. Click Create, and Dreamweaver opens up a fresh, blank web page, as Figure 8-2 shows.

Before you do anything else, save this file. The HTML code that Dreamweaver writes is cleaner when it's working with saved as opposed to unsaved documents. As for the filename, go with *index.html*. This is the default filename for the *home page* of your site—the one that loads when the visitor types your URL into the Address field of the browser. Sure, your new document isn't much to look at now, but eventually it will become your home page.

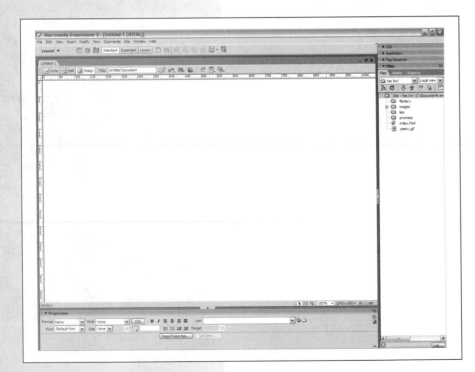

Figure 8-2. A new web page document in Dreamweaver

As to the location, save this page immediately inside your local root folder. Don't put the file into any of the subfolders. Your home page should be at the very top of the structure.

> **TIP**
>
> All the other pages in your site can have descriptive filenames of your choosing, like *products.html* and *aboutus.html,* but your home page should always get the standard *index.html.* Otherwise, the browser might not know which page to load when the visitor lands on your URL.

— HOTKEY —

Press Ctrl-S or Command-S to save the current document.

So choose File→Save from the main menu to get the Save As dialog box, make sure the location is immediately inside your local root folder (which it should be by default), type *index* in the File Name field, and click Save, as Figure 8-3 shows. You don't have to supply the *.html* extension—Dreamweaver does that for you automatically.

> **TIP**
>
> Now that you've named the file, whenever you select File→Save from the main menu, Dreamweaver skips the Save As dialog box and simply saves your file under the original name. From this point forward, if you want to save the document under a different name, choose File→ Save As.

Figure 8-3. Always save your new page immediately after opening it

A Document Window with a View

Dreamweaver provides three different ways of looking at your document window:

Design view

In Design view, Dreamweaver displays your web page similarly to the way that the page appears in a web browser, as Figure 8-4 shows. Use Design view to construct your page visually, but don't rely on it for a completely accurate representation of your page. It's more like a reliable estimate. The best way to see how your page actually looks is to test it in your preview browsers.

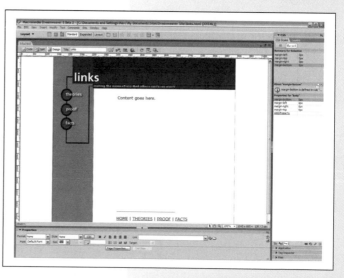

Figure 8-4. Design view gives you a graphical view of your page

Code view

In Code view, Dreamweaver displays the underlying code (e.g., HTML, CSS, JavaScript) of your web page, as Figure 8-5 shows. Code view works like a text editor, in that you can modify the code directly.

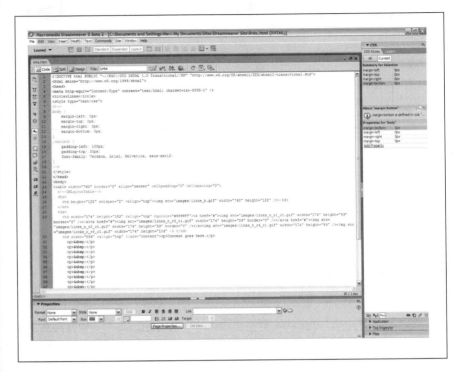

Figure 8-5. Code view shows the underlying code of your page

Split view (Code and Design view)

In Split view, the document window divides into two frames. The top frame shows the underlying code of the page, and the bottom frame gives the visual representation, as Figure 8-6 shows. Split view is a great way to learn HTML. You can draw the layout of your page and add content in the visual frame and then click in the code frame to see what's happening behind the scenes; or you can type HTML directly into the code frame and then click in the visual frame to see the results.

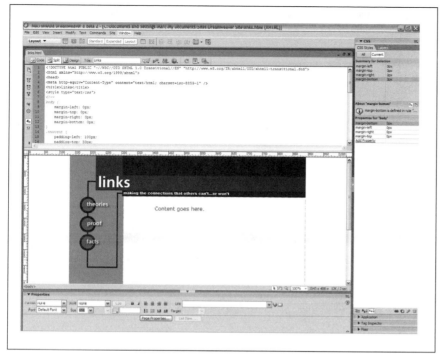

Figure 8-6. Get the best of both worlds with Split view

To switch among the views, use the buttons in the upper-left corner of the document window, as Figure 8-7 shows. For this book, you'll spend most of your time in Design view, which is the default choice.

Setting Page Properties

Now that you have a new document window, you can set up a few basic properties of the page. To do this, go to the main menu and choose Modify→Page Properties. The Page Properties dialog box appears, as Figure 8-8 shows.

Many of the categories on the left side of the Page Properties dialog box don't apply just yet. They're more for the elements that you'll add to your stylesheet in Chapter 12 (and you'll use a slightly different method for adding them). For now, you want to set the most basic appearance attributes of the page, and you'll start with the margins.

By default, when a browser displays a web page, it automatically adds a small amount of padding between the page content and the browser window. This little bit of whitespace can turn into a royal pain, because different browsers add different amounts of it. When you're trying to line up the areas of your design with pixel-perfect precision, as you'll do in the next two chapters, the last thing you need is a variable amount of whitespace throwing off your measurements.

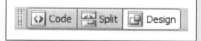

Figure 8-7. These buttons switch among the document-window views

—— **HOTKEY** ——

Press Ctrl-J or Command-J to open the Page Properties dialog box.

For this reason, it's good to remove the browser's default page margins entirely, so that your page fits snugly inside the browser window. If your design ends up feeling a little claustrophobic, you can always go back to the Page Properties dialog box and specify margin values of your choosing, thereby eliminating the x-factor of default browser settings.

To remove the browser's default page margins, click the Appearance category on the left side of the Page Properties dialog box, and skip down to the margins section. Set the Left Margins field to 0, and choose pixels as your unit of measurement from the drop-down menu to the right. Then do the same for the other three margins, so that your Page Properties dialog box looks like the one in Figure 8-9.

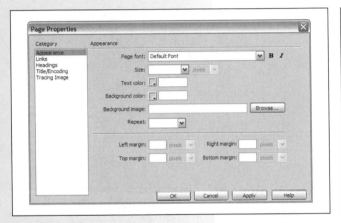

Figure 8-8. Set the appearance attributes of the page

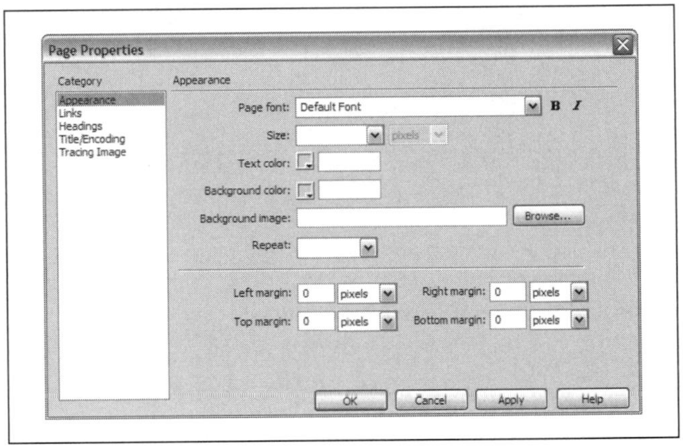

Figure 8-9. Set all four margin values to 0 pixels

Now, set the title of the page. Choose the Title/Encoding category of the Page Properties dialog box.

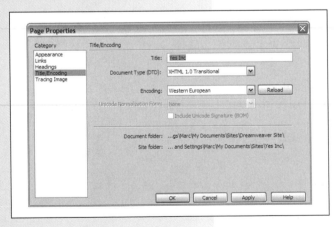

The *title* of a web page appears in the title bar along the top of the browser window. It does *not* appear anywhere on the page itself. You don't add this information so much for the sake of your design as you do for the sake of good coding practice. For now, in the Title field, simply type the name of your web site. Use the same name that you provided in the Site Definition dialog box in Chapter 7, as Figure 8-10 shows. As you create new pages for your site, you'll customize this title to reflect the content of the page.

Figure 8-10. Type the title of your web page in the Title field

Finally, if you created a tracing image for your site in Chapter 6, you may now attach it to the background of the document window.

Choose the Tracing Image category of the Page Properties dialog box. Click the Browse button next to the Tracing Image field, and in the Select Image Source dialog box, navigate to the place where you saved your tracing image. Click the image file to select it, and click OK to return to the Page Properties dialog box.

Notice that you can adjust the transparency of the tracing image with the slider in the Page Properties dialog box. For now, keep the tracing image at 100 percent opacity. If you have trouble seeing what you're doing because the tracing image is too overpowering, you can always come back to the Page Properties dialog box and decrease the opacity.

Click OK in the Page Properties dialog box, and Dreamweaver adjusts the properties of your page accordingly, as Figure 8-11 shows. Choose File→ Save to save your changes.

—TECHTALK—
The title of a web page appears in the title bar along the top of the browser window.

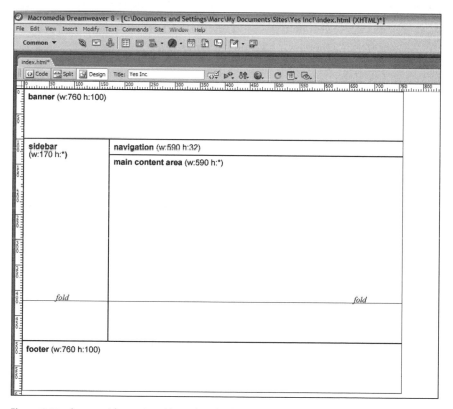

Figure 8-11. A page with margins, title, and tracing image set

Previewing the Page in the Browser

You know from Chapter 7 that when you press F12, Dreamweaver launches your primary preview browser and loads the current page. You launch your secondary preview browser by pressing Ctrl- F12 or Command- F12.

To preview your web page with browsers other than the primary and secondary, go to the Preview/Debug In Browser icon along the top of the document window. Click this icon, and a menu appears, as Figure 8-12 shows. Select a browser, and click.

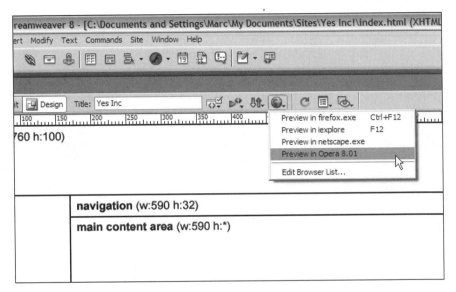

Figure 8-12. Select a preview browser from this menu

TIP

If you want to see the HTML code that Dreamweaver has generated for your page, choose View→Source in IE or View→Page Source in Firefox. Compare this listing with the one in Dreamweaver's Code view, and you should find that they're the same.

Test your page in all your preview browsers, just to make sure that they're all working properly. So far, the browsers do a consistent job with your layout. Notice that your page title is in the title bar, just as it's supposed to be, but there's no tracing image in the browser window. This is because your tracing image is a Dreamweaver-only visual aid. You'll use it to design your layout in the next two chapters, and then you'll remove it from the document window.

Designing with Tables

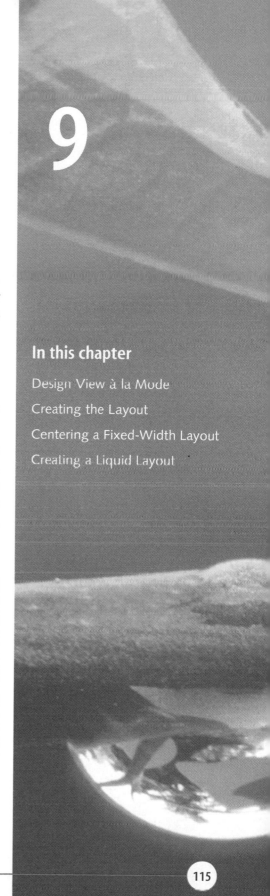

9

So, you're designing with tables, eh? You've opted for the solid choice. Congratulations on your sensible thinking. Tables are very stable, very easy to build, and very easy to convert into a liquid layout. This chapter shows you how it's done.

Design View à la Mode

To begin, go the Files panel, and double-click the file *index.html* from Chapter 8. Dreamweaver loads this file into a document window.

Now, to draw a layout table, you want to enter Layout mode. *Layout mode* is a special mode of Design view that offers table-drawing tools. Normally, when you add a table in Dreamweaver, you get a dialog box that is better suited for data tables—the kind with rows and columns of data. In Layout mode, you literally draw a new table directly in the document window, which makes more sense for page layout.

TIP

Layout mode places a rectangle with an Exit link across the top of the document window, partially concealing the tracing image. The annoyance factor of this notwithstanding, it can throw off the pixel measurements of the layout that you draw.

The heights of your areas aren't as important as the widths, so any distortions in sizing that Dreamweaver enables won't lead to serious problems down the road. At the same time, it *is* a bother, and if it's too much of one for you to overlook, you can remedy the issue easily enough. Go to the top of the document window, and click the Visual Aids button—the one with the eye icon. Choose Hide All Visual Aids from the menu that appears. After you draw the layout, be sure to unhide the visual aids by opening the Visual Aids menu and choosing Hide All Visual Aids again.

To enter Layout mode, go to the Insert panel and select Layout from the menu of objects on the left, as Figure 9-1 shows, and the clickable objects in the Insert panel change. If you don't see the Insert panel, choose Window→ Insert from the main menu.

—TECHTALK—

Layout mode is a special mode of Design view that offers table-drawing tools.

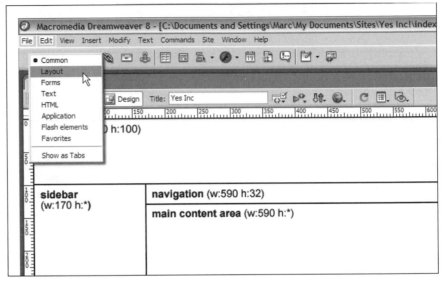

Figure 9-1. Choose Layout from the Insert panel's menu

— HOTKEY —

Press Ctrl- F2 or Command-F2 to toggle the Insert panel.

Now click the button that says Layout, and Dreamweaver enters Layout mode, which Figure 9-2 shows.

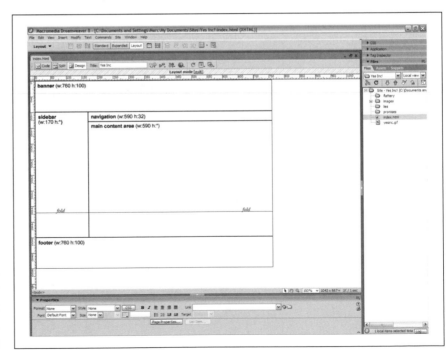

Figure 9-2. Dreamweaver's Layout mode

— HOTKEY —

Press Ctrl-F6 or Command-F6 to enter Layout mode.

Creating the Layout

To be precise about it, you don't actually place the content of your page into the layout table. The table itself is simply a container structure for *layout cells*—rectangular areas that sit inside the table. The cells form the layout, and you place your content inside them.

So drawing a layout table in Dreamweaver is a two-part process:

1. First, you draw the layout table in the document window.

2. Next, you add the layout cells to the table, one at a time.

For most types of layouts, when you draw the cells of your table, Dreamweaver creates *rowspans* and *colspans,* which are HTML attributes that allow the table cells to straddle more than one row (in the case of rowspans) or more than one column (in the case of colspans) in the grid of the table. For instance, in the tracing image in Figure 9-1 and Figure 9-2, the table cell that represents the banner area has a colspan of 2, because the cell straddles two columns: the one with the sidebar and the one with the nav and content areas. The same holds true for the footer area. Similarly, the table cell that represents the sidebar has a rowspan of 2, because this cell straddles two rows: the one with the nav cell and the one with the content cell.

Colspans and rowspans are fine for data tables, the "good" tables by W3C standards, but they're frustrating as anything for layout tables (yet another reason that tables aren't suited for graphic design, many critics point out). When a layout table uses colspans and rowspans, the cells of the table often add space in the least convenient places in the design when you start inserting content.

Fortunately, the technique of nested tables completely eliminates the need for colspans and rowspans in your layout. A *nested table* is a table that appears inside the cell of another table. That's right—the cells of your layout table can hold anything: text, images, Flash movies, and, yes, even other tables. The trick works like this: you divide the layout into rows that stretch across the entire width of the design. (The layout areas inside each row should not contain any colspans or rowspans, either! Otherwise, you're defeating the purpose.) Then, you place a nested table inside every row that requires columns.

This technique is easier to show in a picture than explain in words, so don't worry if the above sounds like babble, and have a look at Figure 9-3 instead. To avoid colspans and rowspans, divide this table into four rows, calling them A–D. The second row (B) divides the sidebar area, but that's unavoidable. Otherwise, you'd have a rowspan in the sidebar cell. Now you can build the columns of the layout in nested tables.

TECHTALK

Layout cells are the rectangular areas inside a layout table into which you place content.

TECHTALK

A rowspan allows a table cell to straddle more than one row, while a colspan allows a cell to straddle more than one column in the grid of the table.

TECHTALK

A nested table is a table that appears inside the cell of another table.

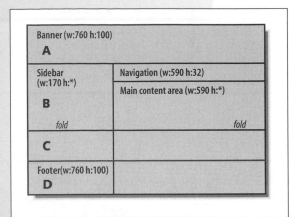

Figure 9-3. The thick grey lines indicate the four rows

A nested table goes into every row that requires columns:

- The top row (A) contains just the banner area. You don't require columns, so you don't need a nested table in this row.

- The second row (B) contains part of the sidebar area and the nav area. That's two columns, so you need a nested table in this row.

- The third row (C) contains part of the sidebar area and the main content area. Again, that's two columns, so you need a nested table in this row.

- The bottom row (D) contains just the footer area. No columns here. No nested table needed in this row.

Drawing the Layout Table

Start with the layout table. Go to the Insert panel again, and click the Layout Table object. This is the one immediately to the right of the Layout button, and looks like Figure 9-4.

Figure 9-4. The Layout Table object icon

Move the mouse pointer into the document window, and the pointer becomes a crosshairs. Position the crosshairs in the upper left corner of the document window, hold down the mouse button, and drag the mouse. Keep the mouse button held down as you draw. When the rectangle looks about the same size as your tracing image in the background, release the mouse button and Dreamweaver adds a green rectangle to your page to represent the layout table, as Figure 9-5 shows.

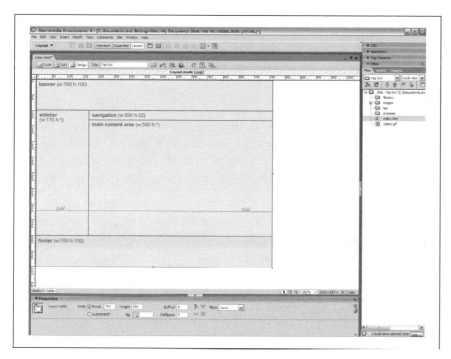

Figure 9-5. The layout table appears in green

Eyeballing the size of the table based on your tracing image is fine, but you want to make sure that the table is exactly as wide as it needs to be. So get out the layout sketch that you drew way back in Chapter 4, and note the page width that you chose: 760 pixels, 955 pixels, or what have you. (If you're planning to create a liquid layout, choose the page width on which you based your initial design.)

Then go to the Property Inspector (or, if you prefer, the Properties panel), which is directly below the document window. If you don't see it, choose Window→Properties from the main menu to get the panel in Figure 9-6.

In the Width field of the Property Inspector, replace the current value with the precise page width, and press Enter or Return. The layout table is now exactly as wide as your design requires (see Figure 9-6). Whatever you do, don't change this number! If you find that you need more height to work comfortably, you can safely increase the Height value to whatever you like. The height of your table isn't as important as the width. In fact, the actual height of the table is subject to change, depending upon the amount of content on your page. But the width should hold firm at its current value.

HOTKEY

Press Ctrl-F3 or Command-F3 to toggle the Property Inspector (also known as the Properties panel).

Figure 9-6. Adjust the layout table in the Property Inspector

Figure 9-7. The Draw Layout Cell icon in the Insert panel

TIP

As you work, you can adjust the position of a layout cell by dragging its border, and you can change the size of the cell by dragging one of the square handles on the border, although these procedures aren't always as easy as they sound. Once you get a few layout cells into the table, moving them and resizing them can get tricky, but not insurmountably so.

Any regions of gray in the layout table represent free space—space into which you can move or resize a cell. If you find that the table is too cramped for you to maneuver, just scale down the adjacent cells. Move or adjust the size of the original cell until you get it the way you want it, and then restore the surrounding cells to their previous positions or sizes.

Adding Layout Cells for the Rows

You have a layout table. Now you're ready to add the individual cells that represent the rows of the layout. Go to the Insert panel, and click the Draw Layout Cell icon, which Figure 9-7 shows.

Move the mouse pointer into the layout table, and the pointer becomes a crosshairs again. Position the mouse pointer in the upper-left corner of the table, hold down the mouse button, and drag the mouse to draw the first cell. Remember, you're drawing the rows that will contain the nested tables, so all your cells should stretch the entire width of the design at this stage of the game.

When the height of the layout cell looks correct based on your tracing image or the layout sketch, release the mouse button, and Dreamweaver adds the cell to the table. You want to confirm the precise size of the cell, so click its outer edge to select it. The table cell turns blue, and the Property Inspector gives you its attributes.

All good? Now go back to the Insert panel, and grab the Draw Layout Cell object again. Move the mouse pointer onto the layout table, and draw the next layout cell. Repeat until you have all the rows of your table, as Figure 9-8 shows. You don't want any channels or corridors of gray between the edges of two adjacent cells, so make sure that all the cells fit snugly against each other.

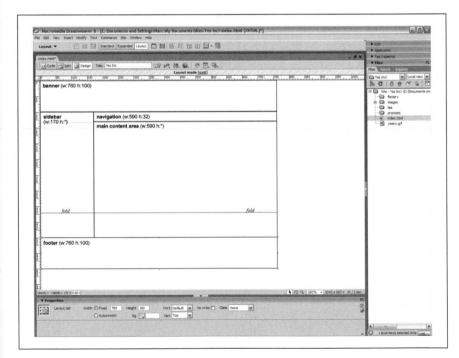

Figure 9-8. Draw layout cells for the rows of the design

Adding Nested Tables

Now that you have the rows, you can add nested tables to those that require columns. Go to the Insert panel, and select the Layout Table object. Move the mouse pointer into the first cell that calls for columns, click the mouse button, and draw the table so that it fills the entire cell.

If you have another row that requires columns, go back and get the Layout Table object again, and draw the next nested table.

Adding Layout Cells for the Columns

The cells for the columns go inside the nested tables. When you drew the nested tables, Dreamweaver automatically inserted a single cell into each, so your first job is to resize the existing cell so that it matches the width of one of the columns. As Figure 9-9 shows, click the border of the cell to select it, and drag the square handle to resize the column, adjusting the Width value in the Property Inspector as needed.

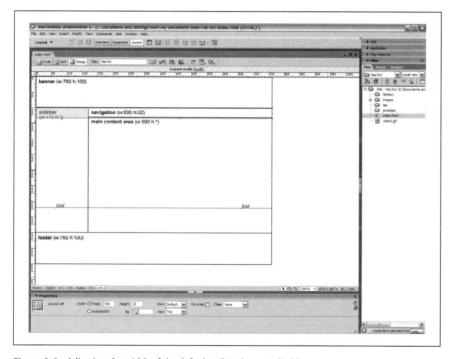

Figure 9-9. Adjusting the width of the default cell in the nested table

Now, with the Insert Layout Cell object, draw column cells to fill the rest of the row, as Figure 9-10 shows.

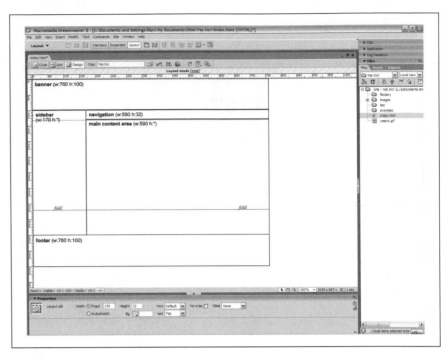

Figure 9-10. Fill in the remaining columns of the row with the Insert Layer Cell object

Continue on to the next row with a nested table. When you're finished adding the columns, your layout now matches your sketch or tracing image, as Figure 9-11 shows.

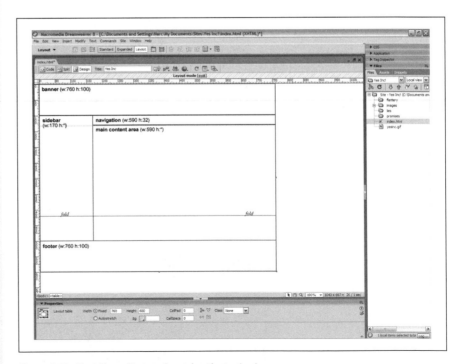

Figure 9-11. Your layout (in green) matches the tracing image

Losing the Tracing Image

Now that you've built your layout, you can safely lose the tracing image. It has served its purpose well.

Choose Modify→Page Properties from the main menu to get the Page Properties dialog box. Select the Tracing Image category on the left side of the dialog box. Then, highlight the contents of the Tracing Image field, and click Delete or Backspace to clear it. Click OK to apply your change and close the Page Properties dialog box, and Dreamweaver removes the tracing image, leaving you with just the green table outlines, as Figure 9-12 shows.

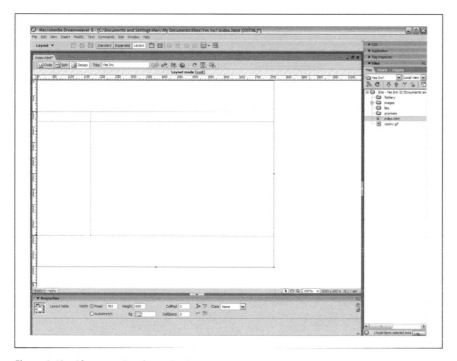

Figure 9-12. After removing the tracing image

TIP

If you want to keep the tracing image around for reference, you don't have to remove it entirely. Simply drag the Transparency slider all the way to the left.

Labeling the Cells

At this point in the process, you might find it helpful to drop short text labels into each table cell for easy identification.

Click the mouse pointer inside a layout cell of your choice, and a blinking cursor appears in the upper-left corner of the cell. Refer to your tracing image or layout sketch, and type the name of the area. Don't press Enter or Return afterwards; just type the name. Then click inside another layout cell, type its name, and repeat until you've labeled all the cells in the layout, as Figure 9-13 shows.

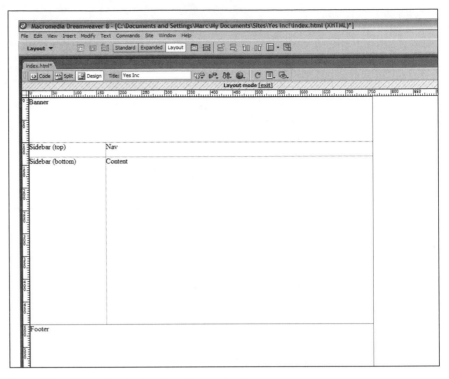

Figure 9-13. After typing short text labels into each cell

Centering a Fixed-Width Layout

You may recall from Chapter 4 that designers often like to center a fixed-width layout in the browser window. This little trick helps to reduce the effect of having too much whitespace, which happens when the size of the visitor's screen is wider than that of the design.

To center your fixed-width layout in the browser window, just follow these steps:

1. Select the layout table by clicking the Layout Table tab in the upper left corner of the table. You'll know you've selected it when the Property Inspector reads "Layout table" instead of "Layout cell."

2. You're currently in Layout mode. Go to the Insert panel, and click the Standard button to switch to Standard mode. The table remains selected.

3. Go to the Property Inspector, and choose Center from the Align menu.

4. Switch back to Layout mode.

Dreamweaver centers your fixed-width layout, as Figure 9-14 shows.

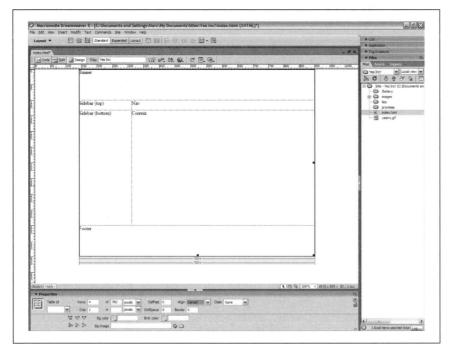

Figure 9-14. Center your fixed-width layout

Creating a Liquid Layout

To create a liquid layout, you convert the liquid areas—the ones with a width of *asterisk* (*), or *whatever*—into *Autostretch* columns. This isn't hard at all. You select a liquid area and click the Autostretch option in the Property Inspector, and then you resize the neighboring columns if necessary.

Give it a try. In the document window, make sure you're in Layout mode, and select the table cell of a liquid area by clicking the edge of the cell. Then go to the Property Inspector, and click the Autostretch option. The Choose Spacer Image dialog box appears, as Figure 9-15 shows.

A *spacer image* is the most humble of all possible graphics files. It's a one-pixel-by-one-pixel transparent GIF. But what it lacks in content, it makes up for in usefulness. The spacer image helps to maintain the widths of your fixed-width cells. Without a spacer, liquid layout tables are subject to all manner of browser mischief. The fixed-width cells don't always stay fixed. They change size in odd ways, and sometimes they collapse entirely. Your visitor can't see the spacer, because it's completely transparent, but to the browser, it's like a brace inside the layout cells, preventing them from collapsing.

TECHTALK

Autostretch is Dreamweaver terminology for a layout table or layout cell that changes width depending upon the width of the browser window.

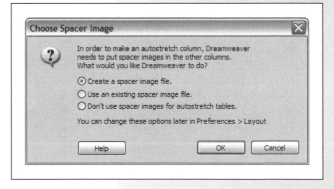

Figure 9-15. The Choose Spacer Image dialog box

TECHTALK

A spacer image is a 1-pixel-by-1-pixel transparent GIF that pads out a liquid layout table and maintains the widths of the fixed-width cells.

In the Choose Spacer Image dialog box, shown in Figure 9-15, choose the Create A Spacer Image option if it isn't already selected, and click OK. The Save Spacer Image File As dialog box appears. Double-click your images folder to open this folder, and click the Save button to create and save the spacer image to this location. Dreamweaver adds the spacer image to your images folder and liquefies the column, as Figure 9-16 shows.

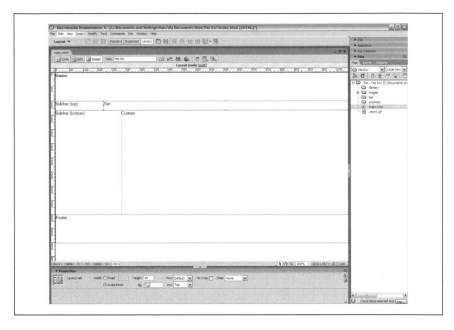

Figure 9-16. Convert the table cells of liquid areas to Autostretch columns

Keep going for all the liquid areas of the design. If at any point the width of a fixed cell gets thrown off, which is highly likely when you're dealing with nested tables, simply resize the cells, as Figure 9-17 shows.

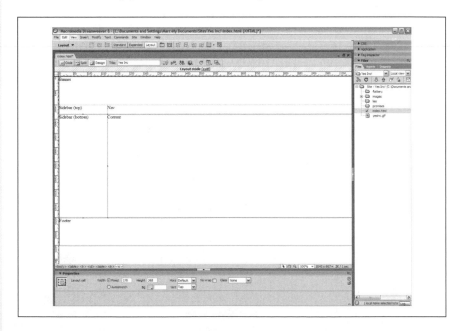

Figure 9-17. Resize cells that happen to get thrown out of alignment

Designing with Layers

10

So, you're designing with layers, eh? You've opted for the cutting edge. Congratulations on your forward thinking. Fixed-width layouts by way of layers are a breeze to build in Dreamweaver (as long as you don't need to center them; see Chapter 4 for a refresher). Liquid layouts require a bit more work, but you knew coming in that layers could be tricky, and if that didn't dissuade you, then you're up to the challenge.

Figure 10-1. Use the Layers panel to view layers and prevent overlaps

Whenever you work with layers in Dreamweaver, do yourself a favor and open the Layers panel from Figure 10-1 by choosing Window→Layers from the main menu. The Layers panel helps you to keep track of the various layers on your page. Also, from this panel you can prevent your layers from overlapping, which comes in handy when you're drawing the areas of your design. Make sure you check the Prevent Overlaps option before you do anything else.

TIP

The Prevent Overlaps option in the Layers panel only applies to layers that you manually drag in the document window. If you modify the positions of your layers from the Property Inspector, you can create layer overlaps that Dreamweaver doesn't catch.

When you have layer overlaps, the border of the overlapped layer appears as a dashed line in the document window. When you're building a page layout, you don't want the dashed line! All your layers should have solid borders.

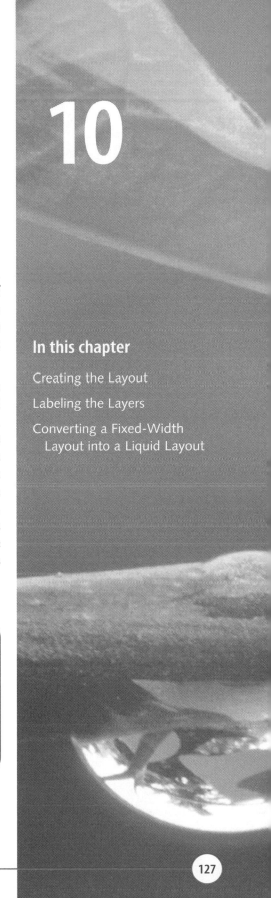

— HOTKEY —

Press F2 to toggle the Layers panel.

You should also go to the Insert panel and choose Layout from this panel's menu, as Figure 10-2 shows. The Layout collection of objects includes the one for drawing layers. If you don't see the Insert panel on screen, choose Window→Insert from the main menu.

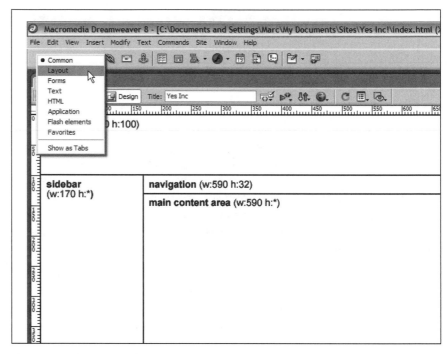

Figure 10-2. Choose Layout from the Insert panel's menu

Finally, if your document window happens to be in Layout mode (see Chapter 9), you want to switch to Standard mode by clicking the Standard button in the Insert panel. When you're in Layout mode, the object for drawing layers is grayed out.

With these settings made, you're ready to draw your layout.

— HOTKEY —

Press Ctrl-F2 or Command-F2 to toggle the Insert panel.

Creating the Layout

To begin, go to the Insert panel, and click the Draw Layer icon, as Figure 10-3 shows. Move the mouse pointer into the document window, and it turns into a crosshairs.

Choose the topmost area to start. Position the crosshairs in the upper-left corner of this area. Then hold down the mouse button, and drag the mouse to draw the layer. When the size of the layer closely matches the one in your tracing image or layout sketch, release the mouse button, and Dreamweaver adds the layer to the page, as Figure 10-4 shows.

Figure 10-3. The Draw Layer icon on the Insert panel

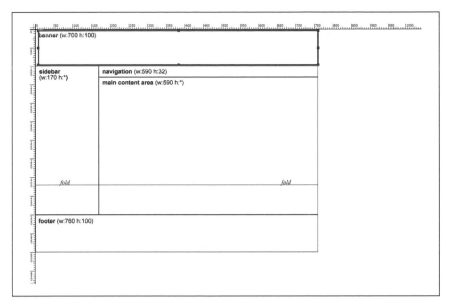

Figure 10-4. Your layer appears with a thick blue border

While this layer is selected, go to the Property Inspector (also called the Properties panel) at the bottom of the screen. If you don't see it, choose Window→Properties from the main menu.

Note four key fields in the Property Inspector: L, T, W, and H. These stand for *left offset*, *top offset*, *width*, and *height*, respectively. The values in the L and T fields control the position of the layer on the screen. For instance, a layer with a left offset of 10 pixels and a top offset of 20 pixels appears 10 pixels from the left side of the browser window and 20 pixels from the top. The values in the W and H fields control the size of the layer, as you might expect.

All the layers that form the topmost row of your layout, such as the one for the banner, should have a T value of 0—that's zero offset from the top, which positions the layer at the very top of the browser window. Similarly, all the layers that form the leftmost column of your layout, like the navigation area in a side-nav design, need to have an L value of 0 to position them snugly against the left side of the browser window. If your layer touches the top of the browser window *and* runs down the left side, then both the T and the L values should be 0.

> **HOTKEY**
>
> *Press Ctrl-F3 or Command-F3 to toggle the Property Inspector (also known as the Properties panel).*

BEST BET

All the layers that form the topmost row of your layout should have a T value of 0 and all the layers that form the leftmost column should have an L value of 0.

Unless you have a very steady hand, your first layer is probably off by a couple pixels. You can remedy this by typing 0px in one, the other, or both the T and L fields of the Property Inspector. Make sure that you add the *px* (for *pixels*) to the end of the value, and don't separate the value and the units with a space. This is the appropriate format for CSS, from which layers derive their appearance attributes.

While you're checking values in the Property Inspector, make sure that the width and height of your layer match the measurements in your tracing image or layout sketch. If they don't, simply type the correct values in the W and H fields. Don't forget to include the *px*.

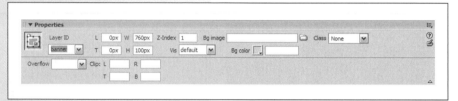

Figure 10-5. Adjust your layer in the Property Inspector

Notice also that Dreamweaver has given your layer the generic ID *Layer1*. The *ID* is exactly what it sounds like: a unique label to identify the layer. Left to its own devices, Dreamweaver simply numbers your layers in the order in which you draw them. While the generic, Dreamweaver-supplied ID is fine, you should probably change it to something more descriptive, like the name of the area that you just drew. This way, you don't have to remember which layer number corresponds to which area of your layout. So, type *banner* or *nav* or something to that effect in the Layer ID field of the Property Inspector, as Figure 10-5 shows. Just make sure that each of your layers has a unique ID. In other words, don't use the same ID more than once.

You've now added the first layer to the layout. Go back to the Insert panel, and click the Draw Layer object again. Move the mouse pointer into the document window, position it, and draw the next layer in your layout. For best results, build the top and left sides of your layout first, and work your way down and right.

BEST BET

Build the top and left sides of your layout first, and work your way down and right.

Always check the positioning and the size of each new layer in the Property Inspector before you move on to the next area in your design. Pay special attention to the T and L values. Your layers should sit snugly against each other on the page. If, for instance, your main content area sits immediately below the banner, and the banner has a height of 100 pixels, you know that the correct top offset for the main content area is exactly 100px. Likewise, if the main content area sits immediately to the right of the navigation area, and the nav layer has a width of 150 pixels, then the correct L value for the content layer is exactly 150px.

As you work, you can resize a layer visually by clicking its edge to select it and dragging one of the small square handles along the sides. Move a layer by selecting it and then dragging its large handle in the upper-left corner. Because you selected the Prevent Overlaps option in the Layers panel, you can't resize or reposition a layer so that it creeps into the territory of another layer, so you might have to change the size and position attributes of the adjacent layers temporarily to give yourself enough room for whatever adjustments you need to make. Just be sure to put the adjacent layers back where you found them.

When you finish, your document window looks something like Figure 10-6.

Congratulations! You now have a fixed-width layers-based layout that's ready for service. To remove the tracing image, so go to Modify→Page Properties, select the Tracing Image category in the Page Properties dialog box, either clear out the contents of the Tracing Image field or drag the Transparency slider all the way to the left, and click OK.

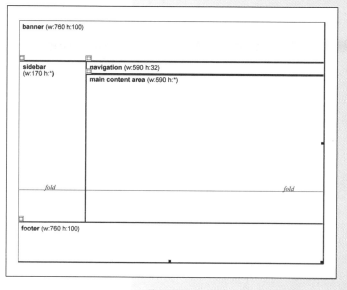

Figure 10-6. Add a layer for each of the areas in your layout

> **BEHIND THE SCENES**
>
> The *z-index* value of a layer determines its stacking order on the page. The layer with the highest z-index value appears in the extreme foreground of the page. The layer with the lowest value appears in the extreme background. The in-between values give you varying degrees of depth. In a page layout, the z-index value doesn't matter so much, because you shouldn't have any overlapping layers.

Labeling the Layers

Now is a good time to add a short text label to each layer in your layout. You already provided IDs for your layers, but IDs are more of a help for the technical side of things. Text labels are strictly for your benefit, so that you can see at a glance what goes where. You'll remove these labels once you add actual content to your page.

To add a text label, click inside a layer and type its name, as Figure 10-7 shows. Don't press Enter or Return afterwards; just move on to the next layer.

When you finish, choose File→Save.

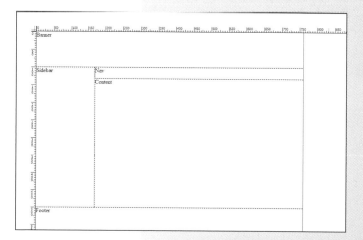

Figure 10-7. Label the layers

Converting a Fixed-Width Layout into a Liquid Layout

If you've leafed through Chapter 9, you may have noticed that creating liquid layouts is relatively easy. This is because all the cells of the table are related. They're all on the same grid, so to speak, connected in the larger framework of the table. When you change one, the rest follow. Think of it as an ecosystem. Think of it as a community. Insert your favorite metaphor from the political left here.

You get no such luck with liquid layers. Each layer is an independent entity on the page, completely autonomous and unrelated to the others. When you liquefy one layer, nothing happens to any of the others. Therefore, you have to select each layer in turn and carefully modify its appearance attributes. Where the layer sits in relation to the other layers of the design determines how you go about positioning it in the context of a fluid layout.

Some of these changes are so picky that the Property Inspector by itself isn't up to the task. For this, you need the help of Dreamweaver's CSS Styles panel, which Figure 10-8 shows. Choose Window→CSS Styles to open it. In fact, make the CSS Styles panel as tall as it can be by collapsing all the other panel groups on the screen. To do this, simply click the name of any expanded panel group.

Begin on the *right* side of the layout, not the left side, and work your way from right to left and then from the top of the design to the bottom. So select the topmost layer that touches the right side of the layout, and ask yourself the following questions:

- Does the selected layer stretch across the entire width of the layout, from the left side all the way to the right side, like the one that's selected in Figure 10-9? If so, see "Executing Plan A."

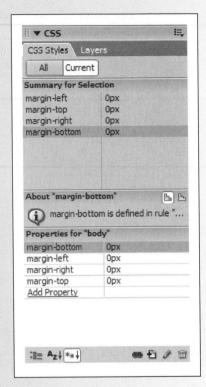

Figure 10-8. The CSS Styles panel

HOTKEY

Press Shift-F11 to toggle the CSS Styles panel.

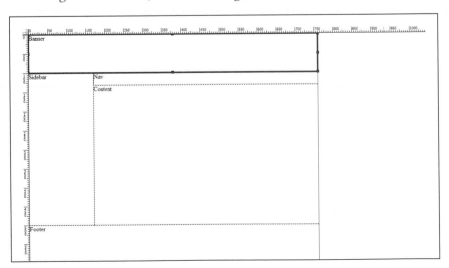

Figure 10-9. The selected layer spans the entire width of the layout

- Is there another layer immediately to the left of the selected layer?

  — Is the selected layer supposed to be fixed-width, like the one that's selected in Figure 10-10? If so, see "Executing Plan B."

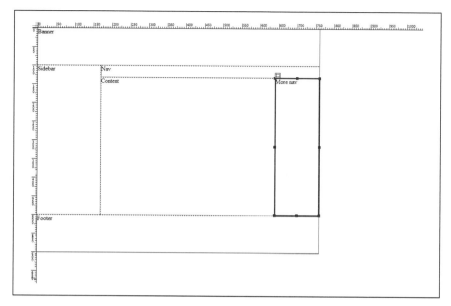

Figure 10-10. *The selected layer is supposed to be fixed-width*

  — Is the selected layer supposed to be liquid, like the one that's selected in Figure 10-11? If so, see "Executing Plan C."

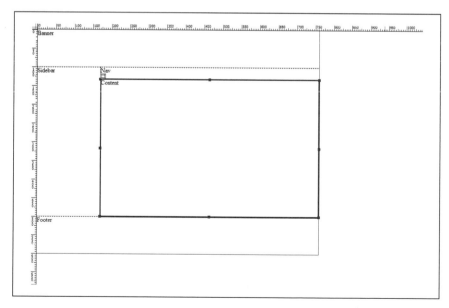

Figure 10-11. *The selected layer is supposed to be liquid*

- Does the layer sit against the left side of the layout, and is there a layer to its immediate right, like the one that's selected in Figure 10-12? If so, do nothing. You don't have to modify the properties of this layer.

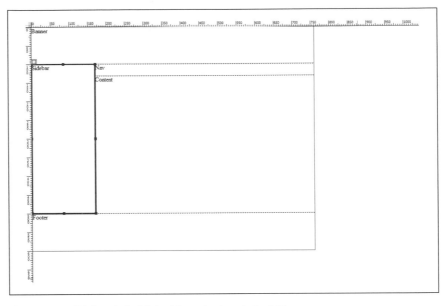

Figure 10-12. This layer is flush left with another layer to its right

Repeat this process for each of the layers in your design. When you're done, choose File→Save from the main menu.

> **TIP**
>
> If this procedure doesn't give you satisfactory results for your particular layout, you may be attempting something that is difficult to express in CSS by way of Dreamweaver. Try building your design with tables instead, or rethink the complexity of your layout.

Executing Plan A

To create a liquid layer that spans the entire width of the layout, follow these steps:

1. In the Properties list of the CSS Styles panel (the lower list, not the upper list marked *Summary*), find the entry for Width.

2. Click in the box to the right of this entry.

3. Type 100 in the first field, and choose % from the menu under the second field, as Figure 10-13 shows.

Do this, and Dreamweaver converts the layer from fixed-width to liquid.

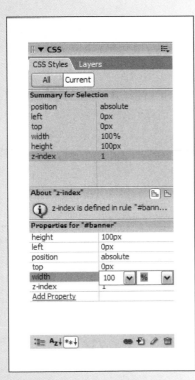

Figure 10-13. Liquefying a layer using the CSS Styles panel

Executing Plan B

If you have a layer on the right side of your layout, and if you want this layer to remain fixed-width, follow these steps:

1. In the Properties list of the CSS Styles panel (the lower list, not the upper list marked *Summary*), find the entry for Left. Select this property by clicking its name.

2. Go to the bottom of the CSS Styles panel, and click the Delete CSS Property button—the one with the trashcan icon. Dreamweaver removes the Left property from the list and repositions your layer with zero left offset.

3. Now click the Add Property link directly under the last item in the list of properties. The link changes to a drop-down menu. Choose Right from this menu, and two fields appear.

4. Type 0 in the first field, and choose Pixels from the second, as Figure 10-14 shows. It Pixels is already selected, simply press Enter or Return.

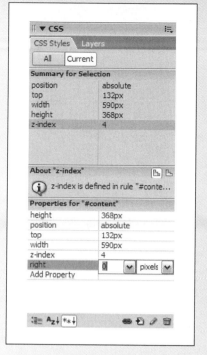

As a result, Dreamweaver pushes the layer to the right side of the document window. Why? Because you have just specified that this layer has no right offset value; that is, its correct position is 0 pixels from the right side of the browser window.

5. Select the layer immediately to the left of the one that you just adjusted.

6. Is the newly selected layer supposed to be liquid or fixed-width? If it's supposed to be liquid, proceed to Step 7. If it's supposed to be fixed-width, go back to Step 1—but instead of setting the right offset to 0 in Step 4, set the right offset to clear the layer (or layers) on the right.

Figure 10-14. Making a flush-right fixed-width layer

So if you want to have two fixed-width layers side by side on the right side of your design, the rightmost layer requires a right offset of 0 pixels to position it on the far right of the browser window. However, the layer to its left needs a right offset so that the two layers don't overlap. If the rightmost layer has a width of 100 pixels, then 100 pixels is the correct right offset for the layer to its left.

7. In the Properties list of the CSS Styles panel, find the entry for Width, and click in the box to the right of this entry. Two fields appear.

8. Choose Auto from the menu under the first field, as Figure 10-15 shows.

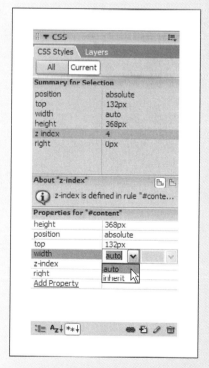

9. Click the Add Property link again, and choose Right from this menu.

10. Set the right offset to the combined width (in pixels) of all the layers on the right side of the design.

Doing this prevents the liquid layer from overlapping the layer or layers on the right.

Figure 10-15. Setting the width of a layer to automatic

Don't be alarmed if the width of your liquid layer shrinks to match the width of its content—in this case, the text label that you typed in the last section. This is a necessary side effect of layer liquefication, Dreamweaver-style. Happily, as you add content to the liquid layer, it'll fill out to its widest possible size.

Executing Plan C

If you have a layer on the right side of your layout, and if you want this layer to be liquid, follow these steps:

1. In the Properties list of the CSS Styles panel (the lower list, not the upper list marked *Summary*), find the entry for Width.

2. Click in the box to the right of this entry. Two fields appear.

3. From the dropdown menu under the first field, choose Auto.

4. Now click the Add Property link directly under the list item in the Properties list. The link changes into a dropdown menu. Choose Right from this menu, and two fields appear.

5. Type 0 in the first field, and choose Pixels from the second. If Pixels is already selected, simply press Enter or Return.

Again, the width of the liquid layer shrinks to fit its current content, and again this is all right. It will expand to fit whatever you put inside it.

Creating Templates

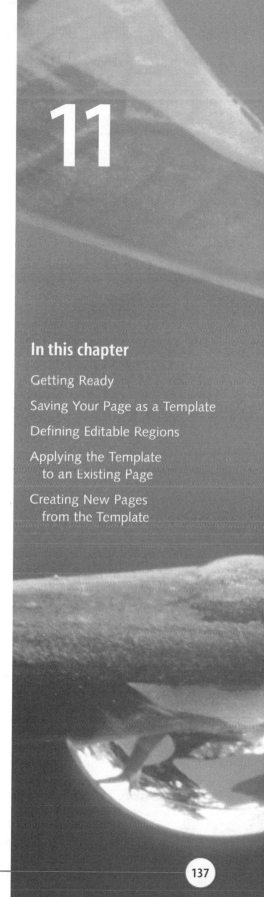

11

If you look at the layout that you created in Chapter 9 or Chapter 10 and think ahead to what these areas will actually contain, you'll realize that many if not most of them will show exactly the same content on every page of your site. For example, your logo or banner isn't likely to change from page to page. Your main navigation probably also falls into this category, as do portions of your main content area, like the space at the bottom for the secondary navigation or a place at the top for second-level or third-level navigation choices. In fact, it's highly likely that the only information that *will* change from page to page is the stuff in the middle of the main content area and the items in the sidebar, if you have one. Instead of adding the very same content to each page of your site over and over again, wouldn't it be nice to add this repeated stuff once and then have Dreamweaver automatically place it in the document window whenever you open a new page for your site?

Wish granted! A Dreamweaver template does exactly this. A *Dreamweaver template* is a special document that contains all the permanent elements of your site, like the layout, the logo, the banner, the main navigation, and whatever else fits into this category for your particular project. You add these elements to the template, and Dreamweaver locks them in. Open a new document window from this template, and Dreamweaver places all the permanent content exactly where you want it.

What about the sections that change from page to page, like the middle part of the main content area? You can easily make room for these in your template by defining them as *editable regions*: variable areas with no fixed content. Inside an editable region, you're free to add whatever content best suits the page in question.

It gets better. Assume that you're halfway through production, and you realize that you need to increase the width of your main content area. This change is easy enough to make in Dreamweaver, but it's still a hassle to go through every page of your site and adjust the same values in the Property Inspector. Or maybe you want to change the image in the banner area. Again, this is a simple Dreamweaver procedure, but to change the same image 70 times on 70 different pages? Who has the time for that? But when you build your site from a template, you can make these kinds of changes once, in the template document itself, and with a click of the mouse, Dreamweaver updates all the pages of your site—*without* affecting any of the variable content in the editable regions.

Dreamweaver templates are so helpful and so conducive to lightning-fast production that one wonders why anyone would build a Dreamweaver site without them. This chapter shows you how to convert your *index.html* document into a template, which you will then use to produce new pages.

> **TIP**
>
> This chapter concentrates on the main design template, or the one that controls the look and feel for the majority of your pages. However, some sites, particularly larger ones, use different layouts for different content areas or different levels of pages. If this describes your site, you can easily create a separate template document for every one of your layouts.

Getting Ready

To begin, fire up Dreamweaver, and open your *index.html* document from Chapter 9 or Chapter 10. This page contains the skeleton layout for your site.

Knowing which content is fixed and which is variable is the secret to designing effective templates, so it's worth reviewing the plan for your site and setting up the template document accordingly. By way of example, Figure 11-1 shows the general mockup for your new client's web site, and Figure 11-2 shows the corresponding tables-based layout that you've created so far and saved as *index.html*. Now, given this design, which areas (or sections of areas) are fixed, and which are variable?

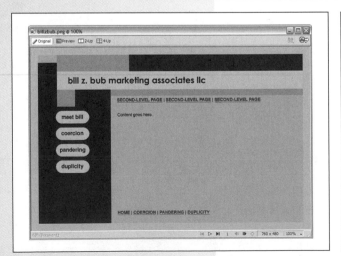

Figure 11-1. The general mockup for your latest client's web page

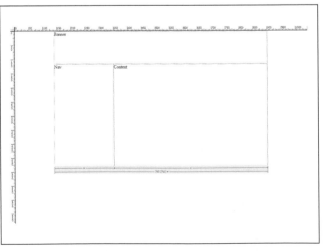

Figure 11-2. The layout that you've created for this site

You decide that the banner is fixed content, because it remains unchanged from page to page. The same goes for the secondary navigation (i.e., the list of links at the bottom of the main content area).

By contrast, the second-level links at the top of the main content area do change from page to page, as does whatever appears in the "Content goes here" section, so these need to sit inside editable regions of the template.

What about the nav bar? Is it fixed or variable? This depends upon the style of nav bar that you plan on building.

Assume that you're planning a nav bar like the one in Figure 11-3, where the buttons of the nav bar don't change their default appearance depending upon the page. In a case like this, the nav bar is fixed content.

A nav bar like the one in Figure 11-4, though, is variable content, because the default style of the button *does* change depending upon the page. In this design, when the visitor lands on the Meet Bill page, the Meet Bill button in the nav bar becomes a simple text label to reinforce the idea of "You are here." By this logic, on the Coercion page, the Meet Bill button reverts to normal, while the Coercion button becomes a text label; a similar behavior happens on all the pages of the site.

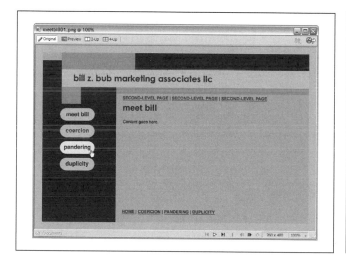

Figure 11-3. An example of a fixed-content nav bar

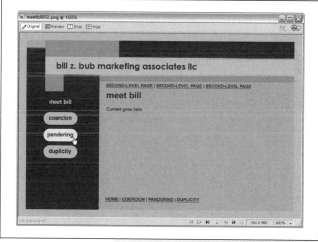

Figure 11-4. An example of a variable-content nav bar

> **BEST BET**
>
> If the buttons in your nav bar don't change their default appearance depending upon the page, then your nav bar is fixed content. If they do, then the nav bar is variable.

For the sake of argument, say that you're planning a nav bar like the one in Figure 11-3, so add the navigation area to your list of fixed elements. Your mental worksheet looks something like this:

- Fixed content
  - — Banner area
  - — Nav area
  - — Secondary navigation (bottom of content area)
- Variable content
  - — Links to second-level pages (top of content area)
  - — "Content goes here" section (middle of content area)

To make the most of your template-building session, you should add a few content placeholders to your Dreamweaver layout. The goal here is to divide the main content area into specific sections so that you can choose which should be editable regions a little later in this process.

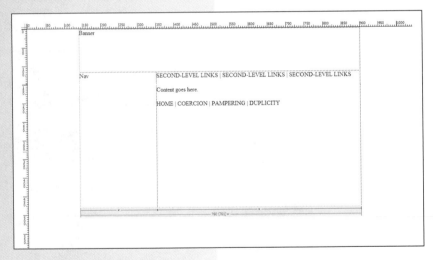

Figure 11-5. Placeholder text indicates the sections of the content area

From the looks of things, your content area has three sections: the second-level links at the top, the "Content goes here" in the middle, and the secondary navigation at the bottom. So go into Dreamweaver, click inside the Content area of your layout, and add these sections, as Figure 11-5 shows. You don't have to position the secondary navigation at the bottom of the Content area. Remember, the height of the content area depends upon the actual amount of content that goes in it. Right now, as long as the secondary navigation appears below the "Content goes here" section, you're in good shape. Likewise, don't worry about turning the items into links or formatting the text the way you want it. Just get the placeholder text into the layout to represent the three sections.

When you press Enter or Return to separate the lines of placeholder text, Dreamweaver automatically marks up the placeholder elements as paragraphs, as you can see by checking the Format menu on the Property Inspector. This is an important point to remember for when you add editable regions to your template (see "Defining Editable Regions" later in this chapter).

Now compare the items in your fixed/variable mental worksheet with the elements that you've added to your Dreamweaver layout, and you find that they're a one-for-one match, which is exactly how you want it.

Saving Your Page as a Template

The next step is to save your modified *index.html* page as a template file. Go to the main menu, and choose File→Save As Template. The Save As Template dialog box appears, as Figure 11-6 shows.

The current Dreamweaver site should appear in the Site field. If it doesn't, open the menu and choose the correct site.

In the Save As field, type a name for the template. This should not be the same as your home page, *index.html*. Come up with something else short and descriptive, such as *main* or *layout*. If you plan on creating several different templates for various styles of pages on the site, you might also leave a short text description of this template in the Description field, although you can also safely leave this field blank.

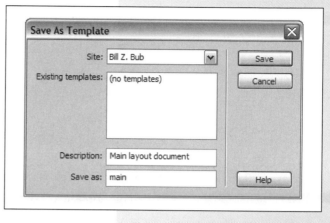

Figure 11-6. The Save As Template dialog box

When you're ready, click Save. The Save As Template dialog box closes, and Dreamweaver adds a new directory to your local root folder called *Templates* and saves your template inside it with the *.dwt* extension, as Figure 11-7 shows.

> **TIP**
>
> When you save your page as a template, you may get a dialog box that asks you about updating links. If so, click Yes. This dialog box appears when your page includes hyperlinks or pointers to external content, such as the spacer image in a tables-based layout.

Figure 11-7. Your template's new home

Defining Editable Regions

Dreamweaver assumes that all the content in the template is fixed unless you specify otherwise, so, now that you have the template file, you can add the editable regions.

There are two editable regions in this layout: the section for the second-level links and the "Content goes here" section. You might as well start at the top. In the template document window, click anywhere inside the section for second-level links. You want the blinking cursor to appear somewhere inside this line of text.

Now go to the Tag Selector, which appears at the very bottom of the document window, as shown in Figure 11-8, and click the `<p>` tag. The `<p>` tag stands for paragraph, as you may recall from Chapter 1. When you do this, Dreamweaver selects the entire paragraph that contains the second-level links.

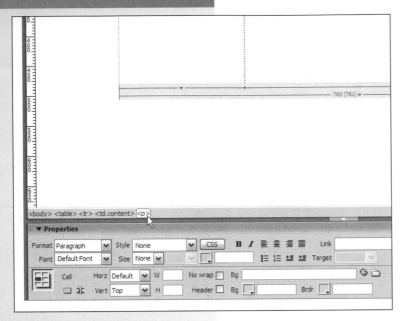

Figure 11-8. Using the Tag Selector to select parts of the document

The Tag Selector helps you to make very specific selections in the document window. If you had selected the text just by dragging the mouse across it, Dreamweaver might not have included the tag as part of the selection.

With the paragraph selected, go to the Insert panel, and set it to the Common category if need be. Then click the inverted triangle to the right of the template objects, as Figure 11-9 shows. Choose the Editable Region object from the menu that opens, and you get the New Editable Region dialog box, which appears in Figure 11-10.

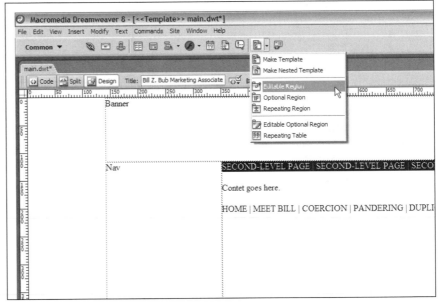

Figure 11-9. Choose the Editable Region from the Insert panel

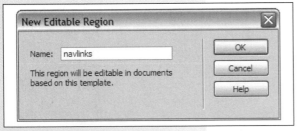

Figure 11-10. Mark off a New Editable Region in your template

Type a short, descriptive name for the editable region in the Name field, such as *navlinks* or *level2nav*, and click OK. Dreamweaver boxes off this paragraph as an editable region, as Figure 11-11 shows.

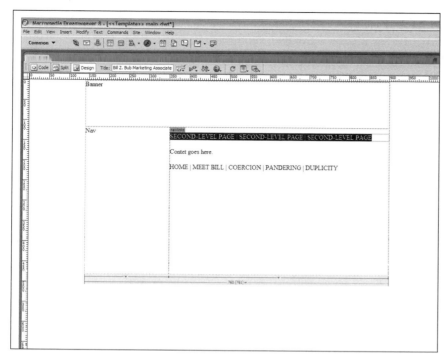

Figure 11-11. *Editable regions are boxed in turquoise*

So much for the first editable region. On to the second! Click anywhere inside the "Content goes here" placeholder. Then go down to the Tag Selector, and choose the paragraph tag, <p>, to select the entire paragraph. Now go up to the Insert panel, and click the Editable Region object to open the New Editable Region dialog box. Type a name such as *content* in the Name field, and click OK. Dreamweaver defines the new editable region, and your document window looks like Figure 11-12.

But what if your navigation bar is variable instead of fixed, or what if the banner area is variable? Not a problem. Simply use the existing text label as the placeholder for an editable region, with one minor modification. When you click inside the Nav or Banner text label, go to the Property Inspector, and choose Paragraph from the Format menu if this text isn't already in paragraph format. (It probably isn't, because when you added labels to the areas of your design, you didn't press Enter or Return. You just typed the label and moved on to the next area.) This gives you a specific <p> tag to click when you go to the Tag Selector and therefore guarantees that you select the entire element. With the paragraph selected, it's just a matter of clicking the Editable Region object, naming the region *nav* or *banner* or whatever makes sense, and clicking OK to add it to the template, as Figure 11-13 shows.

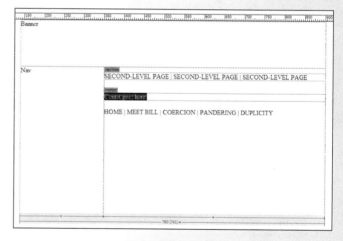

Figure 11-12. *The main content area is marked as an editable region*

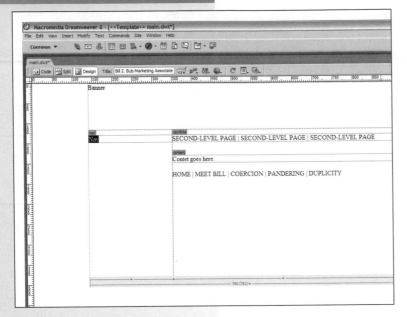

Figure 11-13. A variable nav bar set as an editable region

When you're done adding editable regions, choose File→Save from the main menu to save your template.

Applying the Template to an Existing Page

Your template file and the *index.html* page are now two separate documents. To associate *index.html* with the template, so that the home page receives automatic updates when you edit the content in the template, you must now apply the template to the home page.

To do this, go to the Files panel, and double-click *index.html*. Dreamweaver opens the home page in a new document window. (You don't need to close the template's document window, although you can if you want.) Then, from the main menu, choose Modify→Templates→ Apply Template To Page. The Select Template dialog box shown in Figure 11-14 appears. Click the name of the template that you want to apply, and then click Select.

> **TIP**
>
> On the Select Template dialog box, make sure that you check the option for updating the page when the template changes. Otherwise, when you change the content of the template document, Dreamweaver will keep the old template content on this particular page of your site.

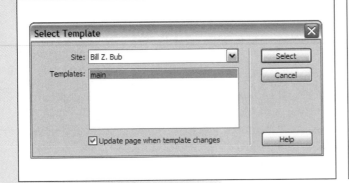

Figure 11-14. Select the template to apply

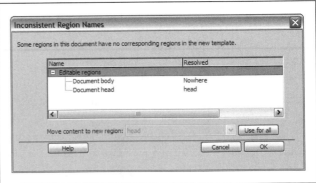

Figure 11-15. Choose what to do with the existing content of the page

In all likelihood, you receive the Inconsistent Region Names dialog box shown in Figure 11-15, which simply means that Dreamweaver isn't sure what to do with the existing content of the home page. It's up to you to explain to Dreamweaver how to handle each inconsistent item, by moving, deleting, replacing, or ignoring it.

- You should replace the current document body content. Select Document Body from the dialog box, and choose Nowhere from the menu.

- You should move the current head content to the appropriate editable region. Select Document Head from the dialog box, and choose Head from the menu.

BEHIND THE SCENES

You don't remember adding an editable region called *head* because you didn't add this region! Dreamweaver did it for you automatically when you created your template.

Click OK, and Dreamweaver applies the template to your home page, as Figure 11-16 shows.

Move the mouse pointer over the layout, and notice that the pointer turns into a "no" sign when you hover over any non-editable region. This is permanent, template-controlled content—you can still change it, of course, but you must change it in the template document itself.

Choose File→Save from the main menu to save your changes to the home page.

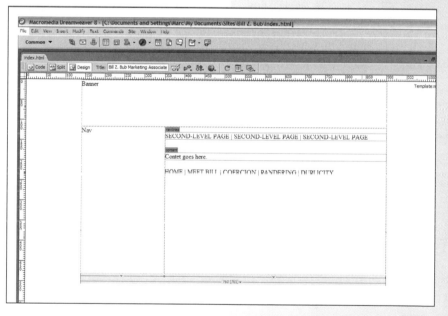

Figure 11-16. Dreamweaver applies the template to the home page

Creating New Pages from the Template

Now that you have a template, it's extremely easy to create new pages based on the template. Suppose you want to start filling out the structure of your site by adding home pages for all the top-level content categories: Meet Bill, Coercion, Pandering, and Duplicity. You created folders for these sections of your site in Chapter 7, but these folders remain empty.

Not for much longer! Go to the main menu, and choose File→New. The New Document dialog box opens, as before. This time, click the Templates tab at the top of the dialog box, and you get new options, as Figure 11-17 shows.

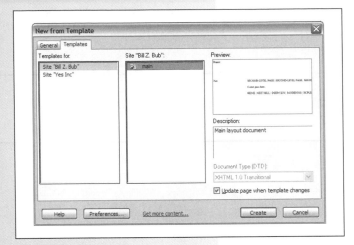

Figure 11-17. The Templates tab of the New Document dialog box

Select the desired template from the list and then click Create. Dreamweaver opens a new document window and automatically fills it with all the content from the template file, as Figure 11-18 shows.

Assume that you want to save this file as the main page under Meet Bill. In the Title field of the document window, indicate that this is the Meet Bill page. Probably the best way is to attach *Meet Bill* to the end of the existing title, separating it with a colon (:) or greater-than symbol (>).

Now go back to the main menu, and choose File→Save. The Save As dialog box appears. This is the Meet Bill page, so navigate to the subfolder for Meet Bill. Supply a suitable name for the file, such as *meet*, and click Save. Dreamweaver adds the new page to the appropriate subfolder of the Files panel.

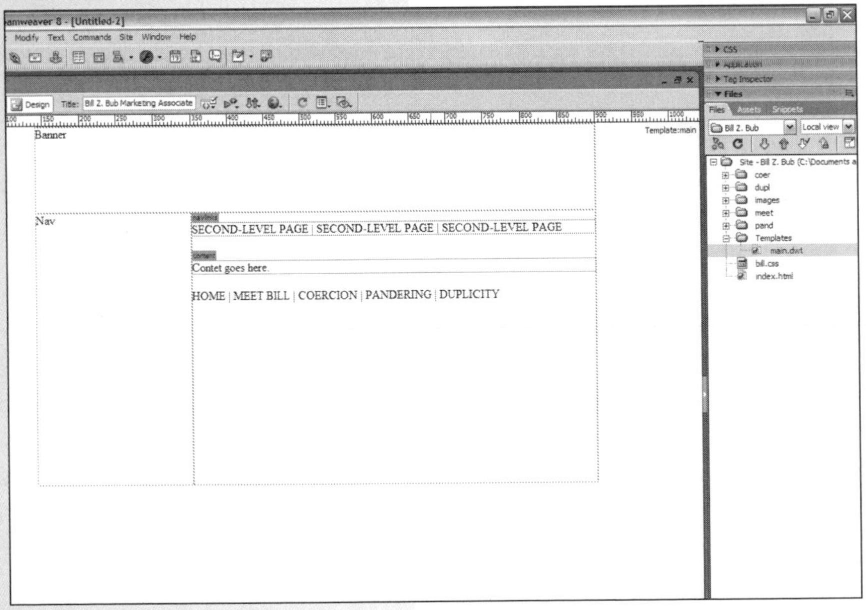

Don't stop there! Edit the document window's Title field to match the next top-level category: in this case, Coercion. Choose File→Save As from the main menu, and navigate to the Coercion subfolder. Save this file as *coer*, and you have another new page. Repeat this procedure for the rest of the top-level content categories, and in no time at all, your site is brimming with pages. These aren't just rinky-dink sample pages, either. They're full-blown production documents. In fact, these are (probably) the very same files that you'll publish to the Web at the end of this book. Because you created them from a template, they'll grow in step with the template document.

Figure 11-18. Create a freshly minted page based on your template

> **TIP**
>
> Remember, if you get a dialog box asking about updating links, click Yes.

Building a Stylesheet

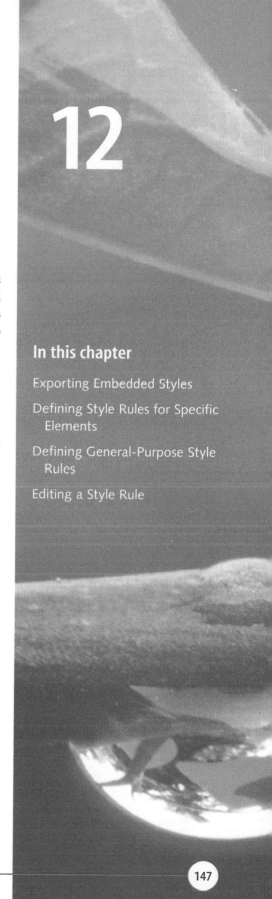

12

In Chapter 11, you created a Dreamweaver template for your site and you used it to spawn an assortment of new pages, but the overall design is still looking rather plain. It's time to start assigning some appearance attributes to the elements of your page, which can mean only one thing: it's time to start building your Cascading Style Sheet. This chapter shows you how.

Exporting Embedded Styles

There are two ways to get Cascading Style Sheets into a web page: embedding and linking. *Embedding* means writing the CSS code directly into the HTML file, either as a separate block in the head section:

```
<html>
<head>
  <title>Hello!</title>
  <style type="text/css">
    p {
      font-family: Arial, Helvetica, sans-serif;
    }
  </style>
</head>
<body>
  <p>Hello, everybody.</p>
</body>
</html>
```

or in the style attribute of a specific HTML tag:

```
<html>
<head>
  <title>Hello!</title>
</head>
<body>
  <p style="font-family: Arial, Helvetica, sans-serif;">Hello,
everybody.</p>
</body>
</html>
```

Linking means writing the CSS code into a separate file and then pointing to this file from the HTML document:

```
<html>
<head>
  <title>Hello!</title>
  <link href="hellostyles.css" rel="stylesheet" type="text/css">
</head>
<body>
  <p>Hello, everybody.</p>
</body>
</html>
```

Embedding and linking produce identical results: the ones that you see in Figure 12-1. So which method is better?

Embedding may seem like the better pick here, because the web page is more self-contained this way, but linking to an external file is usually smarter for the same reason that creating new pages from a Dreamweaver template is usually smarter. Instead of duplicating the same old block of CSS code on every page of your site, you put all the style rules in a centralized location. Then, when you want to make changes to your styles, you simply edit your CSS document, and all the pages that link to the external stylesheet automatically update themselves.

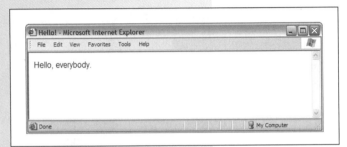

Figure 12-1. External and embedded CSS looks the same

However, by default, Dreamweaver chooses to embed CSS, because embedding is a little easier to automate. The first step toward creating your stylesheet, then, is to export the currently embedded CSS code in your template as an external CSS file. First you delete the embedded block of code, and then you link the template document to the CSS file.

> **BEST BET**
>
> Linking to an external CSS file is almost always better than embedding CSS code directly into the HTML page.

Here's what to do:

1. From Dreamweaver, go to the Files panel, look in the Templates folder for the current site, and double-click the Dreamweaver template that you created in Chapter 11. Dreamweaver opens the template in a new document window.

2. Open the CSS Styles panel by choosing Window→CSS Styles from the main menu or pressing Shift-F11. The CSS Styles panel helps you to navigate the various style rules on the page. You have a few of these already; e.g., Dreamweaver created a style rule when you set the margin values of the page in Chapter 8. And if you designed your layout with layers, each layer has a corresponding style rule.

3. To export the template's currently embedded CSS code as an external file, choose Text→CSS Styles→Export from the main menu. The Export Styles As CSS File dialog box appears. Navigate to the top level of your local root folder, so that you see all the subfolders for the site. This is a good location for your CSS file.

4. In the File Name field, type something brief but descriptive, like *bill* or *billstyles* for the Bill Z. Bub Marketing Associates site, and click Save. Dreamweaver creates the external stylesheet but doesn't yet link the template to this stylesheet.

5. Now remove the existing embedded code. Click the All button in the CSS Styles panel. Then select the <style> item in the panel's list of style rules, and click the trashcan icon in the lower-right corner of the panel. The CSS Styles panel reports that there are no styles defined.

6. Finally, link to the external CSS file. Click the Attach Style Sheet button at the bottom of the CSS Styles panel. (This is the button with the linked-chain icon.) The Attach External Style Sheet dialog box appears, as Figure 12-2 shows.

Figure 12-2. Link to a CSS file with the Attach External Style Sheet dialog box

---

BEHIND THE SCENES

From the Media menu in the Attach External Style Sheet dialog box, you may specify the target medium (or multiple target media), in which case you get a media-dependent stylesheet. As you might suspect, a *media-dependent stylesheet* applies only to the selected medium or media. For instance, to attach a stylesheet that applies only when the visitor prints out your page, choose Print from the Media menu. If you want the stylesheet to apply to both print and screen, type `print, screen` in the Media field. If you want the stylesheet to apply to all media, leave the Media field blank.

To learn more about media-dependent stylesheets, point your browser to *http://www.w3.org/TR/CSS21/media.html/*.

---

7. Click the Browse button, and navigate to the CSS file that you created in Step 3. Double-click this file, and then click OK in the Attach External Style Sheet dialog box. Dreamweaver links to this file and adds its style rules to the list in the CSS Styles panel.

8. Choose File→Save from the main menu. The Update Template Files dialog box in Figure 12-3 appears, showing a list of all the HTML pages that Dreamweaver will modify based on your changes to the template.

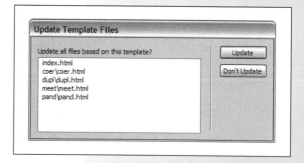

Figure 12-3. These web pages will be modified

9. Click Update. Dreamweaver closes the Update Template Files dialog box and opens the Update Pages dialog box to give you a brief summary of the results, as shown in Figure 12-4. Click Close.

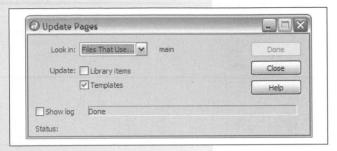

Figure 12-4. A quick status report in the Update Pages dialog box

Congratulations! You have successfully switched from embedded to linked styles. (You have also witnessed the glory of templates for the first time. Each of your existing pages has changed on the basis of a single set of corrections.) You're ready now to begin creating new style rules.

Defining Style Rules for Specific Elements

You can divide the elements of a web page into two broad categories: layout elements, like table cells and layers; and content elements, like text and images. Both types can receive appearance attributes from a Cascading Style Sheet, which may lead you to wonder when to apply a style rule to a layout element and when to apply the rule to the content.

Applying style rules directly to the elements of your layout—that is, your table cells or layers—makes good sense in situations like these:

- You want to set the background color of an area of your layout.

- You want to control the amount of padding in the main content area or sidebar.

- You want to add margins to the main content area or sidebar.

- You want to draw a visible border around an area of your layout.

BEST BET

Create a style rule for a layout element specifically when you want to control the appearance of the layout itself, not the content that goes inside the layout.

Notice that, in all of the above, you're defining the appearance of the layout itself, not the appearance of the content that goes into the layout. These appearance attributes remain the same, in other words, no matter what type of content you happen to place inside the table cell or layer.

By contrast, whenever you want to control the look of the content itself and not its container, you're usually better off creating style rules specifically for the content element. In other words, if the style rule stays the same no matter where the content happens to appear in the layout, then you should attach the style rule to the content element.

Content-type styles are more common overall. However, right now, most of the elements in your Dreamweaver template fall into the layout category. You may have a few content elements, like the list of secondary nav links at the bottom of the main content area, but not many. Rest assured, this number will increase dramatically when you get into Part 3 of this book. For now, you'll look at one example of a content-type style in "Creating a Style for a Content Element" a little further on in this chapter, just so you see how it's done. You'll go on to create styles for other types of content elements throughout the rest of this book.

Creating a Style for a Layout Element

Assume that you want to add some padding to the main content area to prevent the content from sitting snugly against the borders. You experiment with your layout sketch, and you decide upon the following values:

- Along the top and bottom of the main content area, 20 pixels of padding
- Down the left side of the main content area, 60 pixels of padding
- Down the right side of the main content area, 0 pixels of padding

To do this, follow these steps:

1. In the template's document window, click anywhere inside the main content area.

2. Go to the Tag Selector at the bottom of the document window, and select the tag of the appropriate layout element. For a tables-based layout, you want the `<td>` tag, as selected in Figure 12-5. For a layers-based layout, you want the `<div>` tag. Clicking this tag selects the layout element itself, not the content inside it.

Figure 12-5. The `<td>` tag is selected in the Tag Selector

3. With the table cell or layer selected, go to the CSS Styles panel, and click the New CSS Rule button. (This is the one with the page icon.) Dreamweaver opens the New CSS Rule dialog box, as Figure 12-6 shows.

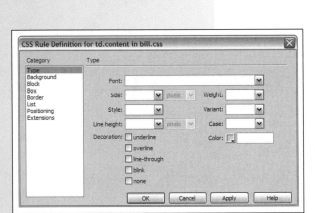

Figure 12-6. Use the New CSS Rule dialog box to add a style rule to your external CSS file

TIP

In the New CSS Rule dialog box, under Define In, make sure that you select the option for your external stylesheet. Otherwise, Dreamweaver embeds the CSS code.

4. If you want your style rule to apply to all table cells on the page, choose Tag under Selector Type, and then choose td or div from the Selector menu, but rarely is this the case. You probably don't want the nav area or the banner area to have the same amount of padding as the content area. Choose Advanced instead, and in the Selector field, type the name of the tag (either td or div), a period (.), and then a brief but descriptive name for the style. Since you're building this style for the main content area, *content* is as good a name as any, so type td.content or div.content.

5. Click OK. The New CSS Rule dialog box closes, and the CSS Rule Definition dialog box in Figure 12-7 opens. Table 12-1 lists the types of attributes that appear under each category in this dialog box.

Figure 12-7. Define new style rules in the CSS Rule Definition dialog

Table 12-1. Appearance attributes by category in the CSS Rule Definition dialog box

Category	Includes
Type	Typeface, type size, font weight (bold), font style (italic), font variant (small caps), line height, type casing, type color, type decorations (underline, strike-through, etc.)
Background	Background color, background image
Block	Word spacing, letter spacing, text alignment, indents
Box	Width, height, padding, margins
Border	Border style, border width, border color
List	List type, leading character

Table 12-1. Appearance attributes by category in the CSS Rule Definition dialog box (continued)

Category	Includes
Positioning (These attributes apply primarily to the layers of a layers-based design.)	Position on screen, clipping regions, stacking order, visibility, overflow behavior
Extensions (These attributes apply to Internet Explorer version 4.0 or later, although many of them aren't supported by any version of any browser.)	Page break, visual effects

6. You want to add padding to the main content area, so you consult Table 12-1 and find that padding is in the Box category. Click the Box category in the CSS Rule Definition dialog box.

7. Under Padding, uncheck the Same For All checkbox. Then type 20 in the Top field, 0 in the Right field, 20 in the Bottom field, and 60 in the Left field. Make sure all the units menus are set to pixels, as shown in Figure 12-8.

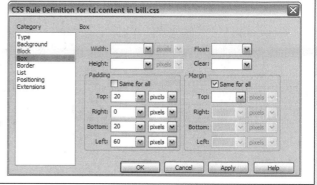

Figure 12-8. Define the padding of the main content area under the Box category

8. Click OK. Dreamweaver opens the CSS file as a separate document window and adds the new style rule to it. Click its tab, and choose File→Save from the main menu to save your changes to the stylesheet.

9. Now switch back to the template's document window, and apply the new style rule to the layout element. With the table cell or layer still selected, go to the Property Inspector, and choose the name of your style from the Style menu. Dreamweaver applies the style to the layout element, as Figure 12-9 shows.

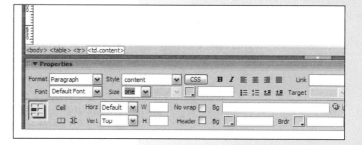

Figure 12-9. Applying the style to the selected layout element

10. Choose File→Save from the main menu, and update the pages of your site.

Creating a Style for a Content Element

Try another style definition, only this time, set the appearance of a content element, like the secondary nav links at the bottom of the main content area. You look back over your notes from Chapter 6, and you decide upon these specifications:

- A typeface of Verdana, Helvetica, or the visitor's default sans-serif font

- A type size of 12 pixels

- Boldface

> **TIP**
>
> Avoid using the menus and buttons on the Property Inspector to set the appearance attributes of text, because Dreamweaver embeds this CSS code into the page.

Here's what you do:

1. In the template's document window, click anywhere inside the paragraph that holds the secondary nav links.

2. Go to the Tag Selector, and click the <p> tag to select the entire paragraph.

3. Go to the CSS Styles panel, and click the New CSS Rule button. The New CSS Rule dialog box opens.

4. Again, you probably don't want this style to apply to all paragraphs on your page, so choose the Advanced option, and type p.secondarynav or something to that effect in the Name field.

5. Click OK. The New CSS Rule dialog box closes, and the CSS Rule Definition dialog box opens.

6. You see from Table 12-1 that various type attributes appear under the Type category, so choose the Type category from the CSS Rule Definition dialog box if it isn't already selected.

7. From the Font menu, choose the font list that reads *Verdana, Helvetica, sans-serif.*

BEHIND THE SCENES

You may recall from Chapter 6 that you specify a list of fonts rather than a single font for the typeface. The fonts appear in order of preference. Take a font list that reads *Verdana, Helvetica, sans-serif.* To the browser, this says, "The preferred font for the element is Verdana, but if Verdana isn't available on the visitor's system, then try Helvetica. If Helvetica isn't available either, then just go with the visitor's default sans-serif font."

Dreamweaver comes prebuilt with several common and reliable font lists, but if you want to create your own, choose Edit Font List from the Font menu, and start choosing fonts. Be sure to conclude your list with *serif, sans-serif,* or *monospaced.* These are generic placeholders that correspond to the visitor's default serif, sans-serif, and monospaced font, whatever they happen to be. This way, if all else fails, the browser picks the default system font in the style of your choosing, and your page looks something like the way you intended it.

---

8. From the Size menu, set the type size to 12 pixels.

9. From the Weight menu, choose Bold. Your dialog box looks like the one in Figure 12-10.

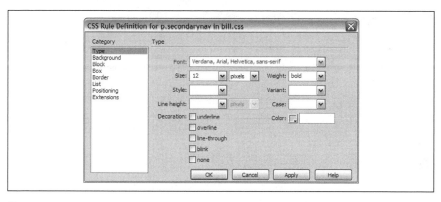

Figure 12-10. Now build a style rule for the secondary navigation text

10. Click OK to add the style rule to the stylesheet.

11. Switch to the stylesheet's document window, and choose File→Save from the main menu.

12. Switch back to the template's document window, and, with the paragraph still selected, choose the name of the style that you just created from the Style menu on the Property Inspector. Dreamweaver applies the style to the selected paragraph, as Figure 12-11 shows.

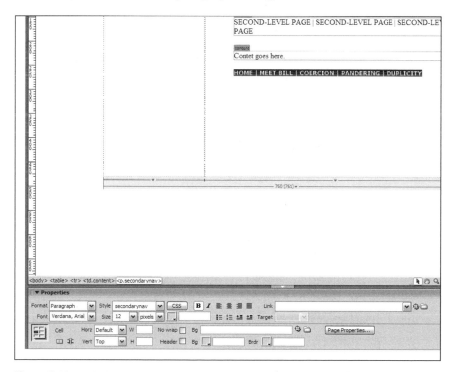

Figure 12-11. Apply the new style rule to the selected paragraph

13. Choose File→Save from the main menu, and update the pages of your site.

Defining General-Purpose Style Rules

Occasionally, you may want to create a general-purpose style rule that applies to more than just one type of element. For instance, you might need a special strikethrough style that crosses out whatever text it happens to format, be it in a paragraph, a heading, or a list.

If so, create a class style, which can apply to any element. Here's how:

> **BEST BET**
>
> Create a class style whenever you want the style rule to apply to more than one type of element or HTML tag.

1. In the CSS Styles panel, click the New CSS Rule button. You don't have to select anything in the document window first. Just click the button, and the New CSS Rule dialog box appears.

2. Under Selector Type, choose Class, and type a brief but descriptive name for the style, like *strikethrough* or *strikethru*, as shown in Figure 12-12.

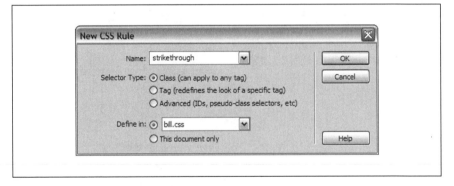

Figure 12-12. Create a class style when you want the style rule to apply to any element

3. Click OK. The New CSS Rule dialog box closes, and the CSS Rule Definition dialog box opens.

4. In the Type category, under Decoration, check the option for line-through.

5. Click OK. Dreamweaver adds the style rule to your external CSS file. Switch to its document window, and choose File→Save. Then switch back to the document window for your template, but you don't have to save, because you didn't change anything in it. You simply modified the external CSS file.

6. To apply this style, select some text in the document window by dragging the mouse across it. Then go to the Style menu on the Property Inspector, and choose your strikethrough style. Dreamweaver dutifully crosses out the text, as Figure 12-13 shows.

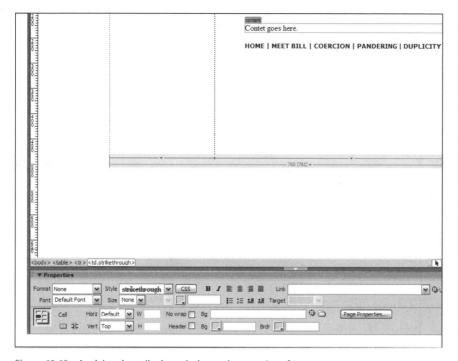

Figure 12-13. Applying the strikethrough class style to a string of text

Editing a Style Rule

Once you've created a style rule, you may edit its definition at any time. You can change the values of the attributes that you defined previously, or you can add or delete attributes from the existing style.

Assume that you want to add a background color to the style for the main content area. Here are the steps:

1. From the CSS Styles panel, click the All button if it isn't already selected.

2. From the list of style rules in the CSS Styles panel, click the name of the style for the main content area.

3. At the bottom of the CSS Styles panel, click the Edit Style button. This is the one with the pencil icon. The CSS Rule Definition dialog box appears, preloaded with the current attributes of the style.

BEHIND THE SCENES

There's a better way to add background colors to layout areas when these areas don't have a specific style rule. See Chapter 13 for details.

4. You want to add a background color, so choose the Background category of the CSS Rule Definition dialog box.

5. Click the color square under Background, and choose a background color from the menu of color swatches that appears.

6. Click OK. Figure 12-14 shows that Dreamweaver adds the style to the stylesheet and simultaneously updates the template document window, because the main content area is already set up to receive this style.

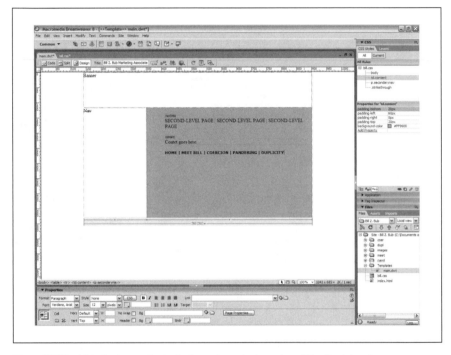

Figure 12-14. Add a background color to the main content area by editing its style rule

7. Switch to the document window for the CSS file, and choose File→Save. Then switch back to the template's document window. You don't have to save the template this time, because not a single byte of code has changed. Your edit affected the CSS file, not the template file.

> **TIP**
>
> To delete a style rule, select it from the list in the CSS Styles panel, and then click the trashcan icon at the bottom of the panel. Be sure to save your external CSS file afterwards.

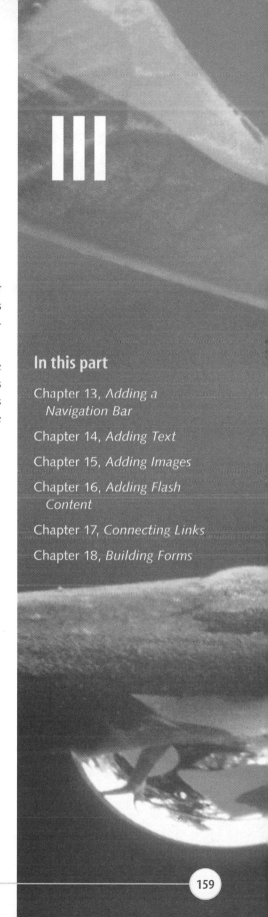

Building Your Site

In Part 2 of this book, you created the essential production documents for your site: the design template and the Cascading Style Sheet. The time has come for you to put these documents to their intended use. As of now, production officially begins.

The next several chapters show you how to add just about anything to the pages of your site. Navigation, text, images, Flash movies, links, forms—it's all here. You're building from the foundation that you laid in Part II, and as you'll soon see, the foundation is strong. Your site will begin to take shape almost immediately. Even your client will be amazed at the results.

In this part

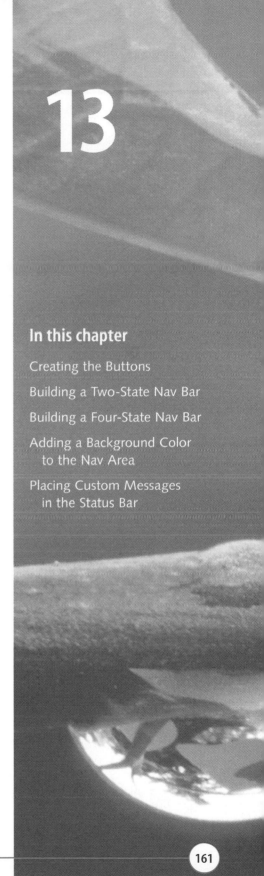

Adding a Navigation Bar

13

Building a navigation bar happens in two distinct phases. First, you create the button graphics in your image editor of choice. Second, you add the buttons to your template document and link them to the pages of your site. As you work, Dreamweaver handles all the necessary HTML code and writes the JavaScript for your rollover effects. This chapter takes you through the entire process.

But first, a program note: this chapter deals with graphical navigation bars—the kind with clickable images and button states. If you're interested in using regular old text links in your main navigation, see Chapter 14 for the low-down on adding text and Chapter 17 for the ins and outs of link connection.

Creating the Buttons

A navigation bar (or *nav bar*) begins life as a mockup in your image editor. Figure 13-1 shows a typical example. Assume that you want this to be a straightforward nav bar with a simple rollover behavior on the buttons, and you don't want the buttons to change their default appearance depending upon the page.

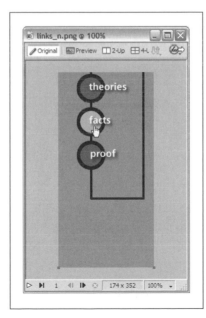

Figure 13-1. This is the nav bar that you want to build

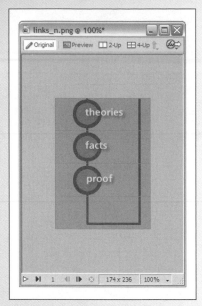

Figure 13-2. Slice the mockup into separate files—one for each button

To break this nav bar into separate buttons, you make use of a technique called *slicing*, which is exactly what it sounds like: you cut up the image into smaller rectangular areas, each of which you save as a separate image file. (In your Dreamweaver template, you'll eventually reconstruct the nav bar from the individual slices, just like putting together a jigsaw puzzle.) Figure 13-2 shows the slices that you make in your image editor after trimming off the excess space at the bottom of the mockup.

This nav bar is going to have a rollover effect. You'll remember from Chapter 4 that a rollover graphic is actually two separate image files—one for the default button or *up state*; and one for the *over state*, or button as it looks when the visitor rolls over it with the mouse pointer. By slicing your mockup, you created separate image files for the up state, but you still need the image files for the over state. Lighten the color of the button face for the rollover effect, and save the slices as separate image files. Figure 13-3 shows what you come up with, all sliced and ready to go. Notice that you don't need to create an over state for the decoration at the bottom of the nav bar, because it doesn't have a rollover effect.

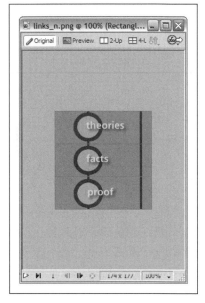

Figure 13-3. Sliced and ready to go

Your nav bar now consists of seven separate image files, shown in Figure 13-4:

- Three up-state buttons
- Three over-state buttons
- One decoration for the bottom of the nav bar

These are for a standard two-state nav bar, which matches your specifications exactly. It's worth noting, though, that Dreamweaver nav bars can have up to four button states. In addition to the up and over states, you can also define a *down state*, which is how the button looks when the visitor is on the corresponding page or section of the site; and the *over-while-down state*, which is the rollover effect for a button in the down state. Figure 13-5 shows the sliced nav-bar mockups for a four-state nav bar: the up state (top left), the over state (bottom left), the down state (top right), and the over-while-down state (bottom right). Figure 13-6 shows the resulting separate image files, which are seventeen in number (four buttons times four states, plus one graphic for the decoration at the top).

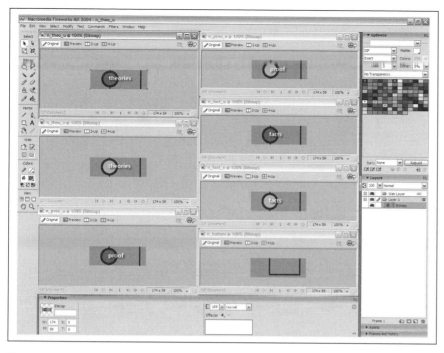

Figure 13-4. Your nav bar now consists of seven separate image files

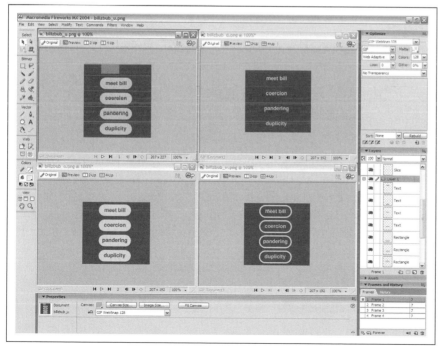

Figure 13-5. The up state (top left), the over state (bottom left), the down state (top right), and the over-while-down state (bottom right)

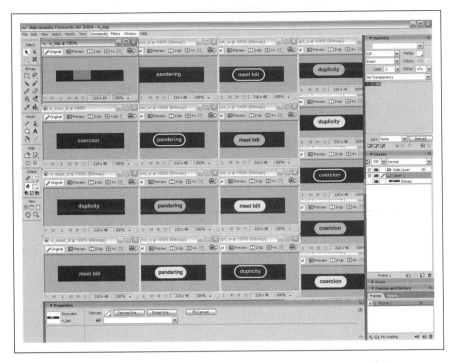

Figure 13-6. Save the slices as separate image files, and you get these seventeen graphics

Building a Two-State Nav Bar

First things first. Before you even think about building the navigation bar,
you need to put all the image files in the *img* or *images* folder of your site. If
you're storing these files somewhere else on your computer, make copies of
them, and move the copies to the *images* folder. This is very essential! If you
use the image files in some other folder, your site is going to generate broken
graphics all over the place when you upload it to the Web.

Do you have your graphics in the right place? Good. The next question is:
where do you build the nav bar? Do you put it in the template document,
or do you put it on the actual pages of your site? By now, you can probably
guess the answer. This is a two-state nav bar, which means that it's fixed
content—the default state of the buttons is always the up state, no matter
where on your site the nav bar appears; and fixed content belongs in the
template document, as you'll recall from Chapter 11.

> **BEST BET**
>
> When the buttons of your nav bar are always in the up state by default, add
> the nav bar to the template document.

You want to work on the template document, so launch Dreamweaver and load the layout template for your site. Click inside the navigation area, remove the text label, and set the Format menu on the Property Inspector to None. The flashing cursor should now be in the upper-left corner of an empty table cell or layer, similar to Figure 13-7.

Go to the Insert panel, click the inverted triangle to the right of the image objects to open their menu, and choose the Navigation Bar object as in Figure 13-8. When you do, Dreamweaver opens the Insert Navigation Bar dialog box shown in Figure 13-9.

Working through this dialog box isn't hard at all. Just take it step by step. In the Element Name field, type a brief but descriptive name for the first button in the nav bar. In this case, it's the Theories button, so *theories* makes sense as a name.

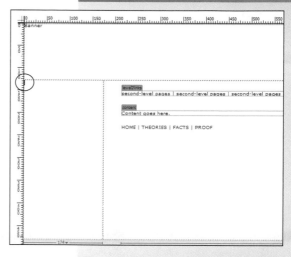

Figure 13-7. Clear out the navigation area so that the flashing cursor is in the upper-left corner of the table cell or layer

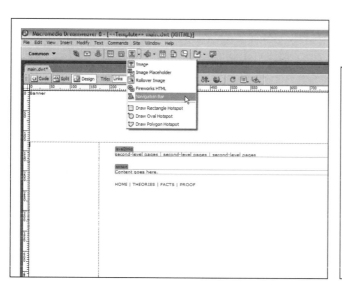

Figure 13-8. Find the Navigation Bar object in the menu of image objects

Figure 13-9. Use the Insert Navigation Bar dialog box to construct your nav bar

Then click the Browse button next to the Up Image field, and navigate to your images folder. Select the image file that corresponds to the up state for the Theories button. You have a two-state nav bar, so repeat this process for the Over Image field, this time choosing your over-state image file for the Theories button. Feel free to skip the states that you don't need. Just leave their fields blank.

In the Alternate Text field, type "Go to the Theories section" or something to that effect. When you're dealing with an interactive element like a button, the alternate text should always start with a verb. Don't just say "Theories." That means nothing out of context. Explain to the visitor who can't see your web page exactly what the button does.

Now click the Browse button next to the When Clicked field, and navigate to the location of the page that appears when the visitor clicks the button. In this case, this is the Theories button, so you want to connect to the main Theories page.

Figure 13-10. Fill in the information for the first button in the nav bar

Under Options, make sure that the Preload Images checkbox is checked for this element. Preloading images helps to make the rollover animation smoother.

Your Insert Navigation Bar dialog box looks much like the one in Figure 13-10.

This takes care of the first nav-bar button. Go to the top of the dialog box, and click the plus button to add a new element to the nav bar. This one is the Facts button, so do exactly as you did previously, only substitute the Facts images for the button states and the main Facts page as the target location.

One nav-bar button remains, so click the plus button at the top of the Insert Navigation Bar dialog box, and fill out the fields.

You're almost done. All that's left is to review the options at the bottom of the dialog box. From the Insert menu, choose the orientation of your nav bar: Vertically for buttons that go top to bottom or Horizontally for buttons that go left to right. For this site, you want a vertical, top-to-bottom nav bar, so your Insert Navigation Bar dialog box should look like the one in Figure 13-11.

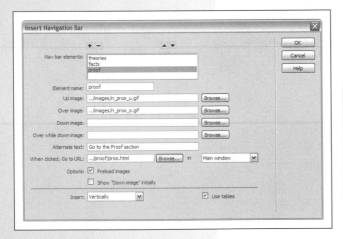

Figure 13-11. These are the fields that should be filled out

Click OK, and Dreamweaver adds the nav bar to the navigation area of your template document, as Figure 13-12 shows.

While the nav bar is selected, glance at the Property Inspector, and notice that it indicates a table. Dreamweaver constructed your nav bar in a table structure, just like you may have done for the general page layout, but even if you built a layers-based page layout, your nav bar still appears in a table.

TIP

If the very thought of using a table for layout of any kind drives you into a foaming frenzy, uncheck the Use Tables option in the Insert Navigation Bar dialog box before you build your table. This isn't recommended, though, because a standalone nav bar may appear with gaps between the buttons or increase the width of the navigation area.

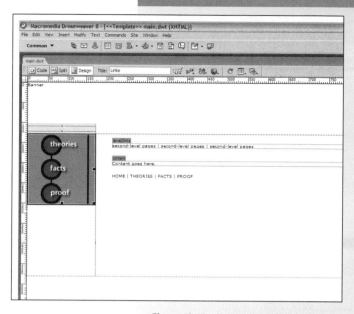

Figure 13-12. Dreamweaver builds the nav bar in the template document

Each nav-bar button occupies its own cell of this table. You still have a decoration for the bottom of the nav bar, so why not add a new cell to the nav-bar table and place the decoration graphic into this cell? Here's what to do:

1. With the nav-bar table still selected, go to the Property Inspector.

2. Find the Rows field. It currently shows the value 3—three rows for three buttons.

3. Type 4 in the Rows field, and press Enter or Return. Dreamweaver adds a new row to the bottom of the table.

4. Click inside this new row in the document window.

5. Choose Insert ›Image from the main menu. The Select Image Source dialog box appears. Navigate to the decoration image, and click OK.

TIP

If you inserted a horizontal nav bar, then adjust the value in the Cols (columns) field, not the Rows field.

6. The Image Tag Accessibility Attributes dialog box appears. Because this is a decoration image that contributes nothing in terms of content to the page, you don't have to specify alternate text or a long description (see Chapter 14 for more information). In other words, a visitor who can't see your web page loses nothing by missing a textual description of this particular graphic. Simply click OK to close the dialog box.

Dreamweaver adds the decoration image to the nav-bar table, as Figure 13-13 shows.

Choose File→Save from the main menu, and update the pages of your site. To test your nav bar, open your home page in Dreamweaver, and press F12 to

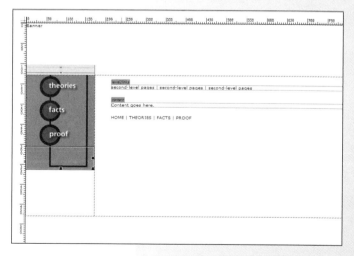

Figure 13-13. Add a new row to the nav-bar table, and insert the decoration graphic

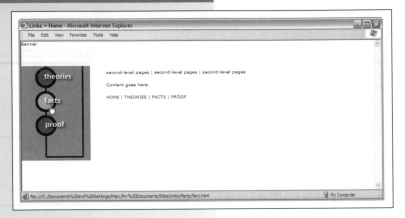

Figure 13-14. Your nav bar works perfectly in a live browser window

preview this page in a live browser window, as Figure 13-14 shows. When you hover over the buttons with the mouse pointer, the rollover effect kicks in, and when you click the buttons, you go to the appropriate pages of your site.

> **TIP**
>
> Don't try to preview your template document in a live browser window. Always open an actual page of your site for previewing purposes.

Building a Four-State Nav Bar

Constructing a four-state nav bar is very much like building the two-state model, although the process from start to finish requires a little more effort. First, you build the default nav bar, where all buttons are in the up state by default. Then you build custom nav bars for each of the top-level content pages (in this case, the Meet Bill, Coercion, Pandering, and Duplicity pages), where the button for each particular page is in the down state by default.

The way you go about doing this depends upon your comfort level with Dreamweaver. You'll look at two different methods: the easier way (which takes more time), and the harder way (which takes less time). Review them both, and choose the one that makes more sense to you.

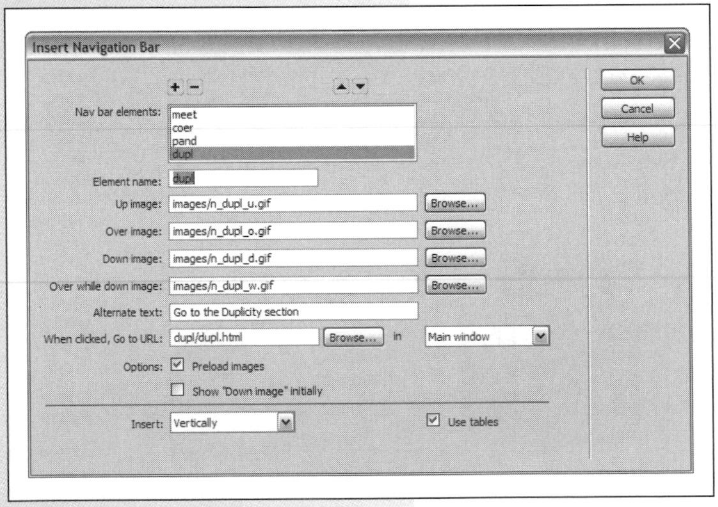

Doing It the Easier (Longer) Way

Open the home page in Dreamweaver, clear out the text label inside the editable region for the main navigation, set the format for this region to None, and choose the Navigation Bar object from the Insert panel. Dreamweaver opens the Insert Navigation Bar dialog box. Fill it out as before, this time adding the images for the other two button states, as Figure 13-15 shows.

Click OK, and Dreamweaver adds the default nav bar to the home page, as Figure 13-16 shows.

Figure 13-15. For a four-state nav bar, fill out all the image fields

While the nav-bar table is selected, go to the Property Inspector, change the number of rows from 4 to 5, and press Enter or Return. This gives you an extra table cell for the decoration image. However, the decoration appears at the top of the nav bar, not the bottom, so a little dragging and dropping is in order. You'll move each button (along with its link) one row down to make room for the decoration image at the top of the nav bar.

In the document window, click the bottommost nav button to select it. Then go to the Tag Selector, and click the `<a>` tag. This tag, which stands for *anchor*, corresponds to the button's link. You don't want to move the button image without its link, so don't skip this important step.

With the button and its link selected, position the mouse pointer atop the button image. Hold down the mouse button, and drag the mouse to the empty table cell. Release, and you've moved the button and its link, as Figure 13-17 shows.

When the top row is empty, click inside it, and choose Insert→Image from the main menu. Select the image file for the decoration, and you're good to go, as in Figure 13-18.

TIP

Don't want to drag images and links around the document window? Who can blame you? Here's a shortcut. Select the nav-bar button that is next to the decoration. Then choose Modify→Table→Insert Rows Or Columns, and you get the dialog box of the same name. Under Insert, choose Rows. Under Number of Rows, type 1. Then, under Where, choose the appropriate location. In the case of Figure 13-18, you would pick Above The Selection. In the case of Figure 13-13, you would pick Below The Selction. Click OK, and Dreamweaver inserts the table row exactly where you want it—no dragging and dropping required.

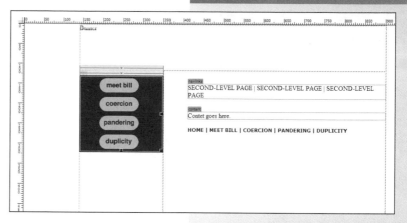

Figure 13-16. Dreamweaver adds the default nav bar to the home page

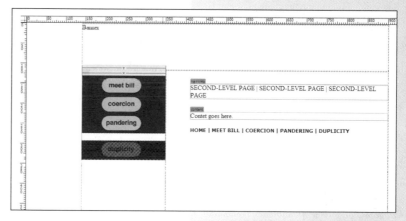

Figure 13-17. Add a new row to make room for the decoration image

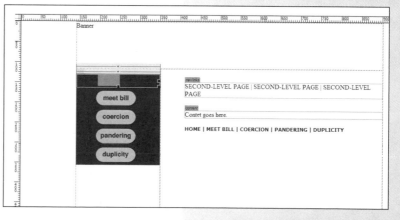

Figure 13-18. Insert the decoration image in the top row of the nav-bar table

Now for the top-level content pages. Tackle each one in turn.

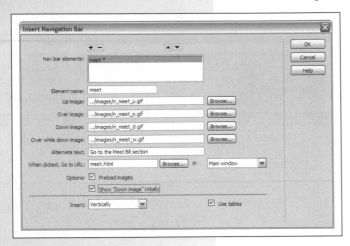

Figure 13-19. Check the "Show 'Down Image' initially" option

Up first is Meet Bill. Open this page in Dreamweaver, clear out the contents of the nav-area editable region, set the format to None, and call up the Insert Navigation Bar dialog box by clicking the Navigation Bar object in the Insert panel. Fill out the dialog box as before. However, for the Meet Bill button, when you come to the Options section, check the "Show 'Down Image' initially" checkbox as in Figure 13-19, because this is the nav bar for the Meet Bill page. All other buttons on the Meet Bill page are in the up state by default, so leave this option unchecked for the remaining nav-bar elements.

When you finish with the Meet Bill nav bar, continue on to the rest of the top-level content pages, always remembering to set the particular button for that page in the down state by default. At this point, the building process can be mind-numbingly repetitive, but it's worth it, as you see when you preview your site in a live browser window. Figure 13-20 shows the fruits of your labor: the Coercion button appears in the down state by default when the visitor is on the Coercion page.

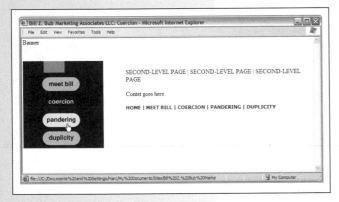

Figure 13-20. Each page's button appears in the down state initially

> **TIP**
>
> Now that you have a custom nav bar on each of the main content-category pages, you never have to build a nav bar for this site ever again. When you create a second-level content page in the Meet Bill section, for instance, simply copy the Meet Bill nav-bar table from the main Meet Bill page and paste it in the navigation area of the new page.

Doing It the Harder (Shorter) Way

In the easier but longer method, you built the same nav bar on several different pages of your site. By this method, you build the nav bar one time only in the template document, even though it's variable content. Then you create new template-based pages for the top-level content categories, replace the original pages from Chapter 11, and modify the nav-bar behavior on each new content page. This is a little tricky and a little technical, so proceed carefully, and you'll do fine.

Begin by opening the template document and building the default nav bar inside the editable region for the navigation area, as Figure 13-21 shows.

Choose File→Save from the main menu, although you don't have to update the pages for your site this time because you're about to delete them. They served their purpose well. They provided you with a page to which to link from the Insert Navigation Bar dialog box, but now they're out of date.

Choose File→New from the main menu, and create a new page based on your modified template. Then choose File→Save, and save this document as *index.html*, overwriting your existing *index.html* page.

Change the title in the document window's Title field to match the name of the first top-level content page (Meet Bill, in this case), and choose File→Save As. Save this file in the same location and with the same name as the previous Meet Bill page, and make sure you click Yes when Dreamweaver asks about updating the links. Repeat this operation for the remaining top-level pages in the site.

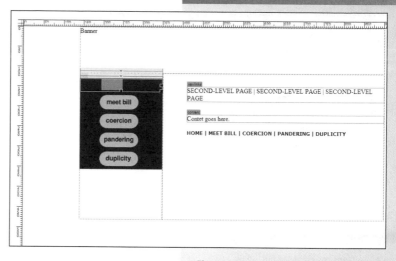

Figure 13-21. Build the nav bar in the template document

You now have brand-new top-level content pages to go with your brand-new home page. What you want to do now is to modify the behavior of the nav bar for each of the top-level content pages. To do this, you need the Behaviors panel, which Figure 13-22 shows, so go to the main menu, and choose Window→Behaviors. The Behaviors panel allows you to browse and edit the JavaScript functions associated with any particular page element. You know from Chapter 4 that the rollover effect happens by way of JavaScript, so what you're about to do, in essence, is rewrite a portion of the rollover script to get the nav bar to show the correct default button state.

Figure 13-22. Browse and edit JavaScript Behaviors of page elements

Start with your first top-level content page (Meet Bill, in this case). If this document window isn't already open in Dreamweaver, open it. Then click the corresponding nav-bar button in the document window, and Dreamweaver lists the associated JavaScript behaviors. This is the Meet Bill page, so the Meet Bill button is the one to click.

Now go to the Behaviors panel, and double-click the gear icon of any one of the Set Nav Bar Image behaviors. It doesn't matter which you choose. They all call up the same Set Nav Bar Image dialog box. In this dialog box, under Options, check the "Show 'Down Image' initially" checkbox, as in Figure 13-23, and click OK. Dreamweaver adjusts the default appearance of the Meet Bill button to the down state, as you see in Figure 13-24.

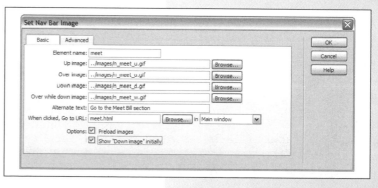

Figure 13-23. Check the "Show 'Down Image' initially" checkbox

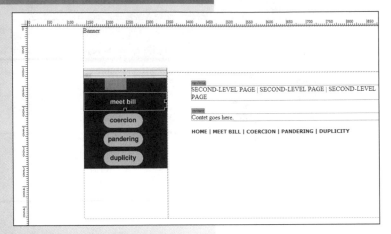

Figure 13-24. Dreamweaver adjusts the default appearance of the button

---

HOTKEY

Press Shift-F4 to toggle the Behaviors panel.

Choose File→Save. Repeat this procedure for the rest of the top-level content pages, and you end up with custom nav bars on each.

Adding a Background Color to the Nav Area

Your nav bar probably doesn't take up the entire space that you allotted for it in your layout. Why not cover up that empty space by coloring in the background of the navigation area? There are two ways of going about it:

HTML attributes

Use this method if your layout is tables-based, you don't already have a style rule for the navigation area, and you want to take a basically harmless shortcut.

CSS attributes

Use this method if you have a layers-based layout or if you want to keep all the color information of your tables-based layout in the external stylesheet. This is the recommended method, but it takes a little more time (unless you already have a style rule for your navigation area).

This section goes through both methods. Compare, choose a favorite, and color away.

Coloring the Nav Area with HTML Attributes

Applying a background color to a table cell using HTML attributes is faster than by way of CSS, although you begin to blur the distinction between content and style that you've worked so hard to maintain. By this method, the color information appears inside the HTML code of the template, not the style rules of the external CSS document. Therefore, if you ever decide to change the color of the nav area, you can't just edit the CSS file, where the color information for everything else resides. You have to get back into the template file to make this one, quirky change. That said, a template-based site in Dreamweaver makes it extremely easy to manage these kinds of edits, so, at the end of the day, it's not that big a deal. Technical purists will want to use CSS, but those who care more about faster results may proceed with these steps:

1. Open the template document.

2. Click anywhere in the navigation area.

3. Go to the Tag Selector at the bottom of the document window, and click the `<td>` tag.

4. Go to the Property Inspector, and click the Bg color box. A menu of color swatches appears. Click any of these, or move the mouse pointer anywhere on the screen, and click to sample a color.

Dreamweaver applies this color to the background of the table cell, as Figure 13-25 shows. Choose File→Save from the main menu to update the pages of your site.

Coloring the Nav Area with CSS Attributes

Keeping the colors with the rest of your styles makes good sense from a technical point of view. If you opt for CSS attributes, here's what you do:

1. Open the template document.

2. Click anywhere inside the navigation area.

3. Go to the Tag Selector at the bottom of the document window, and click the `<td>` or `<div>` tag.

4. Go to the CSS Styles panel, and click the New CSS Rule button—that's the one with the page icon. The New CSS Rule dialog box opens.

5. Under Selector Type, choose Advanced.

6. In the Selector field, type td or div, a period (.), and then a brief but descriptive name for the style. A name like *td.nav* or *div.nav* is perfect.

7. Click OK to proceed to the CSS Rule Definition dialog box. Then, select the Background category.

8. Click the color box to the right of the Background Color field. The mouse pointer becomes an eyedropper.

9. Move the eyedropper onto the nav bar in the document window, and click anywhere on the background of a button image to sample the background color.

10. Click OK. Dreamweaver adds the style rule to your external stylesheet. Switch to its document window, and choose File→Save.

11. Switch back to the template's document window. While the table cell or layer is still selected, go to the Property Inspector, and choose your new style from the Style menu. Dreamweaver applies it to the table cell or layer.

12. Choose File→Save from the main menu, and update the pages of your site.

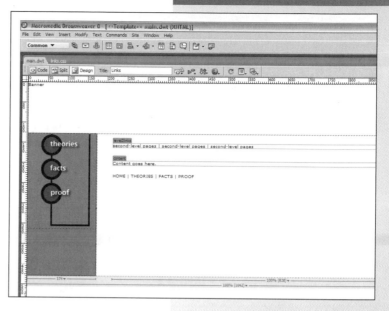

Figure 13-25. Add a background color to the navigation area of the layout template

> **TIP**
>
> If you already have a style rule for the nav area, simply conjure up the CSS Rule Definition dialog box and add a background color to the existing definition.

Placing Custom Messages in the Status Bar

—TECHTALK—

The browser's status bar displays brief messages about what the browser is currently doing or where the selected hyperlink leads.

The *status bar* appears along the bottom of the browser's window. The browser uses it to display brief messages of interest to humans, like what the browser is currently doing (opening the page, downloading images) or where the selected hyperlink leads.

Dreamweaver's Set Text of Status Bar behavior lets you put messages of your choosing into the status bar instead. For instance, when the visitor hovers over one of the buttons in your navigation, you might place "Go to the Theories section" into the status bar instead of the usual esoteric *http:// www.mysite.com/theories/theories.html.*

To place a message in the status bar when the visitor hovers over a nav button, follow these steps:

1. In the document window, click a button in your nav bar.

2. Go to the Tag Selector at the bottom of the document window, and click the <a> tag to select the button's link.

3. In the Behaviors panel, click the plus button, and choose Set Text→Set Text Of Status Bar from the menu that appears. Dreamweaver opens the Set Text Of Status Bar dialog box, which Figure 13-26 shows.

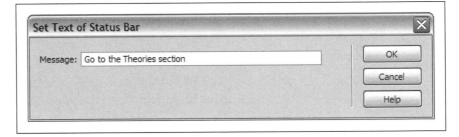

Figure 13-26. Set custom messages in the browser's status bar

4. In the Message field, type the text that should appear in the browser's status bar when the visitor hovers over the button.

5. Click OK. Dreamweaver adds the necessary JavaScript to your page.

6. Choose File→Save from the main menu, and update the pages of your site.

To test your custom messages, view any page of your site in a live browser.

Adding Text

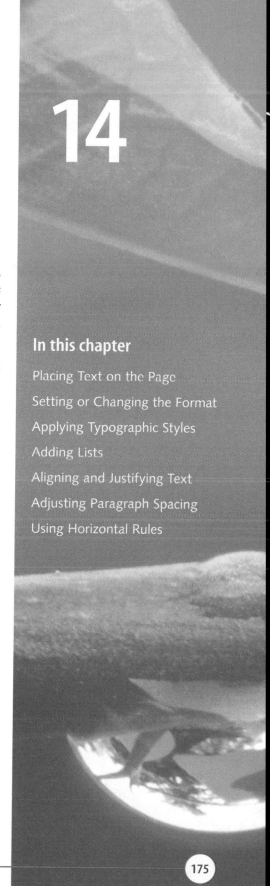

14

If your site is like most, then most of your content comes in textual form, so it makes good sense to get the text in there first. It's easier for you to see what's going on this way, and it gives you a reference point for placing your images and Flash movies, which helps you to work your components into a coherent whole.

This chapter shows you how to add, format, and style the text of your site in Dreamweaver.

Placing Text on the Page

One way to add text is to type it directly into your Dreamweaver page. Typing is convenient for short bursts of wordage. At the same time, Dreamweaver isn't a word processor. It doesn't have many of the features that you might want for serious copywriting. You might also find yourself in this situation: you have a stack of documents from the marketing department that your employer is forcing you to add to the site. Marketing content is never fun in the first place, and retyping marketing content is a form of torture under the Geneva Conventions.

In this chapter

Placing Text on the Page

Setting or Changing the Format

Applying Typographic Styles

Adding Lists

Aligning and Justifying Text

Adjusting Paragraph Spacing

Using Horizontal Rules

> **TIP**
>
> To insert special typographical characters like dashes, curly quotes, the copyright symbol, and the registered trademark symbol, choose Insert→ HTML→Special Characters from the main menu.

Fortunately, Dreamweaver makes it easy for you to paste blocks of text from a word-processor file. If the text is from Microsoft Word, you can even import the Word file directly into your Dreamweaver page.

— BEST BET —

Typing text directly into your page is fine for short sections of copy, but for longer pieces, you're better off composing in a text editor or word processor and then pasting or importing the text into Dreamweaver.

To copy from your word processor or text editor and paste into Dreamweaver, follow these steps:

1. From your word processor or text editor, select and copy the text that you want to use on your page.

2. In Dreamweaver, click the spot on the page where you want to insert the text, or select the placeholder text that you want to overwrite.

3. From the main menu, choose Edit→Paste Special. The Paste Special dialog box shown in Figure 14-1 appears.

BEHIND THE SCENES

The options available under Paste As in the Paste Special dialog box depend upon the application from which you copied the text. The more sophisticated the text editor or word processor, the more options you get.

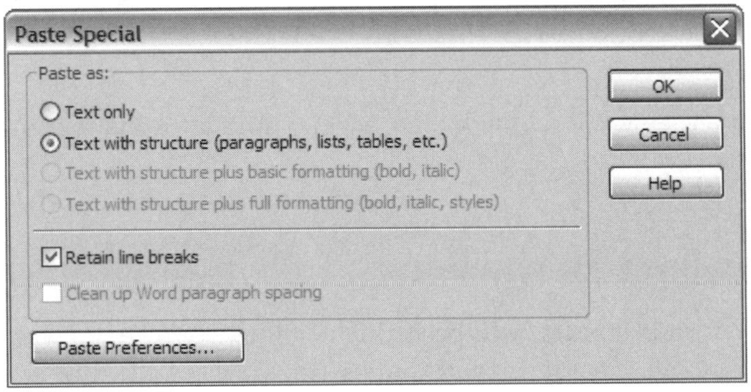

Figure 14-1. Paste Special's options for word processed text

4. Under Paste As, choose Text With Structure or Text With Structure Plus Basic Formatting. You don't usually want the Text Only option, unless the source document has been poorly formatted by someone in the marketing department. You don't usually want Text With Structure Plus Full Formatting, either, because it gives license for Dreamweaver to write embedded style rules into your page. You're better off applying your own, custom-built styles after you paste the text.

5. Click OK, and Dreamweaver pastes the text into the page.

To import a Microsoft Word document, follow these steps:

1. In Dreamweaver, click the spot on the page where you want to insert the text, or select the placeholder text that you want to overwrite.

2. Choose File→Import→Word Document. The Import Word Document dialog box opens.

3. Navigate to the location of the Word document to import, and click this file. Then choose Text, Structure, and Basic Formatting from the Formatting menu at the bottom of the dialog box, and make sure that the Clean Up Word Paragraph Spacing option is checked.

4. Click Open. Dreamweaver imports the document into your page, as Figure 14-2 shows.

Once the text is in the page, you can adjust the format and presentation to suit your needs.

Setting or Changing the Format

When you click a line of text or select a string of characters in the document window, the Format menu on the Property Inspector shows you the format of the text, which in turn tells you the HTML tag that marks it up. To change the HTML tag of the text and thereby change its formatting, simply choose another option from the Format menu, as in Figure 14-3. The paragraph tag is `<p>`, of course, and the six heading tags are `<h1>` through `<h6>`.

As you'll recall from Chapter 6, the paragraph is the catch-all format, so when in doubt, choose Paragraph from the Format menu. The heading formats are specifically for headings—that is, logical divisions in the text, like the headings in this book. You may be tempted to use one of the headings whenever you want a piece of text to appear large and in bold type, but unless this piece of text actually functions as a heading, it's better to create a special paragraph style in your external stylesheet. Figure 14-4 shows the result for the page's title, "the daily gripe."

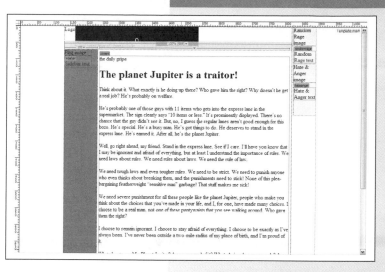

Figure 14-2. Import a Word document directly into your page

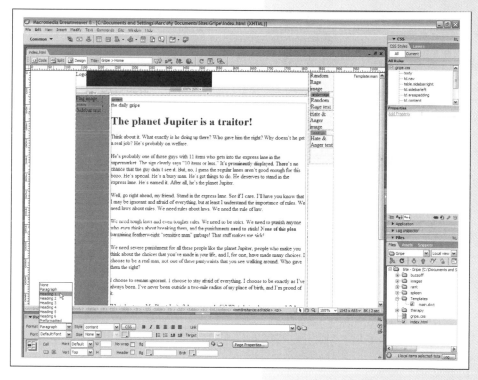

Figure 14-3. Set or change the format of the text from the Format menu on the Property Inspector

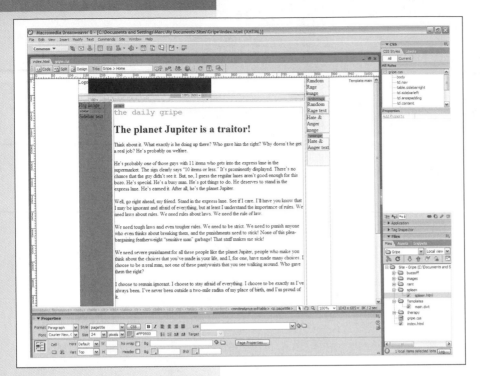

Figure 14-4. "the daily gripe" is styled with CSS, not a heading tag

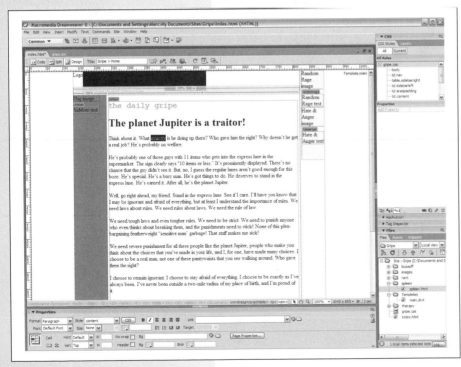

Figure 14-5. Click the B or I buttons on the Property Inspector to apply boldface or italic type styles to otherwise normal text

Applying Typographic Styles

When you're building a site with Cascading Style Sheets, you aren't playing around. You get a host of typographic styles: everything from boldface to small caps. The procedures for adding them vary, though. Sometimes you use the Property Inspector. Other times you go for the CSS Rule Definition dialog box, as the following sections demonstrate.

Adding Boldface and Italics

The B and I buttons on the Property Inspector control boldface and italic type styles, respectively. Normally, this humble tome advises against you clicking the buttons of the Property Inspector whenever it comes to text, because Dreamweaver embeds the corresponding CSS code into your page rather than writing it into your external stylesheet. However, bold and italic type styles are an exception to this rule, because these buttons don't generate CSS code. Rather, when you click them, they insert good old ordinary HTML tags. So feel free to highlight a word or string of text, and click B for bold or I for italic, as Figure 14-5

shows.

That said, it makes good sense to lay off the B and I buttons when you need to apply bold or italic type styles consistently on a particular kind of text, say, for instance, the special paragraph style for the title of your page. In cases like these, simply build the boldface or italics into the style rule when you create it. In the CSS Rule Definition dialog box shown in Figure 14-6, set

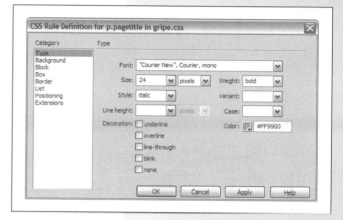

Figure 14-6. The Weight and Style menus are under the Type category

boldface from the Weight menu and set italics from the Style menu.

You'll also discover some interesting choices under both the Weight and the Style menus, like Bolder and Lighter for the weight and Oblique for the style. Currently, no major browser does anything special with these options, so just stick with bold and italic.

Transforming Lowercase Letters to Small Caps

In typographical circles, *small caps* or *small capitals* refer to smaller versions of uppercase letters (A, B, C) that stand in for lowercase letters (a, b, c). Using small caps is a great way to get an

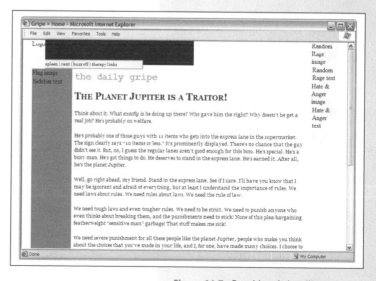

Figure 14-7. For old-style headlines, convert lowercase letters to small caps

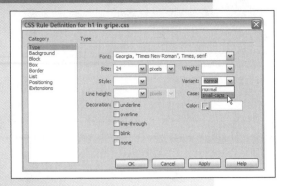

Figure 14-8. Set small caps from the Variant menu

──TECHTALK──

Small caps or small capitals are smaller versions of uppercase letters that stand in for lowercase letters.

Figure 14-9. Change the casing of a block of type from the Case menu

old-style look in headings and heading-like paragraph styles, as Figure 14-7 shows.

To add small caps to a CSS style, set the Variant menu on the

> **TIP**
>
> Avoid using small caps in running text, as this style can be hard on the eyes, particularly at smaller type sizes.

CSS Rule Definition dialog box to small-caps, as shown in Figure 14-8. The browser automatically converts all lowercase letters in text of this style to small caps.

It's important to note that Dreamweaver's document window displays small caps as regular capital letters. You have to preview your page in a live browser to see the small caps in action. All the major browsers support this style.

Transforming Type Casing

Similarly, you can change the way the browser displays the casing of a block of type with the capitalize, uppercase, and lowercase values, all of which appear under the Case menu of the CSS Rule Definition dialog box, as Figure 14-9 shows.

Table 14-1 summarizes the effects of these values when you assign them to a style rule. Note that, in each instance, you aren't changing the actual text of your web page. You're simply changing the way that the browser displays your text. So if you build a lowercase transformation into your default first-level heading style, any uppercase letters in your first-level headings remain uppercase letters in the HTML code. On screen, the browser displays them as if they were lowercase.

Table 14-1. Effects of the casing values

Value	Description	In the code	On the screen
Capitalize	Transforms the first letter in each word to a capital letter	This is sample text.	This Is Sample Text.
Uppercase	Transforms all letters to capitals	This is sample text.	THIS IS SAMPLE TEXT.

Value	Description	In the code	On the screen
Lowercase	Transforms all letters to lowercase	This is sample text.	this is sample text.

Avoiding the Underline Style

Many web designers see that Underline option in the CSS Rule Definition dialog box and go ape. Soon, *everything* is underlined on their web pages. This humble tome urges you to resist the impulse. In fact, it goes so far as to suggest that you forget you ever saw anything about underlines in the CSS Rule Definition dialog box.

Underlines are for links. That's what your visitors expect. If you underline

> **BEST BET**
>
> Don't underline anything that isn't a link.

text that isn't a link, your visitors will try to click it anyway, and then they'll get frustrated when your "links" don't work. If you don't want to underline links on your site, that's your concern, but don't compensate by underlining everything else in sight. It's far better to forego this style altogether than to underline something that isn't a link.

If you want emphasis, don't underline! Use italics or boldface instead.

Adding Lists

If you're typing your text as you go, you can insert a list from the Property Inspector by clicking the Unordered List button for a bulleted list or the Ordered List button for a numbered list, which are shown in Figure 14-10. After the last list item, click this button again to return to normal text.

Occasionally, when you paste text from a text editor, Dreamweaver doesn't format the lists correctly, and you get something like the list in Figure 14-11. To remedy this situation, select the text that you want to convert to a list and click the appropriate button on the Property Inspector. Dreamweaver turns the items into a list, as Figure 14-12 shows.

To modify the appearance of a list, create a style rule:

Figure 14-10. The Unordered List button (left) and the Ordered list button (right)

Figure 14-11. In the document window, highlight the text that you want to convert into a list

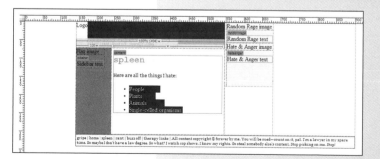

Figure 14-12. Click the appropriate button on the Property Inspector to convert the selected text into a list

- If you want to change the appearance of all lists of a given type on your site, choose Tag as the selector type from the New CSS Rule dialog box. To change all ordered lists, type ol in the Tag field. To change all unordered lists, type ul.

- If you want to change the appearance of a particular list without affecting the others, choose Advanced as the selector type from the New CSS Rule dialog box. In the Selector field, type ol or ul, a period (.), and then a brief but descriptive name for the list, such as hatelist.

The style definitions specifically relating to lists appear in the List category of the CSS Rule Definition dialog box, as shown in Figure 14-13.

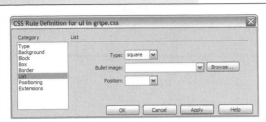

Figure 14-13. Build a style rule for your list under the List category

The values in the Type menu describe the leading character of the list. The Disc, Circle, and Square options work better for unordered lists, while Decimal (1, 2, 3), Lower-roman (i, ii, iii), Upper-roman (I, II, III), Lower-alpha (a, b, c), and Upper-alpha (A, B, C) work better for ordered lists.

For an unordered list, you may also use your own bullet graphic. Click the Browse button, and navigate to the image file that you want to use. Make sure that the image file is in the *images* or *img* folder of your site, or else your custom graphic won't appear properly when you post your site on the Web.

> **TIP**
>
> Choose None from the Type menu to create a bald or bulletless unordered list.

The values in the Position menu determine the placement of the leading character, be it a bullet, number, or letter. The Inside value refers to inside the margin of the list, while Outside refers to outside the margin of the list.

Of course, with CSS, you can change everything else about the presentation of the list, too. Browse the other categories of the CSS Rule Definition dialog box to change the font, the weight, the color, the type size, and so on.

Aligning and Justifying Text

Figure 14-14. Align Left, Align Center, Align Right, and Justify

Figure 14-14 shows four more safe-to-click buttons on the Property Inspector. These control the alignment and justification setting of the currently selected text. So, to align a particular paragraph to the right side of its area, first click anywhere inside the paragraph in the document window, then go to the Property Inspector and click the Align Right button. Likewise, to center a heading or a title paragraph, select the element and click Align Center.

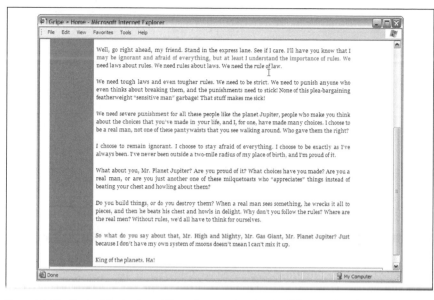

Figure 14-15. Use justification to pad lines of type so that they're all the same length

In *justified* text, the browser pads the lines of type with space so that they're all the same length, except for the last line in a paragraph, as shown in Figure 14-15. This effect doesn't play as well on the Web as it does in print, so be wary of using it.

Adjusting Paragraph Spacing

By default, the browser inserts a line break between paragraphs. You know this. You've seen this. You also know from Chapter 6 that you can use CSS to adjust the amount of space that the browser inserts. Here is how it's done.

As before, the same rules apply:

- If you want to modify the spacing of all paragraphs on the site, choose Tag as the selector type from the New CSS Rule dialog box, and type p in the Tag field.

- If you want to modify the spacing of a particular kind of paragraph, choose Advanced as the selector type. Type p, a period (.), and a brief but descriptive name for the style, such as runningtext.

When you get to the CSS Rule Definition dialog box, go to the Box category, and uncheck the Same For All option under Margin. Then supply values for the Top and Bottom fields, as Figure 14-16 shows. These don't have to be the same value, but for a more balanced look, make them the same.

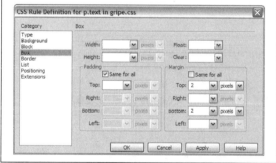

Figure 14-16. To control the space between paragraphs, set values for the top and bottom margins

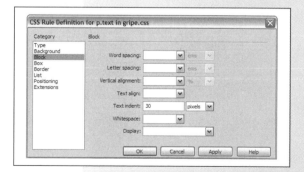

Figure 14-17. Indent the first line of your paragraphs with the Text Indent field

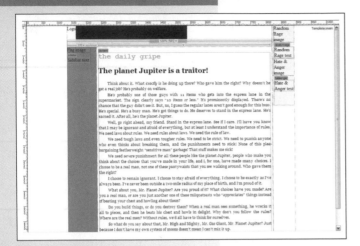

Figure 14-18. The text indent is 30 px, and the vertical margins are 2 px

The less space you insert between paragraphs, the greater the need for you to indent the first line of each

> **TIP**
>
> The spacing trick works for all kinds of elements, including headings (<h1> through <h6>) and the items in a list (<li>). Just be careful about how you apply it. Book-style paragraphs look great in print, but that extra line space between standard HTML paragraphs helps to improve on-screen legibility.

paragraph. Otherwise, your text becomes very hard to read. To indent the first line, go to the Block category of the CSS Rule Definition dialog box, and type a value in the Text Indent field, as Figure 14-17 shows.

The sample values create a paragraph style much like the one in Figure 14-18.

—**TECHTALK**—

A horizontal rule is a browser-generated line that runs from left to right on the page.

Using Horizontal Rules

The often-neglected, always-humble *horizontal rule* is a line that runs from left to right on the page. The browser generates this element entirely by itself—you don't have to build a special image file or create a special style in your external stylesheet.

Horizontal rules are useful for dividing sections of your page. With a little formatting, they make an elegant way of separating your secondary nav from the content of the page,

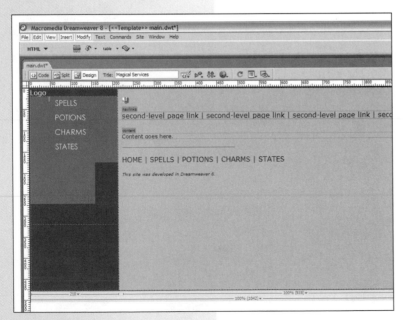

Figure 14-19. A horizontal rule separates the content from the secondary nav

> **TIP**
>
> To insert a horizontal rule by way of the Insert panel, choose HTML from the Insert panel's menu, and then click the Horizontal Rule object.

as Figure 14-19 shows.

To insert a horizontal rule, choose Insert→HTML→Horizontal Rule from the main menu, and then go to the Property Inspector to set its attributes.

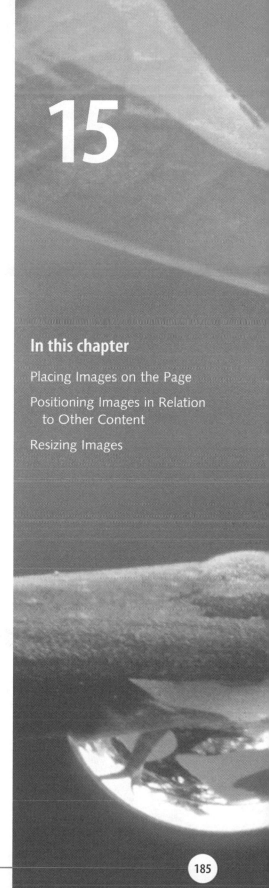

Adding Images — 15

Are you ready for images? Of course you are.

You took a dip in the image pool already in Chapter 13, when you added a graphical nav bar to your template. This chapter covers the static images of your site: the non-clickable, content-bearing images that appear in the body of your page and the trade dress like the logos and banners that go in designated layout areas. (If clickable images of all kinds interest you, then you have only to be patient a little while longer, as they're coming in droves in Chapter 17.)

Along the way, you'll learn about aligning your images in relation to the text that you added in Chapter 14, making your images more accessible to those who can't see them, and resizing and resampling your images for that perfect fit.

Placing Images on the Page

Placing images on your page is easy. First, you click in the document window to set an insertion point (and delete any placeholder text for the image). Then you go to the Insert panel, and you click the Image icon. If the Image icon isn't visible, you choose it from its menu, as Figure 15-1 shows.

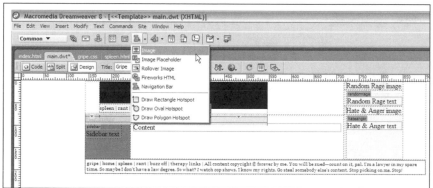

Figure 15-1. Choose the Image object from its menu on the Insert panel

The Select Image Source dialog box appears. Navigate to your *images* or *img* folder, and choose the image file that you want to place. Don't use an image from any other location! All the images for your site should be in this folder. If the image that you want isn't there, click Cancel, leave Dreamweaver for a minute, find the image file, and move it to your site's images folder.

Click OK, and Dreamweaver calls up the Image Tag Accessibility Attributes dialog box (see Figure 15-2). In the Alternate Text field, provide an accurate text description for the image. Don't cheap out here! To improve the usefulness of your images for those who can't see them, the words of your description should paint a clear mental picture of the graphic file. "Mars photo" says little. Try something like this: "In this photograph, the planet Mars shows rocky, rust-red surface features and a pink sky. A range of jagged mountains rolls off in the distance. The gray shadow of the Mars rover appears in the extreme foreground."

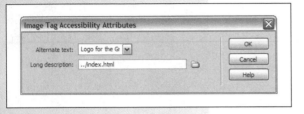

Figure 15-2. The Image Tag Accessibility Attributes dialog box

If you plan to make this image clickable, click the folder icon to the right of the Long description field, and navigate to the page to which you plan to link. The `longdesc` or long description attribute of the image tag gives the location of the page to which the image links. However, keep in mind that you aren't actually linking the image to the page at this stage. See Chapter 17 for information about that. Right now, you're simply embedding this information into the image tag for the benefit of accessibility software like screen readers and text-to-speech converters. You'll add the actual link at a later time. If you don't plan on making this image clickable, then leave the Long description field blank.

BEST BET

If you plan on making your image clickable, fill in the Long description field of the Image Tag Accessibility Attributes dialog box. Otherwise, leave this field blank.

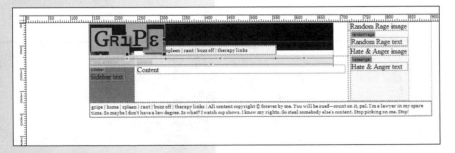

Click OK, and Dreamweaver inserts your image at the insertion point, as Figure 15-3 shows.

Figure 15-3. Dreamweaver inserts the image

Positioning Images in Relation to Other Content

The images of your interface probably all have designated areas, so there isn't anything to position. You click inside the logo area to place the logo, or you click inside the banner area to place the banner, and you insert the image.

Images that appear in the main content area are a different story. Unless the image takes up the entire area, you need to position the image in relation to the rest of the content in the area.

There are two main approaches of doing this. The first is to drop the image directly into the surrounding content and then flow the content around it. The second is to insert a table into the main content area and place the image in one of the cells and the content into another. This section describes both methods.

Using Inline Images

An *inline image* is an image that sits within its surrounding content. In fact, you can think of an inline image as a rather large character in the line of type in which it appears, because that's how the browser handles it.

To place an image inline, choose an insertion point inside the main content area (usually to the left of the surrounding text), and click the Image object in the Insert bar. After you fill out the accessibility information, Dreamweaver drops the image into the mix, as Figure 15-4 shows.

—TECHTALK—

An inline image is an image that sits within its surrounding content.

You might want the liberal amount of whitespace that the inline image creates, although you probably don't. To get rid of it, you can align the image to the surrounding text from the Align menu on the Property Inspector. Select the image and choose an alignment setting, and the surrounding content will flow around the image.

There are several options available, but the ones of most interest are Left and Right. Choose Left from the Align menu, and the image appears on the left side of the area with the surrounding content flowing around it, as Figure 15-5 shows. Choose Right, and you get the reverse situation. The image appears on the right side of the area with the content flowing around it, as Figure 15-6 shows.

Figure 15-4. An inline image sits within its surrounding content

Figure 15-5. The image is aligned left

Figure 15-6. The image is aligned right

To increase the amount of padding between the image and the surrounding content, type values into the V Space and H Space fields of the Property Inspector. The V Space field gives extra padding around the top and bottom of the image and the H Space field gives extra padding around the left and right sides, as shown in Figure 15-7. The units in both cases are pixels, but you don't have to type px. This is an HTML attribute, not CSS.

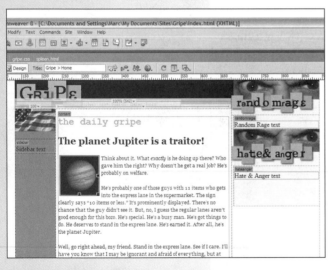

Figure 15-7. This image has a V Space of 2 and an H Space of 4

TIP

To center an inline image, first put it on its own line: Select it, choose Default from the Align menu on the Property Inspector, press the right-arrow key so that the blinking cursor is immediately to its right in the document window, and then press Enter or Return. Then, select the image again, click the left-arrow key so that the blinking cursor is immediately to its left, and click the Align Center button on the Property Inspector.

Using a Table

The alternative to using inline images is to insert a table, much like Dreamweaver did with your nav bar in Chapter 13. The image goes into one cell of the table, and the surrounding content goes into the other.

Standards groups like the World Wide Web Consortium (W3C) can't condone this practice, of course, because it goes against the strict reading of the HTML specifications. Tables aren't for page layout. They're for rows and columns of data. Nevertheless, if you need a two-column effect, tables are the most convenient way to go in Dreamweaver.

To add a table, choose an insertion point in the document window, and go to the Insert panel. Click the Table object shown in Figure 15-8, and Dreamweaver opens the Table dialog box, as Figure 15-9 shows.

You can skip most of the fields in the Table dialog box, as these are more for data tables—tables like the W3C prefers, with information in a grid. You do want to look over the fields under Table Size, though. If you want the image and the content to appear side by side, go for a table with one row and two columns.

Leave the width field empty, because the width of the image and the content will determine the size of the table automatically.

If you want a visible border around the cells of the table, type a value in the Border Thickness field—the larger the value, the heavier the border (in pixels). Otherwise, type 0.

As with inline images, you should add a little padding in the Cell Padding field to improve the image's appearance in relation to its surrounding content. You don't need a lot. A couple of pixels are usually plenty.

The value in the Cell Spacing field controls the amount of space between the cells in the table. Here, zero is usually the best value.

When you're done, click OK, and Dreamweaver inserts the table, as in Figure 15-10.

Now, click inside one of the cells of the table and insert the image into it. Next, select all the surrounding content, drag it with the mouse, and drop it into the other cell. As you can see in Figure 15-11, the shorter column (in this case, the one with the image) is centered vertically against the longer column. To position the image at the top of its column, select the image, go to the Tag Selector, and click the `<td>` tag to select the image's table cell. Then go to the Vert menu on the Property Inspector, and choose Top, as Figure 15-12 shows.

Figure 15-8. The Table object icon on the Insert panel

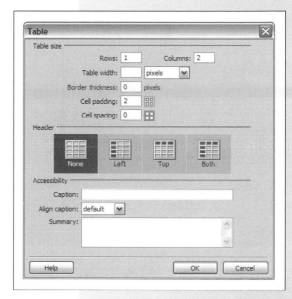

Figure 15-9. Table properties available from the Table dialog box

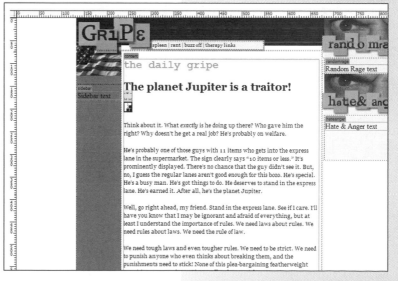

Figure 15-10. Dreamweaver inserts the table

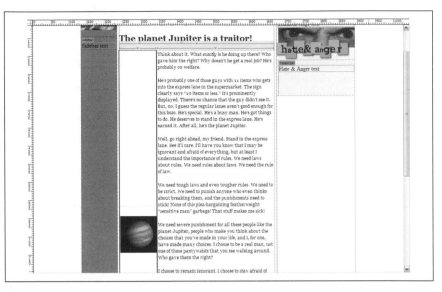

Figure 15-11. The image is centered vertically at first

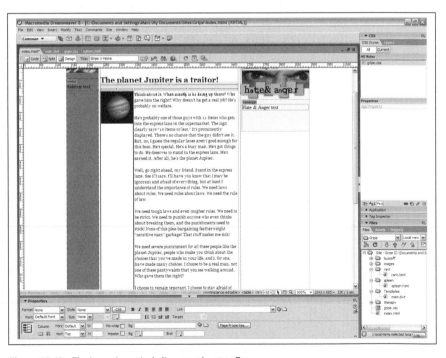

Figure 15-12. The image's vertical alignment is set to Top

Resizing Images

Ideally, images come onto your page at the perfect size. You may not know what this perfect size is, though, until you see it in the context of your page. As you'll recall from Chapter 5, if an image is too large, you can always scale it down and then resample it at its new dimensions.

You can also increase the size of an image, but this is generally less effective than decreasing the size.

Bitmap images such as GIF, PNG, or JPEG contain set amounts of visual information. In other words, there are a specific number of pixels. When you scale an image down, you lose some of the existing information by jettisoning some of the pixels, but Dreamweaver can usually compensate pretty well, and the image looks more or less like it did at the larger size, just smaller. When you scale an image up, however, Dreamweaver has to *add* visual information. It literally increases the pixel count of the image, usually by duplicating neighboring pixels, so you're not really gaining anything new. In fact, you're probably making the image worse, because you're multiplying whatever graininess already exists in the smaller form.

Increasing the size *modestly* is sometimes alright, depending upon the image, but don't count on taking a small icon image and blowing it up to the full size of your page.

Take the image in Figure 15-13. It's too large for its surroundings. It needs to be smaller. You can achieve image reduction in one of two ways:

- Select the image and go to the Property Inspector. The W and H fields represent the width and height of the image. Type smaller values into these fields. To scale the image proportionately, you have to work out the math on your own.

- Select the image, and then drag one of the square handles. Drag the handle along the bottom of the image to scale the height. Drag the handle along the right side of the image to scale the width. Drag the handle in the lower-right corner to scale both width and height. To scale the image proportionately, hold down the Shift key while you drag.

Figure 15-13. This giant image needs to be smaller

TIP

To revert to the original dimensions of the image, click the curved-arrow icon that appears next to the W and H fields on the Property Inspector. Please note that once you resample the image, its new dimensions *are* its original dimensions, so make sure you really like the new size before you commit to it.

Figure 15-14. The Resample button

Once you scale the image to a serviceable size, be sure to click the Resample button on the Property Inspector, as in Figure 15-14. As of now, the rescaled image only looks smaller. The image file itself retains its original dimensions. When you click the Resample button, Dreamweaver saves the image at its new size, but not before warning you that it's a permanent procedure.

Dreamweaver comes with a few other handy image-editing tools, listed in Table 15-1.

Table 15-1. Dreamweaver image-editing tools

Property Inspector button	Icon	Description
Crop		Cuts away a portion of the selected image without resizing it
Resample		Optimizes and saves the selected image at its new dimensions
Brightness and Contrast		Adjusts the brightness and contrast of the selected image
Sharpness		Increases the sharpness or clarity of the selected image

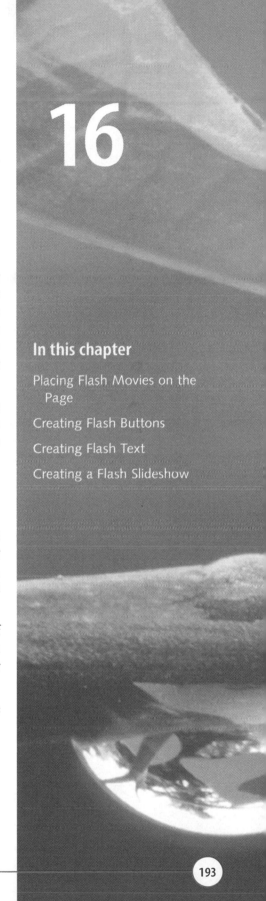

Adding Flash Content

16

Ubiquitous is the word for the Flash multimedia format. The Flash Player plug-in is installed on just about every computer on the Internet, so many a modern web site uses Flash for mission-critical features like navigation and advertising without giving it a second thought. The prevalence of Flash pretty much guarantees it a place of honor among Dreamweaver's site-building tools. The fact that Macromedia produces both Flash and Dreamweaver doesn't hurt, either.

This chapter shows you how to place Flash movies on the pages of your site in an aesthetically pleasing and reasonably accessible form. It also gives you a tour of Dreamweaver's special Flash features, which require no outside authoring tools.

Placing Flash Movies on the Page

For purposes of placing, treat Flash movies just like images. Put them in their predefined areas of your layout, or drop them inline and adjust their alignment in relation to the surrounding content. The main difference is, instead of clicking the Image object on the Insert panel, you click the Flash object shown in Figure 16-1.

When you do, the Select File dialog box appears. Navigate to the location of the Flash movie in your local root folder. Flash movies have the extension *.swf*, so you're looking for SWF files here. You might consider placing your movies in the *images* or *img* directory, just for convenience.

Click OK, and the Object Tag Accessibility Attributes dialog box in Figure 16-2 appears. In the Title field, type a short title for the movie.

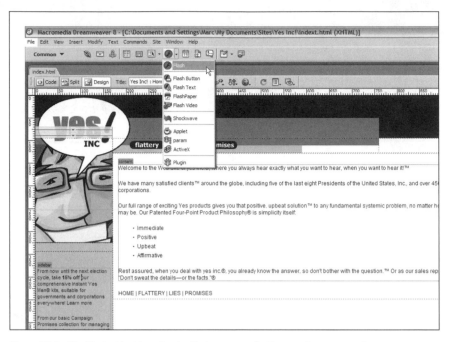

Figure 16-1. The Flash object is under the Flash menu on the Property Inspector toolbar

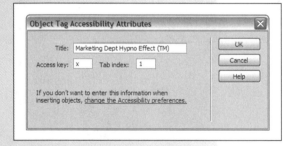

Figure 16-2. Accessibility options for Flash movies

TECHTALK

An access key is a keyboard key that the user presses in conjunction with the Alt key to select an interactive element on the page.

In the Access Key field, type the keyboard key that the visitor may press in conjunction with the Alt key to select the Flash movie in the browser window. For instance, if you type x in the Access Key field, the visitor may press Alt-X to select the movie. The access key works on Windows computers only.

In the Tab Index field, type the tab index of the Flash movie. The *tab index* of an element is the order in which the browser selects the element when the visitor presses the Tab key on a web page. A tab index of 1, therefore, means that the Flash movie is the very first element selected when the visitor tabs through the page. A tab index of 10 means that the movie is the tenth element selected. (For more information about setting tab index values, see Chapter 17.)

When you're finished, click OK, and Dreamweaver inserts the Flash movie into your document window. By default, the movie appears in a gray placeholder box, as Figure 16-3 shows. To align the movie with the surrounding content, choose a value from the Align menu on the Property Inspector. Left and Right are the most useful choices for inline movies.

Finally, to play the Flash movie in the document window, as in Figure 16-4, click the Play button on the Property Inspector. Press Stop to return to the placeholder box.

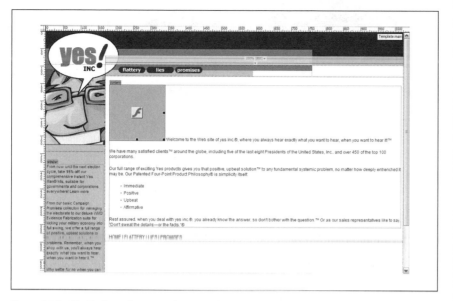

Figure 16-3. The Flash movie appears in a gray placeholder box

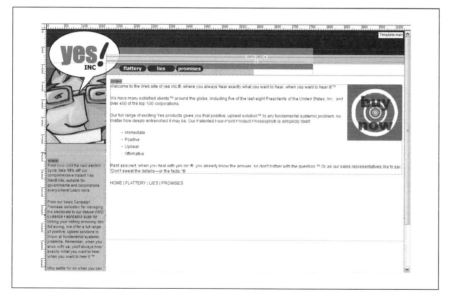

Figure 16-4. The Flash movie is aligned right and is playing

BEHIND THE SCENES

Access keys and tab-index values are important navigational aids for those who don't browse the Web with a mouse. For some visitors, it's a personal preference. For others, it's a necessity. They might log on with nonstandard devices like cell phones, PDAs, or MSNTV, or they might not be able to use a mouse, in which case your access keys and tab-index values improve the accessibility of your site.

TIP

To prevent the Flash movie from playing automatically when the web page loads, uncheck the Autoplay option in the Property Inspector. To prevent the movie from playing repeatedly, uncheck the Loop option.

Multimedia of all kinds pose problems for strict, by-the-book, hard-line accessibility, and Flash movies are no exception. Even when you fill out the Object Tag Accessibility Attributes dialog, you don't completely satisfy the accessibility requirements that the World Wide Web Consortium (W3C) and others recommend.

In Dreamweaver's defense, most of these requirements don't have anything to do with the coding of the Flash movie's placement on the page. Rather, they pertain to the content of the movie itself. Multimedia presentations like Flash movies need to have content equivalents for those who can't see them. In many cases, this amounts to accessible text captions or a spoken-word soundtrack that describes in words what the movie displays visually, and no amount of Dreamweaver coding can do that. You have to build the captions or the soundtrack into the movie file itself, and if you opt for captions, you have to make sure that screen readers can find them and read them.

If you're serious about accessibility, do yourself a favor and review the W3C's multimedia guidelines at *http://www.w3.org/TR/WCAG20/#media-equiv*. See also the Macromedia web site (*http://www.macromedia.com/*) for accessibility recommendations specifically pertaining to the Flash format.

Creating Flash Buttons

As you'll recall from Chapter 4, a Flash button is a short Flash movie that looks and works exactly like a rollover graphic. You can build Flash buttons directly in Dreamweaver—you don't need any outside authoring tools. However, Flash buttons come with some drawbacks in terms of accessibility and performance. If you're hazy on the particulars, see Chapter 4.

If you understand what you're getting into and you still want to add Flash buttons to your site, here's what you do. Click anywhere in the document window to create an insertion point, and then go to the Insert panel. Look in the menu of Flash objects, and choose the Flash Button object, shown in Figure 16-5.

The Insert Flash Button dialog box in Figure 16-6 appears. From the Style menu, choose the graphical appearance of your Flash button, and watch the Sample pane for a preview.

In the Button Text field, type the label that appears on the button face, and choose the font and type size. You don't have to stick with web-safe fonts here. Go with whatever crazy typeface you prefer. In any case, the label should be short enough to fit on the button that you selected. You'll check this in a few steps. The Sample pane won't update itself to show the button with your text, so don't wait around for it to do so.

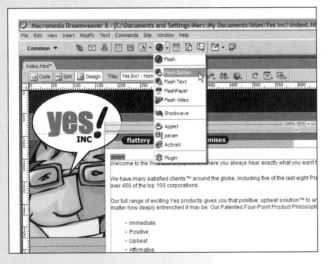

Figure 16-5. The Flash Button object is in the menu of Flash objects

Click the Browse button next to the Link field, and navigate to the page to which you want the button to link.

If you want to color the background of the button, click the Bg Color color box, and select from the menu of color swatches. You can also sample any color on screen.

Finally, type a filename for the button in the Save As field. After the filename, add *.swf*, the Flash file extension.

> **TIP**
>
> Don't save the Flash button in your *images* or *img* folder. Keep it in the same folder as the current page, even if you normally save Flash movies with your images. For the Flash button's link to work correctly, the button file needs to be in the same folder as its page.
>
> The same goes for Flash text, too (see "Creating Flash Text" later in this chapter).

Figure 16-6. Build your Flash button with the Insert Flash Button dialog box

Click Apply to preview your button in the document page. If your label doesn't fit, shorten it, or reduce the type size, and click Apply again. You can also change the button style if you're underwhelmed by the result.

When you finally have the button looking the way you want it, click OK, and fill out the Flash Accessibility Attributes dialog box. Click OK again, and Dreamweaver adds the finalized button to your page. You may then adjust its position on the page with the Property Inspector, as shown in Figure 16-7.

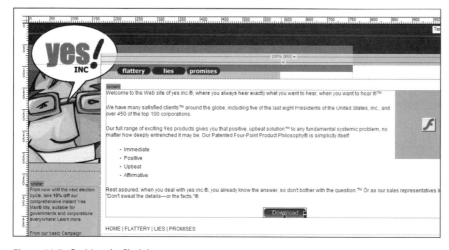

Figure 16-7. Position the Flash button on your page

> **TIP**
>
> Press Play on the Property Inspector to test your Flash button's interactive features, or even better, preview your page in a live browser window. In a browser, you can click the button and follow the link.

To edit your Flash button at any time after you've created it, select it, and click Edit on the Property Inspector.

Creating Flash Text

TECHTALK

Flash text is a short Flash movie that contains clickable text content.

Flash text, much like a Flash button, is a short, clickable Flash movie that you create in Dreamweaver, only Flash text doesn't come with a button background, and it allows you to insert multiple lines of text.

To insert Flash text, choose an insertion point in your document window, and grab the Flash Text object from the Insert panel's Flash menu, as shown in Figure 16-8.

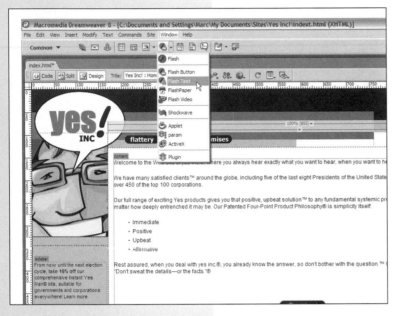

Figure 16-8. Selecting the Flash Text object from the Flash menu

Dreamweaver opens the Insert Flash Text dialog box shown in Figure 16-9. Choose the font and type size from the top fields. As with Flash buttons, you can use the font of your choice, even if it isn't web-safe.

Choose the format, alignment, and colors of the text in the following fields. All the text in the Flash movie shares the same properties, so if you want multicolored text or text with different formats and alignment settings, you'll need to create separate Flash movies.

Type the text itself in the Text field, and press Enter or Return to begin a new line. If you check the Show Font option, the text appears in the field in your selected font. However, the Text field does *not* show your format, alignment, and color options. As before, you'll preview your Flash text before you commit to it, after you've filled out the rest of the dialog box.

Click the Browse button next to the Link field, and choose the page to which the Flash text links. Use the Bg Color color box to set a background color for your Flash text, and then supply a filename for the movie in the Save As field.

You're ready to preview your text. Click Apply, and check the document window. Make whatever changes to the appearance and formatting of your text that you like, and click OK to fill out the Flash Accessibility Options dialog box. Click OK again, and you have Flash text, as Figure 16-10 shows.

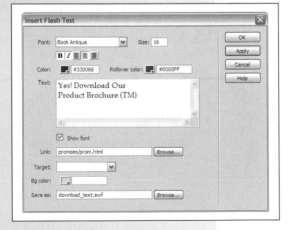

Figure 16-9. Build your Flash text from the Insert Flash Text dialog box

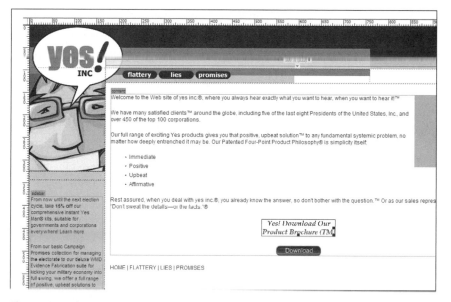

Figure 16-10. Dreamweaver adds your Flash text to the page

TIP

Flash text works best as display copy, like the signage in a store. It isn't searchable or selectable, so be careful about using it too often. The most important text on your site should always appear in regular text form.

TECHTALK

A slideshow is an interactive feature that steps through a sequence of static images.

Creating a Flash Slideshow

A *slideshow* is an interactive feature that steps through a sequence of static images. Dreamweaver comes with a handy, prebuilt, customizable slideshow in Flash format that's just waiting for you to place on your page and use.

To do so, choose an insertion point on your page, and switch to the Flash Elements objects from the Insert panel's menu, as Figure 16-11 shows. Then click the Image Viewer object shown in Figure 16-12.

The Save Flash Element dialog box appears. Navigate to your *images* or *img* folder, and type a name for the slideshow in the File Name field. Click Save, and Dreamweaver adds a large, gray Flash placeholder on the page.

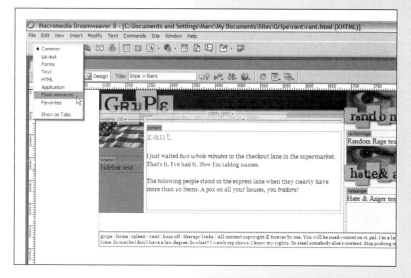

Figure 16-11. Selecting the Flash Elements objects set from the Insert panel's menu

Figure 16-12. The Image Viewer object's icon

▼ Flash element	≡
Flash element	
bgColor	☐ #FFFFFF
captionColor	■ #333333
captionFont	Verdana
captionSize	10
frameColor	■ #333333
frameShow	(No)
frameThickness	2
imageCaptions	[]
imageLinks	['http://macromedia...
imageLinkTarget	_blank
imageURLs	['img1.jpg','img2.jpg...
showControls	(Yes)
slideAutoPlay	(No)
slideDelay	5
slideLoop	(No)
title	
titleColor	■ #333333
titleFont	Verdana
titleSize	10
transitionsType	Random

Figure 16-13. Customize your slideshow from the Flash Element panel

Go to the panel groups, and find the Flash Element panel, as shown in Figure 16-13. Expand this panel. You might also want to collapse the other panels to give you plenty of room to work, because the Flash Element panel is where you customize the slideshow. Click any of the values to edit them. Table 16-1 lists its properties and their meanings.

> **TIP**
>
> With Flash buttons and Flash text, you had to save the Flash movie in the same location as the current page. With a Flash slideshow, it doesn't matter so much. Save it in the most convenient place, which is probably with your images.

Table 16-1. Flash element properties

Property	Controls
bgColor	The background color of the slideshow
captionColor	The color of the image captions in the slideshow
captionFont	The typeface of the image captions in the slideshow
captionSize	The type size of the image captions in the slideshow
frameColor	The color of the slideshow's frame or border
frameShow	Whether the frame appears around the slideshow
frameThickness	The weight of the slideshow's frame
imageCaptions	The text captions for the images in the slideshow sequence
imageLinks	The links for the images in the slideshow sequence
imageLinkTarget	The target for all the links (see Chapter 15)
imageURLs	The images in the slideshow
showControls	Whether a DVD-style control panel appears above the slideshow
slideAutoPlay	Whether the slideshow begins playing automatically when the page loads
slideDelay	The number of seconds between slides
slideLoop	Whether the slideshow repeats with the first image following the final image
title	The title or label of the slideshow
titleColor	The color of the title text
titleFont	The typeface of the title text
titleSize	The type size of the title text
transitionsType	The style of transition between images in the slideshow

Adding Images to the Slideshow

To add images to the slideshow, click the value next to the imageURLs field in the Flash Element panel, and then click the Edit Array Values button to the right. The Edit Array dialog box appears, as Figure 16-14 shows.

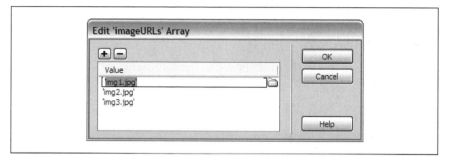

Figure 16-14. Add images to the slideshow from the Edit Array dialog box

Select one of the default images, and a folder icon appears. Click this folder, and navigate to the image file that you want to include. You can add as many images as you like by clicking the plus button. Be sure to remove any images that you don't need by selecting them and then clicking the minus button.

When you're done, click OK.

> **TIP**
>
> It's handy to save the images of your slideshow with the same general file-name plus the number in sequence, as in *slide01, slide02, slide03*, and so on. This helps you to keep them in the proper order when you add them to the slideshow.

Adding Links to the Images

Each image in the slideshow can have its own link. To add the links, click in the imageLinks value field of the Flash Element panel, and then click the folder icon to open the Edit Array dialog box.

Select a link to change its value. Choose a location on your current site by clicking the folder icon and navigating to the desired page, or type the URL of an external web site. If you opt for typing, make sure that the URL appears between single quotes: `'http://www.mysite.com/'` is correct; http://www.my.site.com is not.

The order of the links corresponds to the order of your images, so make sure you're keeping track of which slide is which.

Adding Captions to the Images

Likewise, each image in the slideshow can have its own caption. Click in the
imageCaptions value field of the Flash Element panel, and click the folder
icon to open the Edit Array dialog box. Type the captions in the same order
as your images.

Testing the Slideshow

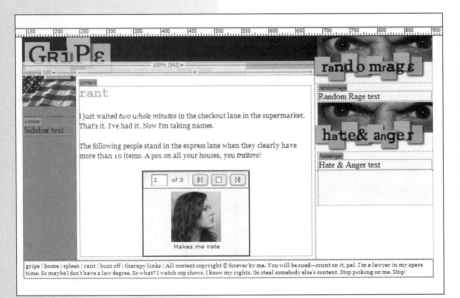

When you're done setting properties,
click the Play button in the Property
Inspector to test your slideshow,
and you will see a slideshow object
as in Figure 16-15. Go back to the
Flash Element panel and tweak the
properties if you like, and position
the slideshow on the page according to the same rules for images and
other types of Flash.

Figure 16-15. Preview your slideshow in the
document window

Connecting Links

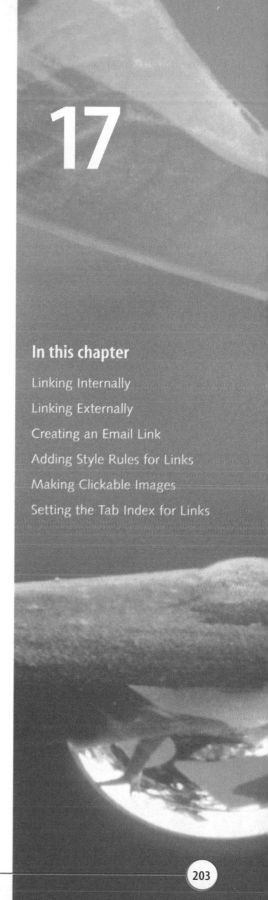

17

Ah, links—the pathways of the Web. By now, you've probably accumulated a mass of template-generated pages. It's time to tie them all together into a fully functional site by way of the small but mighty hyperlink.

This chapter shows you how to create links to any destination, be it strictly local or strange and remote. It gives you methods for creating pop-ups, opening new browser windows, designing link states, and adding rollover effects, and it concludes with a litany of clickable images for virtually any hyperlink need.

Linking Internally

An *internal link* is one that goes from one page of your site to another. You created the most important internal links when you built your nav bar in Chapter 13, but you probably have some more of this kind of linking to do. If nothing else, the secondary nav choices at the bottom of the main content area could use some destination pages.

To create a link to a page of your site, select the string of text that you want to make clickable. For instance, if you're linking the HOME choice in your secondary navigation, select the word HOME. Then go to the Property Inspector and click the folder icon to the right of the Link field. Dreamweaver opens the Select File dialog box. Navigate to the destination page (in this case, the home page of the site, namely *index.html*), and click OK. Dreamweaver turns the selected text into a link to the designated page, as Figure 17-1 shows.

──TECHTALK──

An internal link is one that goes from one page of your site to another.

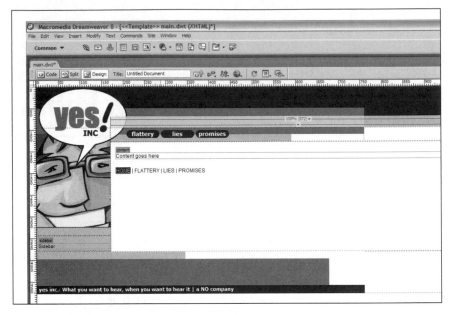

Figure 17-1. Dreamweaver converts the selected text into a link

> **TIP**
>
> When you created your graphical nav bar, you added alternate text to each image. Now, when the visitor hovers over the Flattery button, for instance, a message appears: "Go to the Flattery section" or some such.
>
> You can do the very same thing for non-image, purely textual hyperlinks. First click anywhere inside the text link in the document window, and then go to the Tag Inspector. (If you don't see the Tag Inspector on screen, choose Window→Attributes from the main menu, or press F9.) Then, next to the title attribute, type the alternate text for the link.
>
> When you preview your page in a live browser, hover over the link, and wait a second or two. The alternate text appears, just like it does for an image. This trick works in the latest versions of IE, Firefox, Netscape Browser, and Opera.

> **TIP**
>
> To remove a link, click anywhere inside the link text in the document window. Then go to the Property Inspector, delete the value in the Link field, and press Enter or Return.

If you're working on the secondary nav, go ahead and add the rest of the links. Save your template document when you're done, and update the pages of your site. Then open one of the actual pages in Dreamweaver, preview it in a live browser, and test your links. Nothing makes you feel like you're making more progress than getting the links up and running.

Linking to Named Anchors

Assume that you've written a very long page with several different sections of content, like a Frequently Asked Questions page or something to that effect. You might want to add links from the questions at the top of the page to the answers at the bottom. Is such a thing even possible? Of course it is. You just need a few named anchors.

A *named anchor* is a specific link destination somewhere within the page. Named anchors are invisible elements. The visitor doesn't see them on the page, but just because they're invisible doesn't mean they're not useful. When the visitor follows a link to a named anchor, the browser jumps to the anchor point immediately and positions it as close to the top of the browser window as possible.

If you're building a Frequently Asked Questions page, then, the link for each question goes to a different named anchor. All you have to do is place the named anchors on your page.

Inserting a named anchor

To add a named anchor to your page, choose an insertion point in the document window, usually to the left or immediately above the content to which you want to link. Then click the Named Anchor object in the Insert panel (see Figure 17-2). If you don't see the Named Anchor object, set the Insert panel's menu to Common.

The Named Anchor dialog box shown in Figure 17-3 appears. Type a brief but descriptive name for the anchor, and click OK. (The name can't contain spaces, and it can't start with a number.) Dreamweaver places the anchor in the page as a visible icon, as Figure 17-4 shows, but in the browser, the element is invisible.

Figure 17-2. The Named Anchor object icon

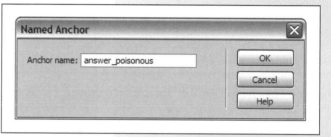

Figure 17-3. Naming an anchor in the Named Anchor dialog box

> **TIP**
>
> All the named anchors on a page should have different names, but you might associate similar anchors by using the same basic name and then attaching a qualifier or number, such as *answer_poisonous*, *answer_ingredients*, and *answer_artificial*; or *answer01*, *answer02*, and *answer03*.
>
> The browser doesn't treat similarly named anchors as any kind of logical group. You do this simply for your own benefit.

Feel free to insert as many named anchors as your page requires. Just make sure they all have different names.

Linking to a named anchor

To link to a named anchor, select the text that you want to make clickable, as before. Then, instead of clicking the folder icon to the right of the Link field in the Property Inspector, hold down the mouse button on the Point To File icon between the Link field and the folder icon.

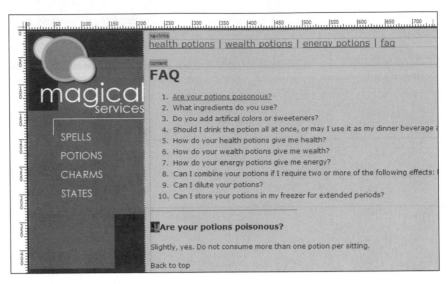

Figure 17-4. The named anchor object looks like an anchor

Still holding down the mouse button, drag the Point To File icon to the named anchor in the document window to which you want to link. When the link appears in the Link field of the Property Inspector, release the mouse button.

Providing a way back

When you're dealing with a dozen or more named anchors on a Frequently Asked Questions page, it's good designer etiquette to include a "Back to top" link after each section of text in the body of the page so that the visitor can jump back to the list of questions at the top without having to scroll.

To do this, follow these steps:

1. Open the template document in Dreamweaver.

2. Click anywhere inside the main content area.

3. Go to the Tag Selector at the bottom of the document window, and click the `<td>` or `<div>` tag.

4. Press the right arrow key to set the insertion point at the very beginning of the main content area.

5. Insert a named anchor called *top* at this location.

6. Save the template document, and update the pages of your site.

7. Open the Frequently Asked Questions page in Dreamweaver. You should see the new named anchor at the top of the main content area, similar to Figure 17-5.

8. Add or select the "Back to top" text at the bottom of an answer section.

9. Go to the Property Inspector, and drag the Point To File icon to the named anchor at the top of the main content area. Dreamweaver adds the link (see Figure 17-5).

10. Repeat steps 8 and 9 for the remainder of the answers on the page.

Opening the Destination Page in a Pop-up Window

Normally, Dreamweaver loads the destination page in the main browser window, replacing the current page. If you prefer, you can load the destination page in a pop-up window instead:

1. In the document window, select the text that you want to make clickable.

2. Go to the Property Inspector, type # in the Link field, and press Enter or Return. The number sign or hash mark stands for a *self-referential link*—a link that goes nowhere.

3. With the link selected in the document window, open the Behaviors panel by choosing Window→Behaviors from the main menu.

4. Click the plus button on the Behaviors panel, and choose Open Browser Window from the menu of behaviors, as shown in Figure 17-6.

> **TIP**
>
> If you plan on using pop-ups frequently on your site, you might consider creating a special template document for pop-up pages. When you need to add a new pop-up to the site, simply create a new page from the pop-up template.

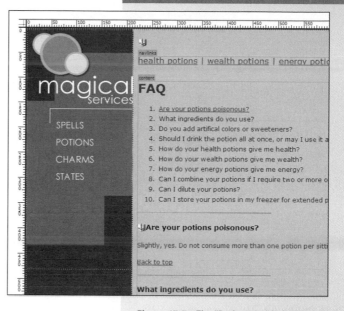

Figure 17-5. The "Back to top" link points to a named anchor at the very top of the main content area

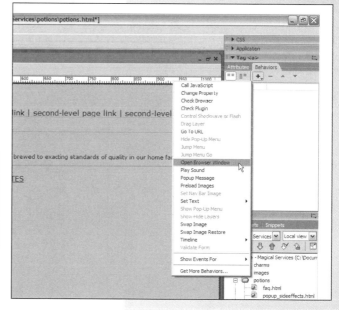

Figure 17-6. Choosing Open Browser Window from the Behavior panel's plus menu

TECHTALK

A self-referential link links to its own page. In other words, it goes nowhere.

HOTKEY

Press Shift-F4 to toggle the Behaviors panel.

5. The Open Browser Window dialog box in Figure 17-7 appears. Click the Browse button to the right of the URL To Display field, and navigate to the page that should open in the pop up.

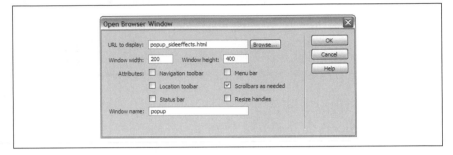

Figure 17-7. Defining the pop-up window

6. Specify a width and height for the pop-up window in the appropriate fields. Both values are in pixels.

7. Under Attributes, check the features that you want to add to your pop up. You don't need to check any of them, although at a minimum the option for scrollbars is a wise choice.

8. In the Window Name field, type a brief but descriptive name for the window. The name *popup* is as good as any.

9. Click OK. Dreamweaver adds the necessary JavaScript code to your page.

To test your pop up, preview the page in a live browser window, and click the pop up's link, as demonstrated in Figure 17-8.

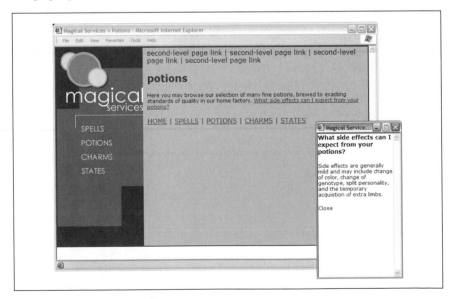

Figure 17-8. Test your pop up in a live browser window

Part III: Building Your Site

One of the drawbacks of pop-up windows is that many visitors find them annoying, so much so that they might install pop-up blocker software on their computers to minimize the likelihood of their seeing the things.

Generally speaking, your visitors hate automatic pop ups the most. These are the pop ups that appear as soon as a web page loads. Most blocker software screens them out, and for good reason. When your visitors land on a web page, they want the information that they requested, not the information that they requested plus a bunch of pop-up ads. If you value your visitors, avoid automatic pop-ups at all costs.

The pop ups that you're creating in this chapter are elective, in that the visitor manually clicks a link to cause the pop up to appear. The default settings of most pop-up blockers allow elective pop ups to squeak through. Even so, given the association of pop-up windows with advertisements, use elective pop ups very judiciously on your site.

A final word of caution: Pop ups often cause problems for screen readers and other accessibility tools.

To add a Close link to the pop-up window, open the pop-up page in Dreamweaver, and select the text that the visitor clicks to close the pop up. Then go to the Property Inspector, and type javascript: window.close(); in the Link field, as shown in Figure 17-9. Be sure to type all the punctuation exactly as it appears. Don't skip the colon, period, parentheses, or semicolon!

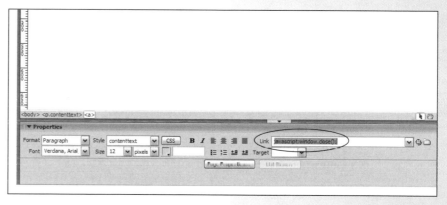

Figure 17-9. Adding a Close link to the pop-up page

Linking Externally

An *external link* is one that goes from your site to some other site. To add an external link to your page, select the text that you want to make clickable, and go to the Property Inspector. In the Link field, type the complete web address of the destination:

- To link to the home page of the site, just type the site's general URL, such as *http://www.macromedia.com/*.

- To link to a specific page of the site, type the URL of the page in question, such as *http://www.macromedia.com/software/dreamweaver/index.html/*.

—**TECHTALK**—
An external link is one that goes from your site to some other site.

- To link to a specific named anchor on a page of the site, type the URL of the page in question, the hash sign (#), and the name of the anchor, such as *http://www.macromedia.com/software/dreamweaver/productinfo/faq/index.html#item-2-1/*.

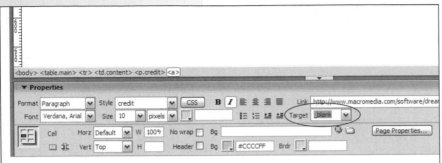

Figure 17-10. Choosing _blank from the Target menu on the Property Inspector

By default, the browser loads the external page in the current browser window, effectively replacing your site. If you would prefer to load the external page in a new browser window, choose _blank from the Target menu on the Property Inspector, as Figure 17-10 shows. This practice is called *targeting* the link.

Generally, it's acceptable to load external sites in a new browser window, but avoid doing so for internal links, unless you're linking to an image or multimedia file that would otherwise interrupt the flow of your navigation. Even so, a pop-up window is probably the better choice, because a pop up feels more secondary and more a part of your site than a separate browser window in full regalia.

BEST BET

Avoid opening internal links in new browser windows, unless the destination is an image or multimedia file that would otherwise interrupt the flow of your navigation.

Creating an Email Link

An *email* or *mailto* link looks like a normal hyperlink, but instead of sending the browser to another page, it opens the visitor's default email program and creates a blank message with the email address of your choice in the To field.

To create an email link, select the text in the document window that you want to make clickable, and then go to the Insert panel. Click the Email Link object shown in Figure 17-11 to open the Email Link dialog box shown in Figure 17-12.

Type the recipient address for the email message in the E-Mail field, and click OK to add the link.

Figure 17-11. The Email Link object icon

Figure 17-12. Entering the link text and the recipient address

Adding Style Rules for Links

You know from Chapter 6 that CSS recognizes four link states: unvisited, visited, active, and hover. For the purposes of your site, you can create one style rule that sets the appearance of all links, regardless of state; or you can create different style rules for different link states, as this section shows.

Creating One Style Rule for All Link States

For a blanket style rule that affects all link states, you want to redefine the appearance of the <a> tag in your stylesheet. Open the New CSS Rule dialog box, and choose Tag as the selector type. Type a in the Selector field, as Figure 17-13 shows, and click OK to go to the CSS Rule Definition dialog box.

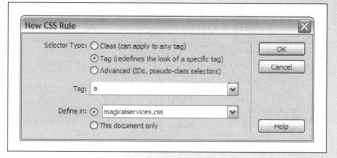

Figure 17-13. Creating a new CSS rule for the <a> tag

Build the rule definition as you normally would, choosing whatever appearance attributes strike your fancy. Under Decoration in the Text category, choose None to remove the underline, as Figure 17-14 shows. If you want to keep the underline, you don't have to select the Underline option—the browser automatically supplies an underline by default.

If you specify a color here, the color applies to all link states. Your links will no longer change color depending upon their state. If you want the links to continue changing color as they normally would, don't specify a color in this style rule.

Click OK when you're finished, and Dreamweaver adds your new style rule to your external stylesheet.

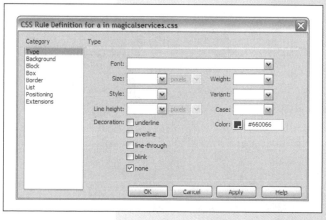

Figure 17-14. Under Decoration, choose None to remove link underlines

Creating Different Style Rules for Different Link States

For specific style rules for the different link states, open the New CSS Rule dialog box, but this time choose Advanced under Selector Type, and select a link state from the Selector menu, as shown in Figure 17-15. The a:link option refers to unvisited links. The rest are exactly what they say they are, although don't choose a:hover just yet—see "Adding a Rollover Effect" later in this chapter for information about rollovers.

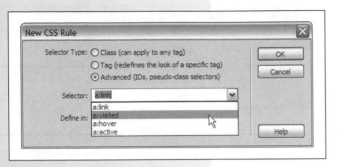

Figure 17-15. Choosing a link state from the Selector menu

In the CSS Rule Definition dialog box, design the appearance of the link state, and then repeat this procedure for the remaining states. Any link states that you omit the browser's default appearance attributes.

Adding a Rollover Effect

Adding a rollover effect to your links is easy, whether you opted for a one-size-fits-all blanket rule or separate rules for separate states. Just follow these steps:

1. Open the New CSS Rule dialog box.

2. Under Selector Type, choose Advanced.

3. From the Selector menu, choose a:hover. Click OK to proceed to the CSS Rule Definition dialog box.

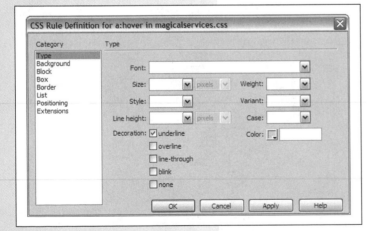

Figure 17-16. When hovered over, links will acquire an underline

4. Design the appearance of the rollover effect. You don't have to duplicate your previous style rules here. Just describe what specifically happens to the link when the visitor rolls over it. For instance, if the link looks exactly the same except that it acquires an underline, check the Underline option under Decoration as in Figure 17-16, and do nothing else. If the link acquires an underline and becomes bold, check the Underline option, and choose bold from the Weight menu. If the link acquires an underline, becomes bold, and changes color, check Underline, choose bold, and set the desired color in the Color field.

5. Click OK. Dreamweaver adds your rollover style rule to the external stylesheet.

Making Clickable Images

Clickable images aren't just about buttons in the nav bar. Resourceful web designers like to squeeze every bit of functionality from the elements on their pages, and an easy way to do this is to turn images into links. One very common practice is to link to the home page of the site from the logo image at the top of the layout.

Happily, turning an image file into a link is simplicity itself. Select the image in the document window, and proceed as if you had just selected a string of text. Follow the steps for internal links, pop-up windows, named anchors, external links, or email links, depending upon what you want the link to do.

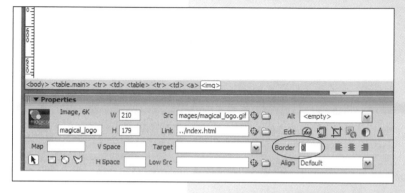

Figure 17-17. The default border of the linked image has a value of 0

By default in the browser, a visible border appears around the clickable image. The color of the border corresponds to the state of the link. However, Dreamweaver automatically turns off this border by setting the value of the Border field in the Property Inspector to 0, as Figure 17-17 shows. If you want to make the border visible, change this value. Generally, a value of 1 is sufficient, but the higher the number, the heavier the border.

There are several other kinds of clickable images that you might want to add to your site. This section goes over the most common types.

Making Rollover Images

Rollover images can sit anywhere on your page, not just in the nav bar. To add a rollover image, create separate graphics for the up and over states, and save these files in the *img* or *images* folder of your site. Then choose an insertion point in the document window, open the menu of image objects in the Insert panel, and grab the Rollover Image object as shown in Figure 17-18.

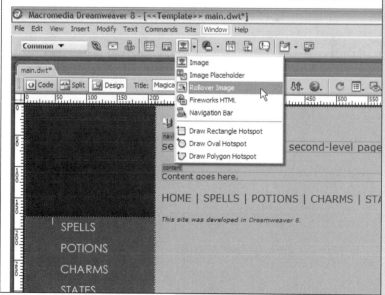

Figure 17-18. Selecting the Rollover Image object from the menu of image objects

Figure 17-19. Add the rollover image with the Insert Rollover Image dialog box

When you do, the Insert Rollover Image dialog box appears, as Figure 17-19 shows. In the Image Name field, type a brief but descriptive name for the image.

Click the Browse buttons next to the Original Image and Rollover Image fields, and navigate to the up- and over-state graphics files, respectively. Also, be sure to check the Preload Rollover Image option for smoother animation.

In the Alternate Text field, supply the textual description of the image. Because this is a clickable image, you want to begin the description with a verb. Tell your visitors what to expect when they click.

Finally, click the Browse button next to the When Clicked field, and navigate to the page to which you want to link. If you're linking to an external site, type the URL in the field instead.

When you click OK, Dreamweaver adds the rollover to the page.

Making Image Maps

An *image map* is a graphic with one or more clickable regions or *hotspots*. Image maps come in handy when the banner for your site is a large, continuous image, of which the logo is a small part. Instead of making the entire banner image clickable, you can define an image map that makes just the logo portion clickable. Here's how:

1. In the document window, select the image to which you want to apply an image map.

2. Go to the Property Inspector, and choose one of the hotspot tools shown in Figure 17-20.

3. Move the mouse pointer onto the selected image and draw the hotspot. If you chose the Rectangular or Oval Hotspot Tool, hold down the mouse button and drag the mouse. If you chose the Polygon Hotspot Tool, you create the hotspot point by point by point. Click the mouse button and release to add a point to the polygon.

——TECHTALK——

An image map is a graphic with one or more clickable regions or hotspots.

Figure 17-20. The hotspot tools available from the Property Inspector

4. Go back to the Property Inspector and grab the Pointer Hotspot Tool. Click the hotspot that you just drew.

5. Back in the Property Inspector, click the folder icon to the right of the Link field and choose the page to which you want to link.

6. Add descriptive text for the link in the Alternate Text field. Remember, this is a clickable image, so start with a verb.

7. Go back to Step 2, and repeat for as many hotspots that you want to add to the image map.

Figure 17-21 shows an image map with a rectangular hotspot over the logo portion of the banner image. The hotspot links to the home page.

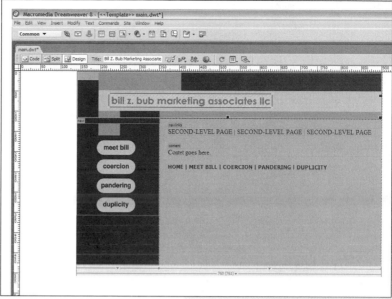

Figure 17-21. A hotspot over the logo in the banner links to the home page

> **TIP**
>
> The best hotspots are the obvious ones: the parts of the image that look clickable, like a logo. If you create a hotspot in an obscure place on the image, don't be surprised if your visitors can't guess where to click.

Making Control Buttons for a Flash Movie

Here's a clever trick for the Flash fanatics among us. By way of Dreamweaver behaviors, you can insert buttons that control the playback of a Flash movie. Here's what you need:

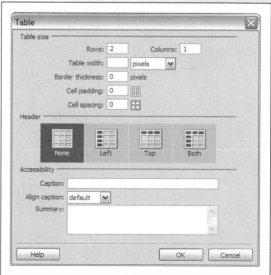

Figure 17-22. Creating a table to house the Flash movie and its control buttons

- A Flash movie

- Button images for any or all of the following: Play, Stop, Rewind, Forward

Start by choosing an insertion point in the document window. Then go to the Insert panel, and click the Table object. What you want to do is create a table that holds the Flash movie and the control buttons, just to keep them together as a unit. If you're against using tables in this way, you don't need the table to make the buttons work, but your design may be less elegant.

In the Table dialog box, specify a table with two rows and one column, as Figure 17-22 shows. The border, padding, and spacing values are up to you. Click OK to insert the table.

Click inside the top cell of the table, and insert the Flash movie. Go back to the Property Inspector to supply a brief but descriptive identifier for the movie and to uncheck the Loop and Autoplay options, as shown in Figure 17-23.

Figure 17-23. Setting the properties of the Flash movie object

Now click in the bottom table cell and insert the button images, as Figure 17-24 shows. If you use a method that asks for a link destination, such as the Insert Rollover dialog box, supply the hash sign (#) to create a self-referential link. When you finish, position the buttons as you prefer and give them self-referential links (if they don't already have them). Select each button in turn, and type the hash sign in the Link field of the Property Inspector.

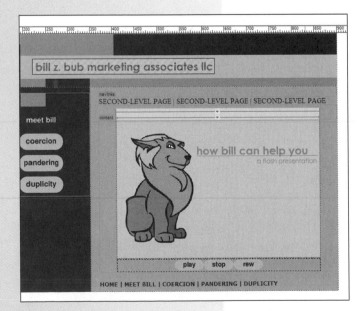

Figure 17-24. Insert the button images in the bottom cell

Select the first button in the document window. Then go to the Tag Selector, and click the <a> tag to select the button's link. Your next stop is the Behaviors panel. If you don't see the Behaviors panel on screen, choose Window→Behaviors from the main menu. Click the plus button on the Behaviors panel, and choose the Control Shockwave Or Flash behavior from the menu that appears, as shown in Figure 17-25.

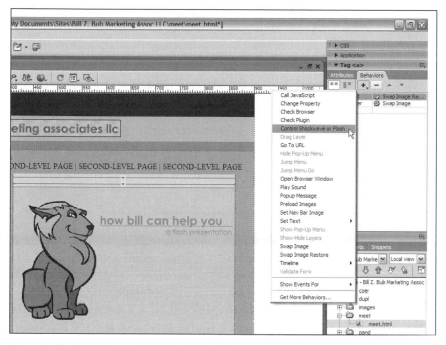

Figure 17-25. Add the Control Shockwave Or Flash behavior to each button in turn

This gives you the Control Shockwave Or Flash dialog box shown in Figure 17-26. From the Movie menu, select the identifier of the movie. Then, do one of the following:

- For a Play button, choose the Play action.

- For a Stop button, choose the Stop action.

- For a Rewind button, choose the Rewind action.

- For a Forward button, choose the Go To Frame action, and supply the frame number to which you want to jump.

Click OK to add the behavior to the button. Repeat this process for the remaining buttons, and you've got your own movie control panel. Save your page, and preview it in a live browser to test the buttons, as in Figure 17-27.

Figure 17-26. The Action field sets the function of the button

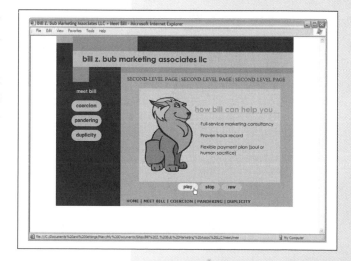

Figure 17-27. Testing the control buttons in a live browser window

Setting the Tab Index for Links

In Chapter 16, you looked briefly at the tab index of page elements, and you learned that the tab index establishes the order in which the elements are selected when the visitor presses the Tab key. This is an important accessibility feature for those who don't or can't browse your web site with a mouse.

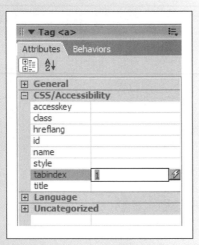

Figure 17-28. Setting the tab index for a link in the Tag Inspector

> **BEST BET**
>
> Set the tab index for all selectable page elements at the same time, when the page is either finished or almost finished.

It's best to set the tab index for all the selectable page elements at the same time, when the page is either finished or close to being finished, so the information here comes a bit out of sequence. Nevertheless, to set the tab index for a link, click anywhere inside the link on the document window, go to the Tag Selector, choose the <a> tag, and then go to the Attributes panel as shown in Figure 17-28, which is also known as the Tag Inspector. If you don't see the Attributes panel, choose Window→Tag Inspector from the main menu.

Look under the CSS/Accessibility category for the tabindex attribute. Then click in the field to the right of it, and supply its value. Remember from Chapter 16 that the tab-index value determines the order in which the element is selected, so a tab index of 1 makes the link the first element selected when the visitor presses the Tab key, while a tab index of 75 makes it the seventy-fifth element selected.

> *— HOTKEY —*
>
> *Press F9 to toggle the Tag Inspector (also called the Attributes panel).*

> **BEHIND THE SCENES**
>
> If you don't specify tab-index values, the browser selects page elements according to the order in which they appear in the HTML code. Likewise for two or more elements that share the same tab-index value.
>
> If you have a tables-based layout, you know from Chapter 4 that the order of the elements on screen doesn't necessarily match their order in the code, so set those tab-index attributes wisely and with pride.

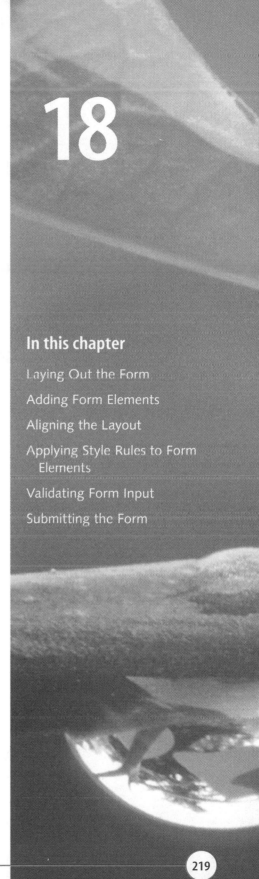

Building Forms 18

Want to collect input from your visitors? An HTML form is the way to go. A *form* is a collection of *fields* (also called *objects* or *widgets*)—little interactive elements that the visitor clicks or types into. When the visitor clicks the form's Submit button, the browser packages the values of the fields and sends them off. In a dynamic site, the form submission often goes to another page for processing, and this page is loaded with server-side code. In a static site, like the kind you're building, you have to instruct the browser to send the submission to an email address.

This chapter shows you how to construct a form in Dreamweaver, align the fields, apply styles, and submit the values by email.

Laying Out the Form

Whenever you build a form, you start by inserting the form container tag, `<form>`. This element groups all the fields of the form into a logical unit so that the browser doesn't get confused. The form container is very easy to forget, because you don't actually see it in the browser window. It's one of those invisible elements that you run across every now and then. The only thing to do is to remember to insert it, so here's what you do:

1. Choose an insertion point in the document window.

2. Go to the Insert panel, and switch to the set of form objects, as Figure 18-1 shows.

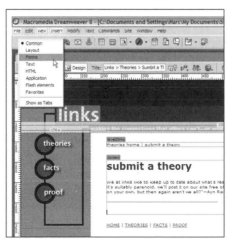

Figure 18-1. Setting the Insert panel's menu to Forms

Figure 18-2. The Form object's icon

3. In the Insert panel, click the Form object (see Figure 18-2).

Dreamweaver adds the form container to the document window as a red rectangle with a dashed border, as Figure 18-3 shows. The rectangle is for your benefit, so that you can see where the form container appears in your layout, but in a browser window the container is completely invisible.

Figure 18-3. Dreamweaver represents the form container as a red rectangle with a dashed border

The best way to lay out a form is to use a table, much to the consternation of standards organizations everywhere. So make a quick sketch of the form that you want to build, and divide it into rows and columns, as Figure 18-4 shows.

To insert the table, click anywhere inside the form container, and then choose Insert→Table from the main menu. In the Table dialog box, set the number of rows and columns to match the rows and columns in your form sketch, in this case 7 and 2 respectively, as Figure 18-5 shows. If you want a visible border around the table cells, type a value in the Border Thickness field. Otherwise, leave it blank. The Padding and Spacing fields can also be blank, or they can take values depending upon your preference.

Click OK, and Dreamweaver places the table inside the form container, as Figure 18-6 shows. You're ready now to insert the fields of the form.

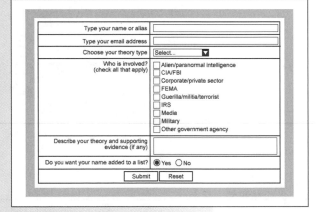

Figure 18-4. Sketch a mockup of your form, and divide it into rows and columns

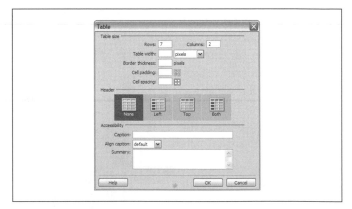

Figure 18-5. Setting the number of rows and columns for the table

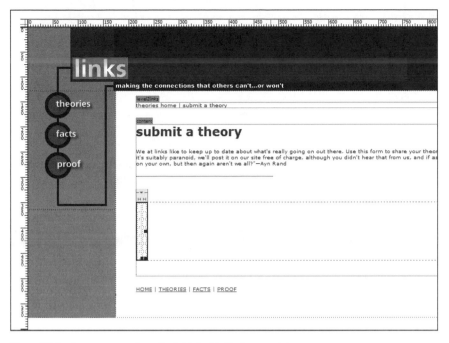

Figure 18-6. Dreamweaver places the table inside the form container

TECHTALK

A form is an HTML structure for collecting visitor input. The form contains one or more fields, which the visitor clicks or fills out.

Adding Form Elements

Click inside the first cell in your form's table, and go to the Insert panel. Choose the form element that you want to insert. You have several options, as Table 18-1 shows.

Table 18-1. Common form elements in Dreamweaver

Insert-panel object	Creates	Best for
Text Field	Single line, multiline, or password text field	Inputting text
Textarea	Multiline text field	Inputting text
Checkbox	Checkbox	A short set of options where the visitor may select none, one, or any
Radio Group	Radio buttons	A short set of options where the visitor may select one and only one
List/Menu	List or menu	A long set of options where the visitor may select none, one, or any (list); a long set of options where the visitor may select one and only one (menu)
Button	Submit or Reset button	Submitting the form (Submit button); resetting the form (Reset button)

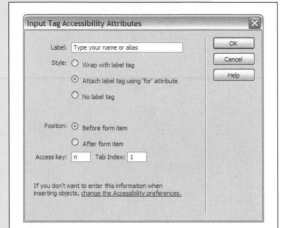

Figure 18-7. The Text Field object's icon

Inserting Text Fields

Looking back at the form sketch in this example, the first item is a text field, so click the Text Field object in the Insert panel, as in Figure 18-7. When you do, the Input Tag Accessibility Options dialog box appears, as Figure 18-8 shows.

> **BEST BET**
>
> When you're laying out a form inside a table structure, attach the label of a form field using the for attribute.

In the Label field, type the label from your form sketch, and under Style, choose the option to attach the label tag using the for attribute. When you're laying out the form in a table, this option works best. Also supply an access key and the tab index for this field. The tab-index value should be 1 here, because this is the first element in the form.

Figure 18-8. Setting the label and accessibility options for the text field

> **TIP**
>
> You know from Chapter 17 that you shouldn't really set tab-index values until your page is finished, but supply them for your form elements anyway, just to determine the order in which they should be selectable. You may have to come back and revise the tab-index values once you have finished the page to make room for other selectable elements like links, but at least this way your form fields are already in the proper order, and you can simply change their tab-index values by the same standard amount. For instance, if you end up having eight links before the first item in the form, change the tab index of the first form field to 9 (1 + 8), the tab index of the second form field to 10 (2 + 8), the tab index of the third form field to 11 (3 + 8), and so on.

> **TIP**
>
> Set the access key of a form field to match the first letter of the most important word in the label. So for the label "Type your name or alias," a good choice for the access key is *n*—*n* for *name*.

Click OK, and Dreamweaver adds the text field to the table, as Figure 18-9 shows.

Now click the text field itself, and drag it into the table cell next door, as Figure 18-10 shows. Leave the label in its current table cell.

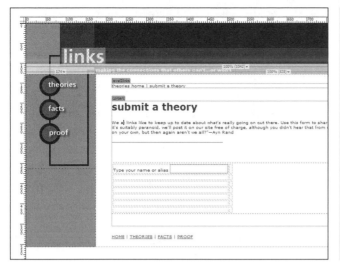

Figure 18-9. Dreamweaver adds the text field to the table

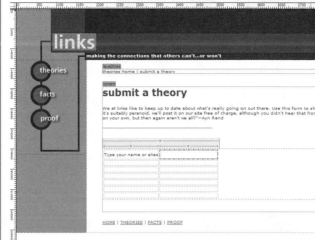

Figure 18-10. Drag the text field to the adjacent table cell

Click the text field to select it, go to the Property Inspector, and fill out the attributes of this element, as Figure 18-11 shows:

Figure 18-11. Setting the attributes of the text field

- In the field under the TextField label, type a short but descriptive name for the element.

- In the Char Width field, type the width of the element on screen (in characters, not pixels).

- In the Max Chars field, type the maximum number of characters that the visitor may enter into this field. This value doesn't have to be the same as the character width, although it's generally helpful to give the same value for both.

- Under Type, choose Password if you want the text field to conceal the characters that the visitor types.

- In the Initial Val field, type the text that should appear in the field by default (if any).

Inserting Text Areas

A *text area* is a multiline text field. To insert a text area, click the Textarea object on the Insert panel, as Figure 18-12 shows. Dreamweaver opens the Input Tag Accessibility Options dialog box again. Fill out the label and accessibility options for this field, as Figure 18-13 shows.

Figure 18-12. The Textarea object's icon

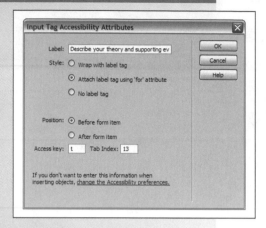

Figure 18-13. Setting the accessibility options for the text area

Drag the text area into the adjacent table cell. Then select the text area and fill out the attribute fields in the Property Inspector as in Figure 18-14:

- Under the TextField label, type a short but descriptive name for the text area.

- In the Char Width field, type the width of the element on screen (in characters, not pixels).

Figure 18-14. Supplying the attributes for the text area

BEHIND THE SCENES

By default, the same character width applied to a single-line text field and a multiline text area produces form fields of two different sizes. You can help to minimize this inconsistency by applying the same font and type size to these fields with CSS.

- In the Num Lines field, type the number of lines visible at once in the text area.

- In the Max Chars field, type the maximum number of characters that the visitor may enter into this field. This value doesn't have to be the same as the character width, although it's generally helpful to give the same value for both.

- The Wrap menu controls the setting for automatic *word wrapping*, or moving incomplete words from the end of one line to the beginning of the next. Under Wrap, choose Off if you don't want automatic word wrapping in the text area. Choose Virtual if you want word wrapping on screen but not in the form submission. Choose Physical if you want word wrapping on screen and in the form submission.

Inserting Checkboxes

You add checkboxes one at a time to your form. Instead of inserting them into the left column of your form table and then moving them to the right, you can insert them directly into the right column.

---TECHTALK---

A text area is a multiline text field.

---TECHTALK---

Word wrapping is moving incomplete words from the end of one line to the beginning of the next.

To insert a checkbox, click the Checkbox object on the Insert panel, as Figure 18-15 shows, which gives you the familiar Input Tag Accessibility Options dialog box shown in Figure 18-16. The caption for a checkbox works better when it comes after the form element, so be sure to choose the After option under Position. Click OK to add the checkbox to the document window.

Figure 18-15. The Checkbox object's icon

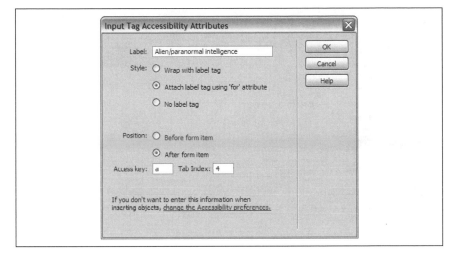

Figure 18-16. Positioning the caption after the checkbox

Now select the checkbox, and go to the Property Inspector to fill in the attributes as in Figure 18-17:

- In the Checkbox Name field, type a name for the checkbox. For your convenience, all the checkboxes of a particular type can have the same name.

- In the Checked Value field, type the value that the form submits for this checkbox if the visitor happens to check it.

- Under Initial State, choose Checked if you want the browser to check the checkbox by default when the page loads.

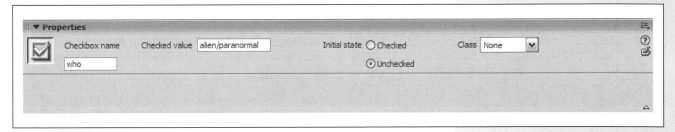

Figure 18-17. Supplying the attributes for the checkbox

To insert the next checkbox in the table cell, hold down the Shift key and press Enter or Return to insert a line break rather than a new paragraph. This gives you the insertion point that you want. When you finish, your document window looks something like Figure 18-18.

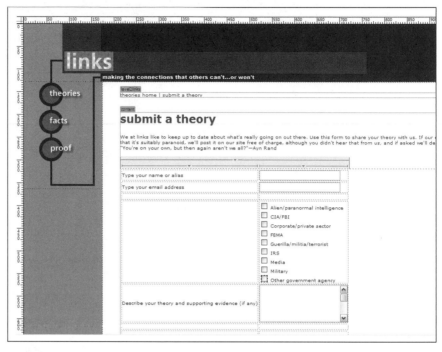

Figure 18-18. The checkbox options are separated by line breaks

Inserting Radio Groups

Unlike checkboxes, which you add one at a time, you can insert an entire group of radio buttons simultaneously. To do so, choose an insertion point in the right column of your table, and click the Radio Group object in the Insert panel, as Figure 18-19 shows. Dreamweaver opens the Radio Group dialog box, as Figure 18-20 shows.

In the Name field, type brief but descriptive name for the radio buttons. All the buttons in the group get the same name.

Under Radio Buttons, supply labels and values for all the buttons in the group. The label is the text that appears on screen, while the value is what goes into the form submission when the visitor selects that particular radio button. Use the plus and minus buttons to add and remove radio buttons from the group and use the arrow buttons to rearrange their order.

Figure 18-19. The Radio Group object's icon

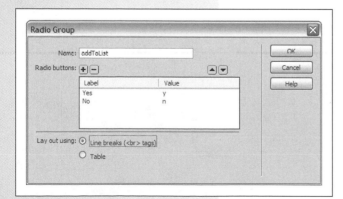

Figure 18-20. Building the group of radio buttons and their attributes

Under Lay Out Using, choose either Line Breaks or Table. Line breaks are easier to modify when you want the radio buttons to sit side by side rather than in a column, but the choice is yours.

Click OK, and Dreamweaver adds the radio group to the document window, as Figure 18-21 shows.

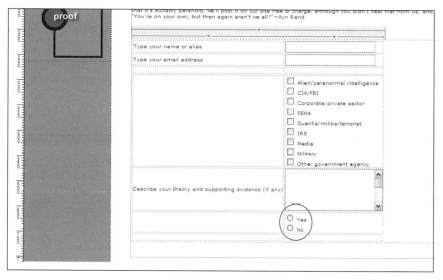

Figure 18-21. Dreamweaver adds the radio group to the document window

To remove the line break after the top radio button's label, position the cursor at the end of the line, and press the Delete key to get the result shown in Figure 18-22.

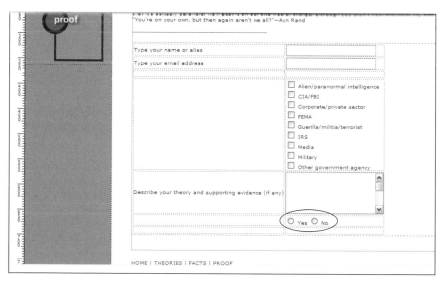

Figure 18-22. Without the line break, the radio buttons sit adjacent

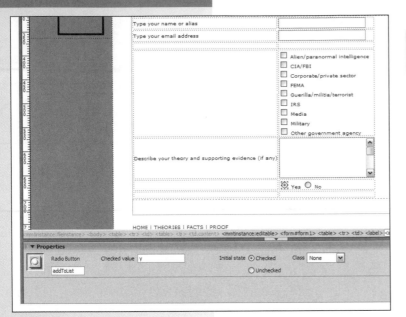

Figure 18-23. Setting one of the radio buttons to be preselected

Figure 18-24. The List/Menu object's icon

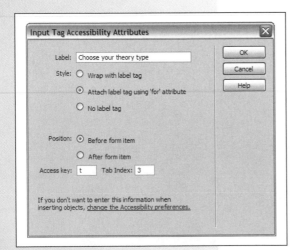

Figure 18-25. Supplying the label and accessibility options

Every radio group should have a preselected option, so select the radio button that you want to make the default choice, go to the Property Inspector, and choose Checked as the initial state, as Figure 18-23 shows.

Inserting Lists and Menus

The difference between lists and menus is subtle but important. Both are for displaying sets of options. The difference is that a list shows several options at once, which encourages the visitor to make multiple selections, while a menu shows one option at a time, which encourages the visitor to select one option only.

To insert a list or menu, choose an insertion point in the left column of your form table, and click the List/Menu object in the Insert panel, as Figure 18-24 shows. As you probably expect, Dreamweaver calls up the Input Tag Accessibility Attributes dialog box. Fill out the dialog box, as Figure 18-25 shows.

Click OK, and Dreamweaver inserts the form field on the page in menu format. Drag the menu to the adjacent table column. Then select the menu, and go to the Insert panel. Type a brief but descriptive name for the element in the field under List/Menu, and choose the List option if you want this item to appear in list format.

To supply the choices for the list or menu, click the List Values button, and the List Values dialog box in Figure 18-26 appears. For each option, type a label, which is the text that appears on screen in the list or menu, and a value, which is the text that the form submits when the visitor chooses this particular item. Add and subtract menu items with the plus and minus buttons, and change the order of the items with the arrow buttons.

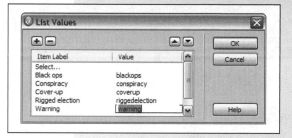

Figure 18-26. Building the options set for the list or menu

Click OK, and Dreamweaver adds the items to the list or menu. If you're creating a menu, then in the Initially Selected field on the Property Inspector, choose the item that the browser should preselect. Normally, this is the first item in the menu, as Figure 18-27 shows.

Figure 18-27. Choosing an option to be preselected in the menu

Inserting Buttons

Buttons come in three types, but the first two are the most relevant to the current discussion. These are the Submit button and the Reset button. A *Submit button* sends off the fields of the form and a *Reset button* restores them to their default values.

Figure 18-28. The Button object's icon

To insert a button, click the Button object on the Insert panel, as Figure 18-28 shows, and fill out the Input Tag Accessibility Attributes dialog box as in Figure 18-29. You don't need to specify a separate text label, because you'll add the label directly to the button once you've created it.

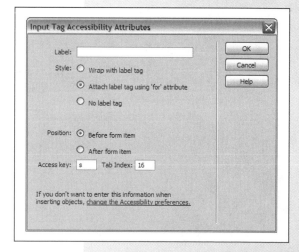

Figure 18-29. You don't have to give a separate text label for the button

Click OK to insert the button. Now select it in the document window, and then fill out the Property Inspector as Figure 18-30 shows:

- Under Action, to create a Submit button, choose Submit Form. To create a Reset button, choose Reset Form.

- Type the label of the button in the Value field. The labels don't have to be *Submit* and *Reset*, although to keep with the *s* and *r* theme of your access keys, you might choose similar-sounding labels such as *Send Form* and *Restore Form*.

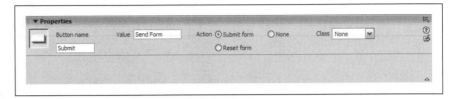

Figure 18-30. Supplying the attributes of the button

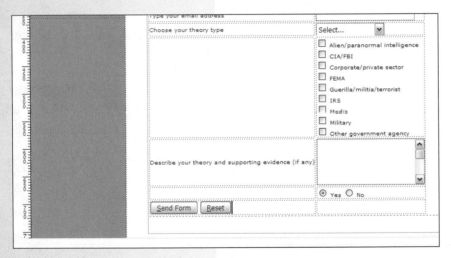

Figure 18-31. There's nothing in the table cell to the right of the one with the buttons

Your form should definitely include a Submit button. If it doesn't, the visitor has no way of sending you the form input! A Reset button, on the other hand, is optional. If you want both types, simply insert another button in the table cell.

When you're finished, notice that the cell to the right is empty, as in Figure 18-31. There's no reason to keep the right table cell, so you can join the cells of this row. Here's how:

1. Click anywhere inside the cell with the buttons.

2. Go to the Tag Selector at the bottom of the document window, and choose the <tr> tag to select the entire row. (The <tr> tag stands for "table row.")

3. Go to the Property Inspector, and click the merge icon shown in Figure 18-32.

Figure 18-32. The merge icon

Dreamweaver merges the selected cells, as Figure 18-33 shows.

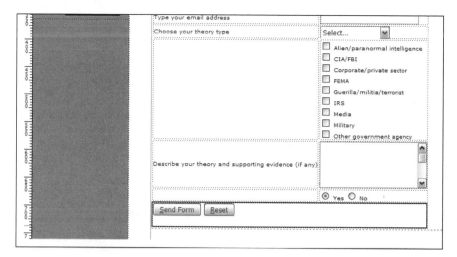

Figure 18-33. Dreamweaver merges the table cells

Aligning the Layout

Now that you've inserted the form fields and labels, you can tinker with the alignment of the various cells:

- To align the label against the right side of its cell, click anywhere inside the label's cell, and choose Right from the Horz menu on the Property Inspector.

- To center the buttons in their merged cell, click anywhere inside the button's cell, and choose Center from the Horz menu on the Property Inspector. To push them all the way to the right, choose Right.

- In single-line rows, align the label and its field vertically on the field's baseline. Click anywhere inside the row, choose <tr> from the Tag Selector, and choose Baseline from the Vert menu on the Property Inspector.

- In multi-line rows, align the label at the top of its cell. Click anywhere inside the cell with the label and choose Top from the Vert menu on the Property Inspector.

- To center the entire form table on the screen, click anywhere inside the table, click <table> in the Tag Selector, and choose Center from the Align menu on the Property Inspector. If you do this, you should also balance the widths of the columns. Select the entire left column, and type 50% in the W field of the Property Inspector. Do the same for the right column.

Making these adjustments gives you a layout like the one in Figure 18-34.

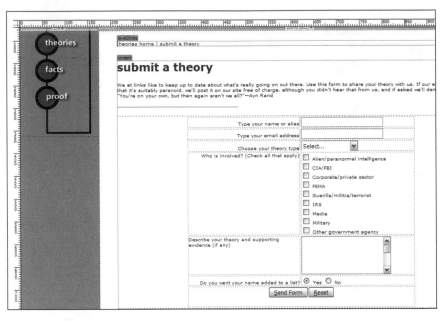

Figure 18-34. After adjusting the alignment of the form content

Applying Style Rules to Form Elements

The default appearance of HTML form elements is enough to induce catatonia. If any element needs the CSS treatment, it's these, so click that New CSS Rule button on the CSS Styles panel and get busy.

For the purposes of style rules, the <input> tag controls single-line and password text fields, checkboxes, radio buttons, and Submit and Reset buttons. The <textarea> tag controls textareas and the <select> tag controls lists and menus, so there isn't an especially high level of consistency here.

As a further complication, browsers don't apply the same style definitions to the various <input> elements consistently. For instance, in Internet Explorer, adding a text color and background color to a text field, Submit button, or Reset button has the expected results: the text acquires the text color and the background of the field acquires the background color. However, the same attributes applied to a checkbox or radio button gives you a white checkbox or radio button against a field of the specified background color, while the check mark or radio bullet inside the element retains its default color. (In Firefox, the text field, Submit button, and Reset button appear much as they do in IE, while the style rule has no effect at all on radio buttons and checkboxes.)

TIP

You can create a style for the text labels of your form by redefining the appearance of the <label> tag.

Your best approach here is to create class styles—styles that aren't tied to a specific HTML tag. You can have a single class style that applies equally to text fields, text areas, lists, menus, Submit buttons, and Reset buttons; or you can define several different class styles: say one for text fields and text areas, another for lists and menus, and a third for Submit and Reset buttons. Because of the disappointing and inconsistent effects of CSS on radio buttons and checkboxes, don't bother including them in your class style. Also, for this reason, don't redefine the appearance of the <input> tag in general, because your style rule will affect the "good" elements like text fields along with the "naughty" elements like checkboxes.

> **BEST BET**
>
> Feel free to create one or several class styles for text fields, text areas, lists, menus, Submit buttons, Reset buttons. Don't bother with radio buttons or checkboxes, and stay away from tag styles.

By way of example, the following procedure gives you a general-purpose class style for all the "good" form elements:

1. On the CSS Styles panel, click the New CSS Rule button. The New CSS Rule dialog box appears.

2. Under Selector Type, choose Class.

3. In the Name field, type formElements or some such. Click OK to proceed to the CSS Rule Definition dialog box.

4. From the Font menu in the Text category, choose a font list for the form elements to use.

5. From the Size menu, choose a type size.

6. From the Weight menu, choose bold.

7. Click the Color color box, and choose a color for the text.

8. Switch to the Background category, click the Background Color color box, and choose a background color for the fields.

9. Click OK. Dreamweaver adds the style to your external stylesheet. Switch to its document window and choose File→Save.

10. Switch back to the document window that contains your form.

11. Click the first form field. Then go to the Property Inspector, and choose formElements (or whatever you named the style) from the Class menu.

12. Repeat Step 11 for the remainder of the "good" form elements: text fields, text areas, lists, menus, Submit buttons, and Reset buttons.

When you finish, your document window looks something like Figure 18-35.

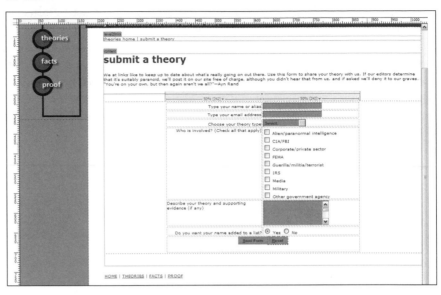

Figure 18-35. Applying a class style to the form fields

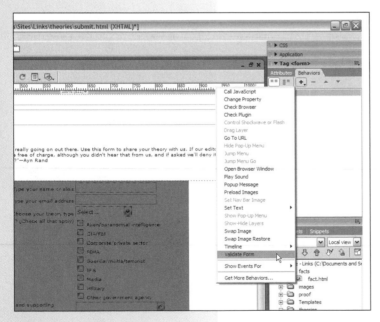

Figure 18-36. Choosing Validate Form from the Behaviors panel's plus button menu

Validating Form Input

Validating the input of a form means checking the fields of the form for technical errors before the browser submits them. Dreamweaver's Validate Form JavaScript behavior performs this feat admirably.

To attach the Validate Form behavior to your form, click anywhere along the red border of the form container. This selects the entire form. (You can also click the <form> tag in the Tag Chooser.) Then go to the Behaviors panel. If the Behaviors panel isn't open, choose Window→ Behaviors from the main menu. Click the plus button on the Behaviors panel and choose Validate Form from the menu that appears, as Figure 18-36 shows.

When you do, Dreamweaver opens the Validate Form dialog box, as Figure 18-37 shows. Under Named Fields, select a field in the form and check the Required option if this field is required for submission. Then, under Accept, choose a value type. If the visitor doesn't type anything into this field or if the value doesn't match the required value type, then validation fails and the script sends an error message to the visitor. In Figure 18-37, the name, email, and description fields are all required, and the email field requires an email address.

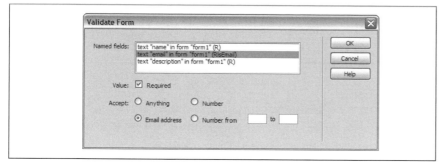

Figure 18-37. Choosing required fields and setting their value types

TECHTALK

Validating the input of a form means checking the fields of the form for technical errors before the browser submits them.

HOTKEY

Press Shift-F4 to toggle the Behaviors panel.

> **TIP**
>
> You might consider marking required fields with an asterisk (*) on your page. You might even create an Advanced CSS style called `label.required` or something to that effect to change the appearance of the text labels of these fields, maybe by making them bold if the others are in normal type.

When you're finished, click OK, and Dreamweaver adds the behavior to your form. Test the validation script by previewing the page in a live browser window.

Submitting the Form

Usually, the submission of a form goes to a web application for processing. (The app almost always resides on another page of the site, built into the code with server-side markup aplenty.) Web applications mean dynamic sites, and your site is a static one, which unfortunately limits your options in terms of what you can do with the data that your visitors submit.

Your only option, in fact, is to send the form submission to your email address. When sent from Internet Explorer, the submission comes as a file attachment to an empty email. You have to save this attachment and then open it up in a text editor like Microsoft Notepad to see the information that the visitor submitted. When sent from Firefox, the submission comes in the body of the email message, so you don't need to launch your text editor to see the contents of the submission.

Either way, the data package comes in a rather technical form, as Figure 18-38 shows. Take it slowly, and you can figure out what it's saying.

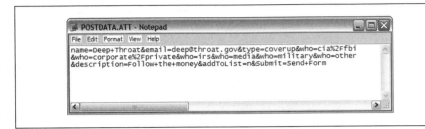

Figure 18-38. The form submission comes in a rather technical form

> **TIP**
>
> To cut down on the technical mumbo-jumbo in the form submission, stick to alphanumeric characters in the values of your radio buttons, checkboxes, lists, and menus. The browser converts anything that isn't a letter or number into a character code. For instance, the slash character (/) becomes %2F. By eliminating the non-alphanumeric characters, you eliminate the character codes.

Still, some form submission is better than no form submission, so here's how to set up your form so that it delivers the submission to your email address:

1. In the document window, click anywhere along the red form container to select the entire form.

2. Go to the Property Inspector. In the Action field, type mailto: plus the email address to which you want to submit the form data (for instance, *mailto:me@mysite.com*).

3. From the Method menu, choose POST. This method bundles the form submission as a kind of email message, which is exactly what you want in this case. The other option, GET, sends the form submission as a series of attribute/value pairs attached to the end of a URL, which is helpful for certain kinds of web applications but not especially useful in this case.

Publishing Your Site

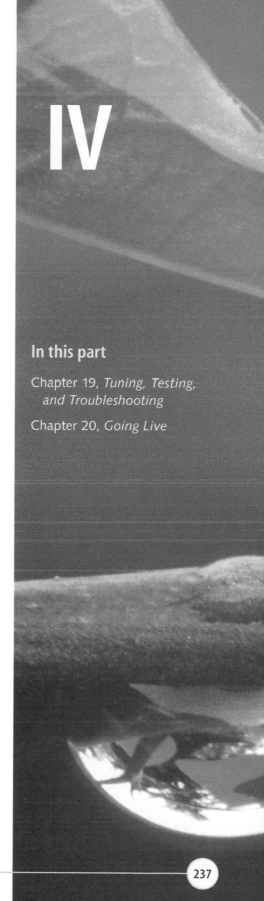

In Part III of this book, you tackled production—no small feat. You placed your content. You linked your pages. You previewed your site in a live browser, and everything is running smoothly.

Your site is running, yes, but it isn't *up* and running. The last two chapters of this book help you to take the working prototype that exists on your computer and publish it to the Web for all the world to see.

In this part

Chapter 19, *Tuning, Testing, and Troubleshooting*

Chapter 20, *Going Live*

Tuning, Testing, and Troubleshooting

19

Before you publish your site to the Web, take a few minutes to assess the work so far, just to make sure that your pages are ready. Add some meta tags. Run a few reports. Your task is to find the last lingering bugs; "isolate and eliminate" is your modus operandi. This chapter shows you how.

Remembering What Everyone Forgets

When you're cranking out pages at blinding speed, it's easy to forget some of the less obvious (but no less important) details, the ones that ooze professionalism, both for the site and its designer. Nobody's blaming anybody here. You were *supposed* to focus on the big picture items: content, style, navigation, and usability. It's understandable that the little things may have slipped through the cracks here and there. But now that you've achieved the first finished, working version of your site, the big stuff is behind you. You can afford to turn those considerable powers of observation to the microscopic level.

Now is an excellent time to go back through your pages with an eye for the following points:

Do all your pages have a title?

Point your browser to your favorite search engine, and search for "Untitled Document." At last count, Google returned about eleven million results. That's eleven million web pages where the designer forgot to go back and supply a page title in the Title field at the top of the document window. After all the work that went into crafting your pages, don't you think they deserve to be in some other (more relevant) set of search results?

Are all your page titles unique?

In a template-based web site, it's easy to put a generic page title in the template document. When you create new pages based on the template, it's equally easy to forget to change or modify the generic title that the template document supplies. Make sure that all your page titles accurately and specifically describe the content of their pages.

— HOTKEY —
Press Shift-F7 to check spelling.

Have you checked spelling?

Dreamweaver comes with a spell checker, so the only reason that Dreamweaver designers don't check spelling is because they don't feel like it. Don't make this silly mistake. For the love of Pete, think of all the poorly written, poorly spelled content you got from the marketing department! Load up your pages, and choose Text→Check Spelling from the main menu.

Have you supplied alternate text for all images that convey information?

Alternate text is the best way to make your images useful for those who can't see them. Using alternate text consistently and correctly also improves the ranking of your pages in search engines, and it makes your pages easier for the search engines to index. You can safely omit alternate text for purely decorative images like the little connector graphics at the bottom of your nav bar and the spacer images in your layout, but any image that contributes to the content on your site needs a textual description.

Have you set the tab order for selectable elements?

Selectable elements include all the interactive goodies on your page: your links, nav-bar buttons, clickable images, image-map regions, form fields, and Flash movies. Make sure you give them logical tab-index values, especially if you built your design with tables. A good way to check this is to view a page in a live browser window and cycle through the elements with the Tab key. If the items aren't selected in a sensible order, you definitely need to go back and tab index them. To set the tab index for an element, select it in the document window and go to the Tag Chooser (also known as the Attributes panel). Look under the Accessibility category, and type a value in the tabindex field.

Have you deleted style rules that you're no longer using?

Carrying obsolete style rules around in your external CSS file isn't that big a deal, unless you have so many of them that it adds noticeable amounts of time to the download. That said, if you don't need these style rules, you don't need them, so you might as well get rid of them. Go to the CSS Styles panel, select your unused styles, and then click the trashcan icon at the bottom of the panel.

Are all the images, movies, scripts, and stylesheets for your site located somewhere in your local root folder?

This is crucial. If they aren't (or if they are, but you placed the ones from some other location onto your pages instead of the ones from your local root folder), these items won't show up on your published pages. A quick way to check this is to search the source code for *file://* using Dreamweaver's Find and Replace feature. Choose Edit→Find And Replace, and set the search to look in the source code of the entire local site. Now, in Dreamweaver, you can set the scope of the search to the page text only, ignoring the underlying code—a handy feature, but not in this case. For this operation to work correctly, you have to include the code in the search, so in the Find And Replace dialog box, be sure to choose Source Code from the Search menu.

Have you cleared the cell heights of your layout tables?

This one is optional. It appeals to those who don't like bits of extraneous HTML floating around their pages. Way back in Chapter 9, when you first built your tables-based layout, this humble tome advised you not to worry so much about the heights of the cells, because the browser determines the proper heights based on the content that goes into the cells. Now that your site is finished, the arbitrary height values that you originally specified are no longer valid. Leaving them alone isn't harming anything, but if you don't need them anymore, and if they're not accurate, why keep them around? You can simply get rid of them if you choose. To do this, open up the template document, and select each table of the layout in turn. For each, choose Modify→Table→Clear Cell Heights from the main menu. When you're done, save the template, and write your changes to all the pages of your site.

> **TIP**
>
> If you decide to get rid of table attributes, clear the cell heights only, not the widths. The widths are far more important to the proper layout of your page, so be careful that you don't choose Modify→Table→Clear Cell Widths from the main menu by mistake.

Adding Meta Tags

Meta tags are invisible elements that provide high-level information about the content of a web page, mostly for the benefit of search engines. A good set of meta tags can improve the placement of your pages in search results, so it's never a bad idea to add some meta information to your site, especially when it's as easy as Dreamweaver makes it.

There are three kinds of meta tags of interest here. The first two—keywords and description tags—are the ones that make the most difference to search engines. The third type—the refresh tag—doesn't have anything to do with search engines, but it does produce a most excellent refresh or redirect effect.

Adding Keywords

Keywords are the subject headings of your web page. Imagine that you're the visitor, and you point your browser to your favorite search engine, and then type a word or short phrase into the Search field. What words or phrases would you expect to search for and get your web page as a result? These, in essence, should be the keywords that you build into your page.

---TECHTALK---
Meta tags provide high-level information about the content of a web page, mostly for the benefit of search engines.

---TECHTALK---
Keywords are the subject headings of your web page.

For once, quantity isn't necessarily the deciding factor as to what makes a good set of keywords. Every search engine is different, of course, and the owners of the search engines like to guard their trade secrets as if they were a matter of national security, but more often than not, it generally works as follows. First, the search engine compares the keywords in your meta tag with the text of the page. It then performs some kind of analysis, and if it looks like the keywords have something to do with the page content, the ranking of your page goes up in the search engine's database. If, on the other hand, it doesn't appear that the keywords match the content, your page might actually go down in the ranking. Be sure to explain this at least three times to any member of the marketing department who insists that you use every word in your native language as a keyword. It's far better to choose a few really accurate keywords than an entire lexicon of tangentially related ones.

> **BEST BET**
>
> It's far better to choose a few really accurate keywords than to embed a dictionary or two into your page.

You have a template-based site, so a good strategy for keywords goes something like this:

- In the template document, add keywords that apply to all pages on your site.

- In each page of your site, supplement these general keywords with ones specific to the page in question.

Start with the template document. Open it in Dreamweaver, and then go to the Insert panel and choose HTML from its menu, as Figure 19-1 shows.

Now look under the menu of head objects, and choose the Keywords object shown in Figure 19-2. The Keywords dialog box appears, as Figure 19-3 shows.

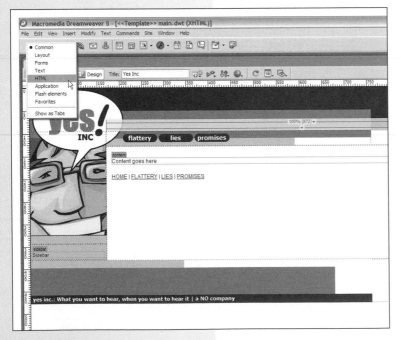

Figure 19-1. Choosing HTML from the Insert panel's menu

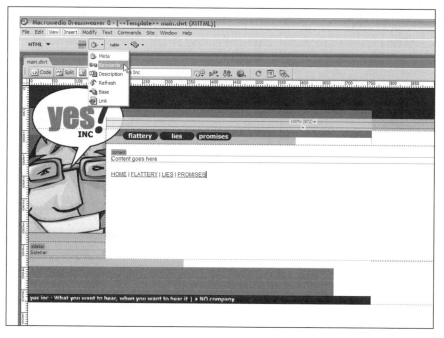

Figure 19-2. Choosing the Keywords object from the menu of head objects

In the Keywords field, simply type the list of general keywords, separating each with a comma, and click OK. Dreamweaver adds them to the template document. Choose File→Save, and update the pages of your site. Then, take each individual page in turn, and add a second list of keywords targeted specifically to that page, as Figure 19-4 shows.

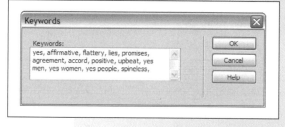

Figure 19-3. A general list of keywords, comma-separated

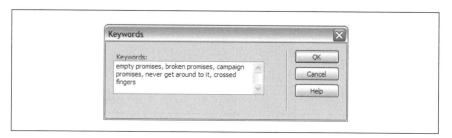

Figure 19-4. Adding keywords specific to the current page

Adding Descriptions

A *description* is a short, one-paragraph summary of the content of a page. Some search engines use your description as the text that appears in the results next to the link to your page.

Because all the pages of your site are different, don't bother inserting a general description in the template document. It's better to write a specific

—TECHTALK—

A description is a short, one-paragraph summary of the content or purpose of a page.

Figure 19-5. Choosing the Description object from the menu of head objects

description for each page of your site. Also, brevity is the key. Try to use no more than three short sentences.

To add a description, choose the Description object from the menu of head objects on the Insert panel, as Figure 19-5 shows. Dreamweaver opens the Description dialog box shown in Figure 19-6. Type the page description and click OK.

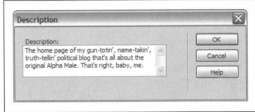

Figure 19-6. Typing a three-line page description

Refreshing the Page or Redirecting the Browser

The refresh meta tag causes the browser to reload the current page to jump to another page entirely after a certain number of seconds.

To add a refresh meta tag, choose the Refresh object from the menu of head objects on the Insert panel, as shown in Figure 19-7. When you do, the Refresh dialog box appears, as Figure 19-8 shows.

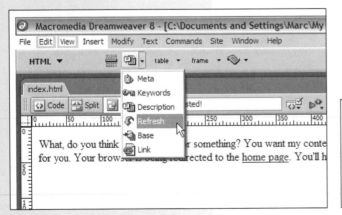

Figure 19-7. Choosing the Refresh object from the head objects menu

Figure 19-8. Setting the attributes of the refresh meta tag

TIP

Want to keep people from snooping inside your *img* or *images* folder? Drop a page called *index.html* inside this folder, and put a refresh meta tag on the page that redirects the browser to some other page of your site. As a courtesy, also provide a direct link to the same page, just in case something goes wrong.

In the Delay field, give the number of seconds before the refresh or redirect kicks in. Then, under Action, choose what should happen. If you want to redirect the browser, click the Browse button and choose a page of your site, or type the URL of the destination in the Go To URL field. If you want to refresh the current page, choose Refresh This Document. Click OK to add the refresh meta tag to your page.

Running Reports

Dreamweaver gives you a number of ways to check the soundness and integrity of your pages before you publish them. You can see where certain browsers are likely to choke. You can clean up the code to standards-police standards. You can find and fix broken links, and you can locate stranded files and either use them or lose them. This section shows you how.

Running a Browser Check

You know from experience that different web browsers interpret the same web code differently. Many times, these differences are benign, if somewhat aggravating. Other times, they can cause problems. A *browser check* calls attention to these peculiarities specifically as they relate to your site. It scans your pages and flags the bits and pieces of code that a particular browser doesn't like.

Choosing target browsers

The *target browsers* are the browsers against which you're checking the code of your site. You don't need to have these browsers installed on your computer. Dreamweaver has a built-in browser-check database.

To select target browsers, open any page of your site, and click the Target Browser button at the top of the document window. Choose Settings from the menu that appears in Figure 19-9, and Dreamweaver opens the Target Browsers dialog box shown in Figure 19-10. Select the make and model of the browsers that you want to use as your targets, and click OK.

----TECHTALK----
A browser check scans your pages and flags the code that a particular browser doesn't like.

----TECHTALK----
Target browsers are the browsers against which you check the code of your site.

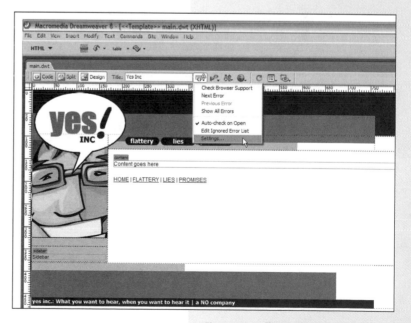

Figure 19-9. Choosing Settings from the Target Browser menu

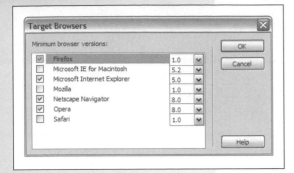

Figure 19-10. Choosing target browsers and minimum versions

The perfectly coded web page that passes inspection in all browsers is exceedingly rare in this time-space continuum, and such a page isn't usually much to look at anyway. For most pages, the more target browsers you check, the more likely you'll run into situations where fixing a coding faux pas in one browser *creates* a coding faux pas in another browser. You're better off limiting the target browsers to those that your visitors are most likely to use.

Running the check

By default, Dreamweaver runs a browser check whenever you open a document window. To see the results of the check, click the Browser Check button and choose Show All Errors from the menu. Dreamweaver opens the Results panel along the bottom of the workspace. You can increase the size of the panel by dragging the bottom border of the document window toward the top of the workspace, as Figure 19-11 shows.

HOTKEY

Press F7 to toggle the Results panel.

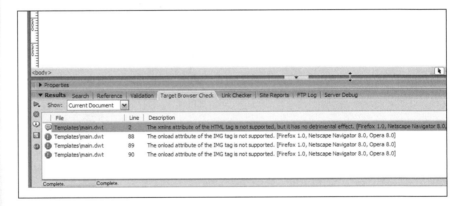

Figure 19-11. Increasing the size of the Results panel

Look specifically for the red caution icons in the list and note which browsers Dreamweaver predicts will experience the problems. On this web page, Dreamweaver identifies Opera, Netscape, and Firefox in each case. To see what specifically is causing these problems, double-click an entry in the Results panel. Dreamweaver switches to Split view and highlights the problematic code, as Figure 19-12 shows.

The warning message says that Firefox, Netscape, and Opera don't support the `onLoad` attribute of the `<img>` tag. Now look at the code:

```
onLoad=""
```

Nothing is happening during the `onLoad` event, so it's safe to delete this bit of code completely. The same holds true for the other two warnings in the Results panel. So after removing the offending bits of empty code, go to the

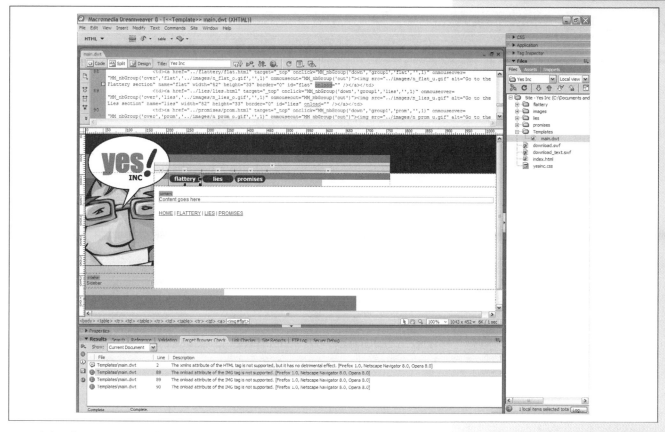

Figure 19-12. Dreamweaver highlights the
problematic code in the top panel

top of the document window, click the Browser Check button, and choose
Check Browser Support from the menu. You find to your relief that the page
passes inspection in the target browsers.

Now, what happens if you get a warning message like this:

```
The tag name: "embed" Not found in currently active versions. [XHTML
1.0 transitional]
```

You find to your horror that this tag marks up a Flash movie or some other
form of multimedia on your page. Do you scrap the Flash movie? Not necessarily. Double-check to make sure that the page works correctly in the target
browser, and if it does, you don't have to worry.

So much for the current page. On to the
next! Or, better yet, on to all of the next.
To run the browser check on the entire site
at once, click the green arrow button at the
top left of the Results panel and choose
Check Target Browsers For Entire Current
Local Site from the menu that appears, as
Figure 19-13 shows.

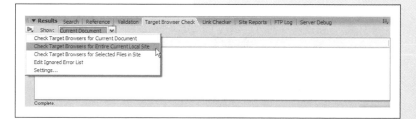

Figure 19-13. Running a browser check on
the entire site

Validating Markup

Aside from checking your code against target browsers, you can *validate* your pages (i.e., check their code against the official standards).

A word to the wise: a standards-compliant web page doesn't necessarily look the same in all browsers. A standards-compliant web page might not even *work* correctly in certain browsers, especially in the case of Cascading Style Sheets. Plenty of official style definitions have yet to receive support in any browsing device. Likewise, a web page that fails standards checks miserably might look spectacular, maintain a decent level of accessibility, and work respectably well in all the biggie browsers. If you have to choose between passing the browser check and passing validation, this humble tome recommends the browser check every time.

This is not to say that standards compliance doesn't have its place. To a certain degree, the Web needs standards. Code that adheres to them is less dependent upon the idiosyncrasies of particular browsers and is therefore less subject to change when Microsoft puts out a new version of Internet Explorer. Officially sanctioned code also tends to work better in a wider cross-section of devices (some of which haven't been invented yet). Yet we live in the present, not the future, and the vast majority of all web browsing on planet Earth at this time comes by way of Microsoft Internet Explorer version 6 for Windows. Your site would appeal to a greater percentage of the overall online audience if you forgot about standards compliance entirely and simply designed your site for this browser, but not even this humble tome suggests that you go that far. By all means, validate. Just don't give up on web design and go back to beauty school if your markup isn't officially sanctioned by the coding cabal.

To validate the markup of your site, switch to the Validate tab of the Results panel, click the green arrow icon, and choose Validate Entire Current Local Site from the menu.

Finding and Fixing Broken Links

Broken links are links that can't find their destination pages. Either the pages don't exist or they aren't at the location that the link is pointing. Dreamweaver locates broken internal links for you but doesn't find broken external links. You should periodically check your external links to make sure they're all still pointing to the right pages and sites.

To check for broken links in the current site, go to the main menu, and choose Site→Check Links Sitewide. Any broken internal links appear in the Results panel under the Link Checker tab, as Figure 19-14 shows. Double-click an entry in the list to open the page with the broken link, and make the necessary corrections.

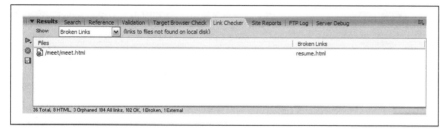

Figure 19-14. The Link Checker tab shows broken internal links

If the same broken link comes up again and again, you can change all occurrences of the link at once. From the main menu, choose Site→Change Link Sitewide, and the Change Link Sitewide dialog box in Figure 19-15 appears. In the Change All Links To field, type the broken link exactly as it appears in the Results panel, with the slash at the beginning. Then click the folder icon next to the Into Links To field and navigate to the page to which the broken link should go. Click OK to make the change.

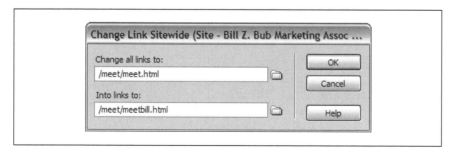

Figure 19-15. Changing a recurring broken link

Finding Orphaned Files

Orphaned files are files in your local root folder that don't appear on any page of your site. You can safely move these files out of your local root folder, but don't delete them unless you're absolutely sure you won't need them in the future. Remember, your data are valuable and storage is cheap.

To check for orphaned files, go to the Link Checker tab of the Results panel and set the Show menu to Orphaned Files, as Figure 19-16 shows.

─TECHTALK─

Orphaned files are files in your local root folder that don't appear on any page of your site.

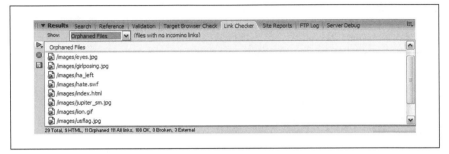

Figure 19-16. Checking for orphaned files in the Link Checker

> **TIP**
>
> One of the few certainties in the game of web design is that, as soon as you delete an orphaned file, within twenty-four hours you'll wish that you hadn't. As such, the author of this humble tome creates a special folder called *work* for every web project. Into the work folder go all orphaned files, along with production files for Fireworks, Flash, Photoshop, Illustrator, and so on.

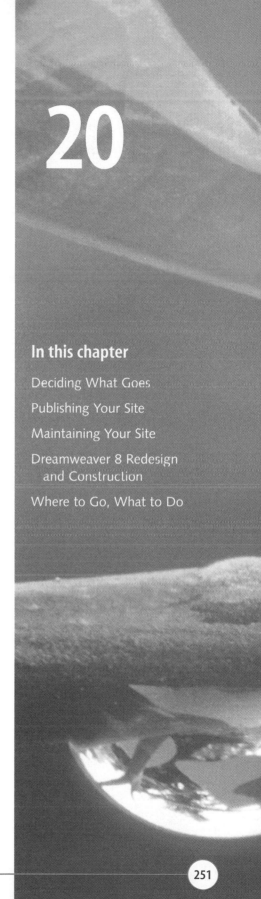

Going Live 20

Publishing your site is a very simple procedure in Dreamweaver, and after all the work that you put into building your site, you deserve to coast to victory.

But a web site is never really finished. There are updates to contend with. Maybe you add new pages. Maybe you retire old ones. Then there's the dreaded R word—no, not Reaganomics. Even worse: *redesign*. But Dreamweaver designers have nothing to fear. Because you decided to use templates and an external stylesheet way back when, even a complete redesign of the entire look and feel loses most of its legendary sting.

This chapter shows you how to publish your site to the Web and how to make site updates—even redesigns—go smoothly.

Deciding What Goes

Most of the stuff in your local root folder belongs on the Web for everyone to see and enjoy, but not all of it. Your *Templates* folder, for instance, is crucially important to you, the designer of the site, but it has nothing to do with your site in its published form, because none of your pages actually link to the template document. The same is true for a *work* or *miscellany* folder that you keep inside the local root folder for convenience's sake. It's great to store your notes, prototypes, experiments, outdated pages, orphaned files, and production files in the same folder as your site, but you don't want to post these files to the Web.

Remember the cloaking feature from Chapter 7, where you hid certain types of files from Dreamweaver? As it turns out, you can also cloak entire folders to prevent Dreamweaver from publishing them to the Web.

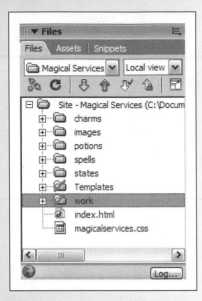

Figure 20-1. Cloaking designer-only folders in your site

——TECHTALK——

Putting your site means uploading it from your computer to your web host's computer for publication on the Web.

> **TIP**
>
> Cloaked files appear in the Files panel with a red line through them, but don't let the red ink fool you. Cloaking doesn't mean that you can't open and edit these files. It simply means that they're skipped during the publishing process.

To cloak a folder in your site, select it in the Files panel. Then right-click for the context menu, and choose Cloaking→Cloak. Dreamweaver draws a red line through the folder's icon, as Figure 20-1 shows. To uncloak a previously cloaked folder, select it in the Files panel, right-click, and choose Cloaking→Uncloak from the context menu.

> **TIP**
>
> When you cloak your *Templates* folder, Dreamweaver informs you that this operation only affects Get and Put commands—in other words, the publishing of your site. This is exactly what you want, so click OK.

Publishing Your Site

Now that you've sorted out what's going and what isn't, you can publish your site. This is a two-part process. First, you connect to your web host from Dreamweaver. Next, you *put*, or upload, the files of your site from your computer to the host's computer. Two clicks of the mouse will do it, as this section shows.

Connecting to the Host

Now that you've sorted out what's going and what isn't, you can connect to your web host. You supplied and tested your connection information when you defined your site in Chapter 7, so you know that everything is working fine.

> **TIP**
>
> Dreamweaver won't know where to publish your site if you omit the information about your hosting service, so if you skipped this part of your site definition for whatever reason, go back and do it now! Choose Site→ Manage Sites, select your site in the Manage Sites dialog box, and click the Edit button.

To connect to your web host, click the Connect button in the Files panel, as Figure 20-2 shows). The Background File Activity dialog box in Figure 20-3 appears and shows you what's happening behind the scenes as Dreamweaver negotiates the connection with your web host. This might take a couple seconds, so be patient.

Figure 20-2. The Connect button in the Files panel

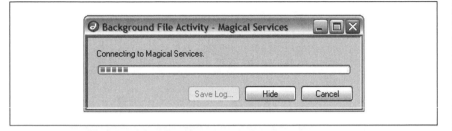

Figure 20-3. The Background File Activity dialog box

If you're working behind Windows Firewall, you may receive the dialog box in Figure 20-4 when you use Dreamweaver's connectivity features for the first time. Make sure you click the Unblock button, or Dreamweaver won't be able to publish your site to the Web.

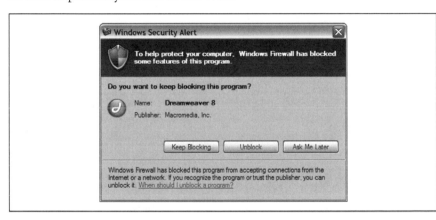

Figure 20-4. Unblocking Dreamweaver in the Windows Firewall

If you're working behind the firewall built into Mac OS X, you may also have trouble connecting to your Web host through Dreamweaver, but for better or worse, you won't get a dialog box warning you about it. Some Mac users solve the connectivity problem by setting Dreamweaver for Passive FTP mode. To do this, choose Site→Manage Sites from the main menu. The Manage Sites dialog box opens. Click Edit for the Site Definition dialog box. Switch to Advanced view, choose the Remote Info category, and check the Use Passive FTP option. If you manage more than one site, and if this fix works for you, make sure you go through and edit the definitions of all your sites for Passive FTP.

Other Mac users get good results by tweaking the settings of the firewall itself. From Sharing in System Preferences, click the Services button, and check the FTP Access option, as Figure 20-5 shows. Then click the Firewall button, and enable FTP access to and from your ISP's server, as in Figure 20-6.

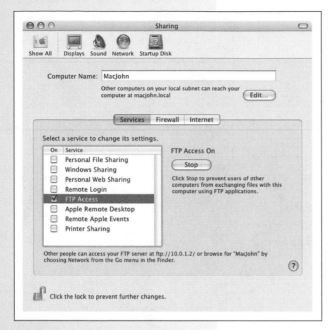

Figure 20-5. First enable FTP Access under Mac OS X Services

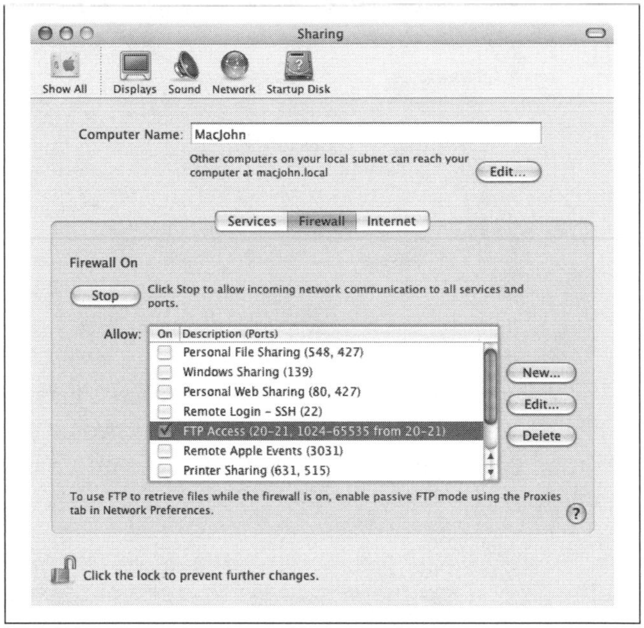

Figure 20-6. Then check FTP Access under Firewall

When Dreamweaver makes the connection with your host, the Background File Activity dialog box closes, and the Connect button in the Files panel lights up, as Figure 20-7 shows. Congratulations! You're online.

Figure 20-7. The Connect button lights up to show you're connected

---

TIP

If all else fails, you can turn off the Mac OS X firewall entirely, and you'll probably—*probably*—be all right. Security is a lucrative business, and horror stories are classic sales motivators. With all the sensationalized tales of cyber-woe and identity theft on the nightly infomercials that pass as news, it's easy for consumers to get overprotective about their computer security. But unless you're Bill Gates, the IRS, a bank, or a credit card company, the hackers aren't out to get you. (And if they are, a firewall isn't going to stop them for long.) That said, if you don't have to turn off your personal firewall, don't, just to be on the safe side. The author of this humble tome has been known to keep his firewall on.

Figure 20-8. Selecting the local root folder in the Files panel

Putting Your Files

The time has come to publish your site's files, or to *put* them, to use the technical jargon. Select the local root folder in the Files panel, as Figure 20-8 shows, and then click the Put button shown in Figure 20-9. Dreamweaver asks if you're sure about putting the entire site. Of course you are. Click OK.

Figure 20-9. The Put button on the Files panel

The Background File Activity dialog box returns as Dreamweaver sends your pages to the web host. Click the arrow button next to Details to see exactly what's happening, as Figure 20-10 shows.

Figure 20-10. Expanding the Details frame to see what's happening

When Dreamweaver finishes, the Background File Activity dialog box closes. Your site is now live! To prove it, switch to Remote view on the Files panel, as in Figure 20-11. You're looking now at your web host's computer, and your folders and files are exactly where you want them.

> **TIP**
>
> To see your remote files and local files side by side, click the Expand button in the Files panel. Click this button again to return to normal view.

Figure 20-11. Switching to Remote view to see your published site

You know what this means: fire up your favorite web browser and point it toward your domain. You are now officially the first visitor to your first published web site. Once again, congratulations! That satisfying taste on your tongue is victory, pure and sweet. Enjoy it. The author of this humble tome wishes you a superabundance of success.

Maintaining Your Site

A live site is a living site. It isn't a static thing like a cinder block. It grows and evolves. As you add new content and new pages, you want to keep the published version of your site up to date. This section shows you some easy methods for doing just that.

> **BEHIND THE SCENES**
>
> An old scrap of web wisdom says that you should update your site as often as you want the visitors to come back. So if you want your visitors to come back once a week, you should make updates once a week. If you want your visitors to come back every day, you need daily updates. If you want them to come back every hour, you need to give them a reason, every hour on the hour. By the same logic, a web site that sits untouched for months on end probably has a similarly unenthusiastic audience base.

Synchronizing Your Site

You now have two versions of your site: the local version, which is the one on your personal computer; and the remote version, which is the live, published version, the one that your visitors see when they go to your URL. Right now, the two versions are exactly the same—they're *synchronized*, or *in synch*. However, as you make changes to your local files—adding new content, removing old content, moving the files to different folders—their remote counterparts don't automatically update themselves. Your updated local version no longer matches the version that you originally published, so your sites are *out of synch*.

Figure 20-12. Publish your latest changes to the remote site

This situation is very easy to remedy. In the Files panel, connect to your site and switch to Local view so that you see the files and folders on your personal computer. Then select the local root folder, right-click, and choose Synchronize from the context menu. The Synchronize Files dialog box appears, as Figure 20-12 shows.

From the Synchronize menu, choose the option for your entire site, and choose Put Newer Files To Remote from the Direction menu. If you've deleted or renamed files in the local site, check the Delete Remote Files Not On Local Drive option. Click Preview to review the changes.

The Background File Activity dialog box opens as Dreamweaver compares the two versions of your site. Upon completion, you get the Synchronize dialog box, as Figure 20-13 shows.

Review the changes that Dreamweaver plans to make. If you don't want to make a specific change at this time, select it in the list and click the Ignore button.

When you're ready to go, click OK, and Dreamweaver performs the requested operations. Your published site is now up to date.

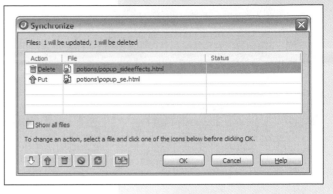

Figure 20-13. Reviewing the update in the Synchronize dialog box

BEHIND THE SCENES

You may notice a mix of backward slashes and forward slashes in the File column of the Synchronize dialog box. This can be confusing, but it isn't a cause for concern. Whether a path appears with forward or backward slashes depends upon the preference of the operating system. Windows prefers the backward slash, while Unix—the operating system, in one form or another, for most of the Web—prefers the forward slash. Both mean the same thing in this context, in that they separate the folders or directories of a file's path.

If you want a quick (but not always accurate) rule of thumb, you can say that a path with backward slashes points to a local file on a PC, while a path with forward slashes points to a remote file on a web server somewhere, but don't rely too heavily on this distinction. The real root of the issue is OS syntax, and unless you're in charge of a complex network, you don't need to worry about which way the slashes are tilting.

Getting Remote Files

Occasionally, you may want to retrieve the remote version of a file. Maybe you made some substantial changes to the local version of the file that you've since thought better of, or maybe someone from the marketing department logged onto your computer and, being attracted to all those bright, shiny Dreamweaver buttons, ended up deleting a local page or two. You can just as easily *get* files, or download them from the remote site to your local site.

To get remote files, connect to your web host and switch the Files panel to Remote view. Select the files or folders that you want to retrieve, and click the Get button in Figure 20-14 to retrieve the remote versions of your files or folders.

—TECHTALK—

Getting files means downloading them from your web host's computer to your computer.

Figure 20-14. The Get button in the Files panel

Figure 20-15. Dreamweaver asks if you want to overwrite your local version of the file

If the file or folder that you selected appears in some version on your local site, Dreamweaver tells you about it, as Figure 20-15 shows. Click Yes to proceed, or click Yes To All if you're getting more than one file and you know that you want to overwrite them all.

> **TIP**
>
> Getting a remote file doesn't delete the file from the remote computer. It simply makes a copy of that file on your local machine (or overwrites the existing local file of the same name).
>
> To delete a remote file, select the file in Remote view of the Files panel, right-click, and choose Edit→Delete from the context menu.

Dreamweaver 8 Redesign and Construction

Fast forward six months. Your site has grown. You've fine-tuned the content and the structure. You're getting good visitor feedback, so you know where your site is succeeding, and you have a pretty good idea about what you can do to make it even better. You're also getting a little tired of the same old look and feel. The more you think about it, the more certain you become that now would be an excellent time for *mysite.com* Version 2.0.

Redesign. The very word makes some web designers cringe. They think about all the shortcuts they took, knowing that they'd have to pay for them eventually. For their sites, that bill is coming due. But you built your site with Dreamweaver templates and external stylesheets, so you're out of the red and into the black before you even start the process. You might even catch yourself having fun.

Assume that you're managing the Magical Services site, and you decide that it's time for a change of graphical scenery. A few concept sketches and layout measurements later, and you come up with the redesign in Figure 20-16. From this mockup, you derive the tracing image that appears in Figure 20-17.

Figure 20-16. Here is the redesign mockup for the Magical Services site

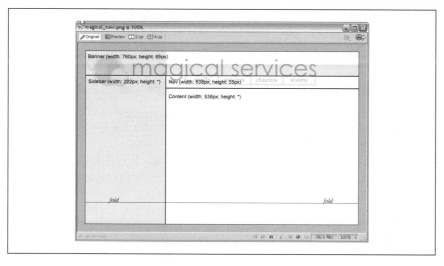

Figure 20-17. Here is the tracing image for the redesign

If you flip back to Chapter 17 for the original design of this site, you see that you're definitely shaking things up. You're going from a side-nav layout to a top-nav layout, for one, and you're gaining a sidebar area where there was none before, not to mention that you're replacing the original's liquid layout with one of fixed width. By any normal standards, this redesign could get ugly. But here is where your decision to use Dreamweaver templates and external stylesheets pays dividends like you never thought possible. You build a single new template document that contains the redesigned layout, and then you attach it to the pages of your site. Dreamweaver replaces the original layout from the original template document with the new layout from the new template document. In a matter of minutes, your entire site has a brand new look. Even better, everything in the editable regions—that is, the content on all your pages—remains exactly as it was. Your pages gain a new layout but keep their content. It's the very best kind of win-win.

Here's what you do:

1. Launch Dreamweaver, create a new page called *new.html* and save it in your local root folder.

2. Attach the tracing image to this page and draw the layout.

3. Type text placeholders into the areas.

4. Attach the current stylesheet.

5. Save the page as a template: *new.dwt* or something to that effect.

6. Insert editable regions. The editable regions can be in completely different locations in the new template. Just make sure that the new regions have the same names as the old ones. Otherwise, Dreamweaver won't

be sure which region corresponds with which. You can also add entirely new editable regions—regions that don't correspond to anything in the old template—and name them anything you like.

> ### TIP
>
> What happens if you have, say, a sidebar area in the current site but no sidebar area in the new site? What does Dreamweaver do with the existing sidebar content on your pages?
>
> What happens is up to you. When you apply the new template to the pages of your site, Dreamweaver gives you the Inconsistent Region Names dialog box, telling you in effect that it doesn't know what to do with the stuff in the current sidebar area because there isn't a corresponding sidebar area in the new design. You can choose to move the sidebar content to another area in the layout or simply delete this content.

7. Add the nav bar.

8. Add other images and text. Don't worry about the content inside the editable regions. Just add the content that goes specifically in the template.

9. Add and connect the links.

10. Apply styles from the style sheet to the elements on the page, modifying the styles as needed to match your new design.

When you're done, you have something that looks like Figure 20-18.

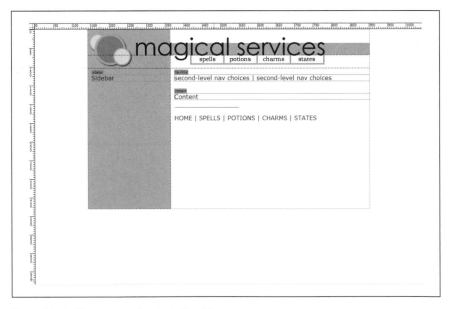

Figure 20-18. Your new template looks like this

Now all you have to do is apply the new template to the existing pages of your site:

1. Open an existing page in Dreamweaver. Don't be alarmed if the styles of the new design appear in the layout of current design. In fact, be alarmed if the new styles *don't* appear. The whole point of having an external CSS document is that you make the changes once, and they propagate themselves throughout your site.

2. Choose Modify→Templates→Apply Template To Page from the main menu. The Select Template dialog box in Figure 20-19 appears.

3. Choose your new template, and click Select.

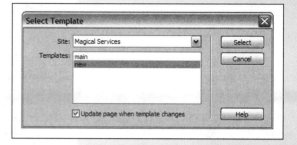

Figure 20-19. Choosing your new template

Just like that, the page is redesigned, as Figure 20-20 shows. Magical Services indeed! Choose File→Save from the main menu and close the document window.

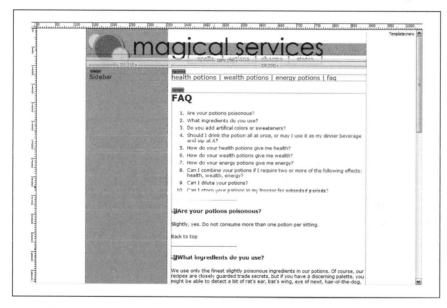

Figure 20-20. Dreamweaver adds the new template to the page and moves all the original content

Now, just follow the same three steps for the rest of the pages in your site, and you can consider your redesign done. Connect to your host and synchronize your sites, and your fresh, new pages are live on the Web.

Where to Go, What to Do

This humble tome offers one perspective about how to use Dreamweaver to design and build a Web site. It has introduced you to a wide variety of topics, most of which it has hardly exhausted, some of which it has only mentioned in passing. It does not claim to be the final authority on the subject of web design and construction. Any tome that does is not so humble.

If, after you've built a few sites with the methods presented here, you find yourself craving more, wondering what else is waiting for you, then congratulations are in order, because you're well on your way to becoming an advanced web designer. You might expand your horizons in the pages of the following volumes.

For an in-depth reference guide to Dreamweaver 8, explaining in great detail and with clarity the many features that this book omits for space considerations, you can do no better than *Dreamweaver 8: The Missing Manual* by David McFarland (Pogue Press). Macromedia's own Training from the Source series also comes highly regarded. Start with *Macromedia Dreamweaver 8: Training from the Source* by Khristine Annwn Page (Macromedia Press), and if you're interested in building dynamic, database-driven sites using server-side technology, move on to *Macromedia 8 with ASP, ColdFusion, and PHP: Training from the Source* by Jeffrey Bardzell (Macromedia Press).

In the area of usability and user-centered design, *Designing Web Usability: The Practice of Simplicity* by Jakob Nielsen (New Riders Press) is a modern classic, as is *Don't Make Me Think: A Common Sense Approach to Web Usability, Second Edition* by Steve Krug (New Riders Press).

If standards compliance is your thing, then be sure to have a look at *Build Your Own Standards Compliant Website Using Dreamweaver 8* by Rachel Andrews (SitePoint).

For the coders among us, a wealth of material exists for your reference and delight. Not all of it is good, but the consistently praised Definitive series by O'Reilly hasn't earned its reputation by mere hype. Try *Cascading Style Sheets: The Definitive Guide, Second Edition* by Eric Meyer (O'Reilly), *Dynamic HTML: The Definitive Reference, Second Edition* by Danny Goodman (O'Reilly), *HTML & XHTML: The Definitive Guide, Fifth Edition* by Chuck Musciano and Bill Kennedy (O'Reilly), and *JavaScript: The Definitive Guide, Fourth Edition* by David Flanagan (O'Reilly).

If a heavy-duty coding manual turns you off at first, and at the risk of becoming an honorary member of my own marketing department, it has been said that *Web Design Garage* by Marc Campbell (Prentice Hall PTR) succeeds at building a bridge between beginning and intermediate web design while having a jolly good time doing it.

Appendixes and Glossary

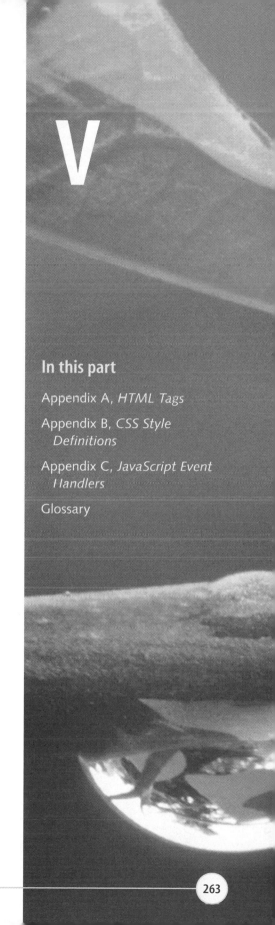

HTML Tags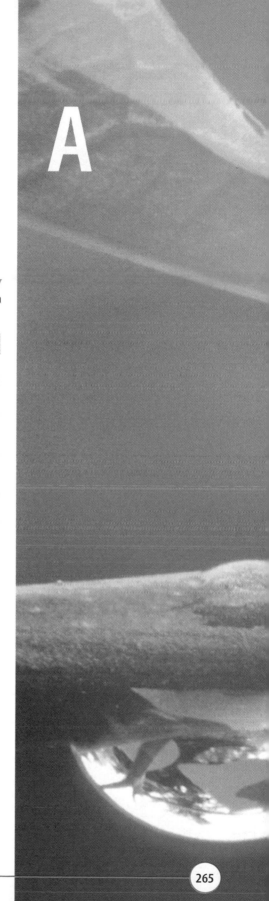

When you mull over HTML elements in the Tag Selector, this table may come in handy. It tells you what the various tags in the code represent on the page.

Tag	Marks up
`<a>`	A hyperlink or a named anchor
`<acronym>`	An acronym
`<address>`	A street address
`<applet>`	A Java applet
`<area>`	A clickable region in an image map
`<b>`	Boldface (deprecated; use `<strong>` or CSS instead)
`<base>`	The path to the current document
`<basefont>`	The default typeface for the text on the page (deprecated; use CSS instead)
`<big>`	Text one size larger than the surrounding text
`<blockquote>`	An offset, indented paragraph
`<body>`	The body section of the page, containing everything that appears inside the browser window
` `	A line break
`<button>`	A clickable button, particularly for freestanding button elements that are not in a form
`<caption>`	The caption of a data table
`<center>`	Centered text (deprecated; use CSS instead)
`<cite>`	A citation
`<code>`	A block of computer code
`<col>`	A table column
`<colgroup>`	A group of related table columns
`<dd>`	Definition of a term in a definition list

Tag	Marks up
`<del>`	Content to be deleted; used by editors and proofreaders to tell the page author which pieces of content to delete before publishing the page to the Web
`<div>`	A division of the page; a layer
`<dl>`	A definition list
`<dt>`	The term to be defined in a definition list
`<em>`	Emphasized text; creates italic in all major browsers
`<embed>`	A multimedia file
`<fieldset>`	A logical group of fields in a form
`<font>`	The typeface of the text (deprecated; use CSS instead)
`<form>`	A form
`<frame>`	A frame in a frameset
`<frameset>`	A system of frames
`<h1>`	A first-level heading
`<h2>`	A second-level heading
`<h3>`	A third-level heading
`<h4>`	A fourth-level heading
`<h5>`	A fifth-level heading
`<h6>`	A sixth-level heading
`<head>`	The head section of a page
`<hr>`	A horizontal rule
`<html>`	An HTML page
`<i>`	Italic text (deprecated; use `<em>` or CSS instead)
`<img>`	An image file
`<input>`	A form object
`<ins>`	Content to be inserted; used by editors and proofreaders to tell the page author which pieces of content were added during the editing process
`<kbd>`	Text that the visitor should type
`<label>`	A label, such as the text describing the function of a form object
`<legend>`	The label of a fieldset
`<li>`	A list item
`<link>`	A link to an external file; used in the head section of the page
`<listing>`	A block of code
`<map>`	An image map
`<meta>`	Head content

Tag	Marks up
<nobr>	A block of content that should not break at the right margin
<noframes>	Content to display if the visitor's browser does not support frames
<noscript>	Content to display if the visitor's browser does not support client-side scripting or has client-side scripting turned off
<object>	A multimedia file
<ol>	An ordered (numbered) list
<option>	An item in a list or menu
<p>	A paragraph
<param>	A parameter to be passed to an applet or embedded multimedia file
<plaintext>	Unformatted text
<pre>	Preformatted text; preserves the spacing and line breaks of the text as it appears in the source code
<q>	An inline quotation, such as the dialog of a character in a novel
<s>, <strike>	Text that is crossed out or "struck through" (deprecated; use CSS instead)
<samp>	Sample output from a computer program
<script>	An embedded or linked client-side script
<select>	A list or menu form object
<small>	Text one size smaller than the surrounding text
<span>	A range of content
<strong>	Strongly emphasized text; displays boldface in all the major browsers
<style>	An embedded or linked stylesheet
<sub>	A subscript
<sup>	A superscript
<table>	A table
<tbody>	The body section of a data table
<td>	A table cell
<textarea>	A multi-line text field in a form
<tfoot>	The foot section of a data table
<th>	A cell that functions as a row or column header in a data table
<thead>	The head section of a data table
<title>	The title of the page
<tr>	A table row

Tag	Marks up
`<tt>`	Teletype or terminal-style text
`<u>`	Underlined text (deprecated; use CSS instead)
`<ul>`	An unordered (bulleted) list
`<var>`	A variable
`<wbr>`	A point within a `<nobr>` element where the browser may break the content if the width of the browser window requires it
`<xmp>`	A block of computer code presented as an example

CSS Style Definitions

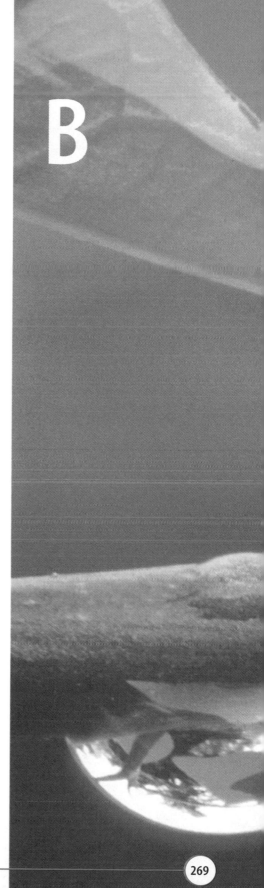

When you examine a style rule in Dreamweaver, you might not be familiar with the names of the style definitions that appear in the CSS Styles panel. The following table lists them and explains them for your convenience.

Style definition	Controls
background-attachment	The behavior of a background image when the page scrolls
background-color	The background color
background-image	A background image
background-position	The position of a background image
background-repeat	The tiling or repeating of a background image
border-collapse	Whether adjacent borders merge or remain separate
border-color	The color of a border
border-spacing	The space between a border and the content it surrounds
border-style	The style of a border
border-width	The width or thickness of a border
border-bottom-color, border-bottom-style, border-bottom-width	The color, style, or width of the bottom border
border-left-color, border-left-style, border-left-width	The color, style, or width of the left border
border-right-color, border-right-style, border-right-width	The color, style, or width of the right border
border-top-color, border-top-style, border-top-width	The color, style, or width of the top border
bottom	The bottom position of an element
clear	How a block of content positions itself in relation to surrounding blocks; cleared blocks move down to the next available horizontal line

Style definition	Controls
clip	The region around a block of content that the browser clips or makes invisible
color	The foreground color
cursor	The shape of the cursor when the visitor hovers over the element
float	How a block of content positions itself in relation to surrounding blocks; floating blocks appear on the same horizontal line
font-family	The typeface
font-size	The type size
font-style	Italic or oblique type
font-variant	All-capped or small-capped type
font-weight	Bold type
height	The height of an element
left	The left position of an element
letter-spacing	The amount of space between characters in a line of type
line-height	The amount of space between lines of type
list-style-image	The image to be used as the leading character in a list item, such as a graphical replacement for the standard HTML bullet
list-style-position	The position of the leading character in a list item
list-style-type	The type of leading character in a list item
margin-bottom	The location of the bottom margin
margin-left	The location of the left margin
margin-right	The location of the right margin
margin-top	The location of the top margin
overflow-x	How the element handles horizontal overflow content
overflow-y	How the element handles vertical overflow content
padding-bottom	The amount of padding along the bottom of the element
padding-left	The amount of padding on the left side of the element
padding-right	The amount of padding on the right side of the element
padding-top	The amount of padding along the top of the element
position	How the browser positions the element on the page, either by relative or absolute units
right	The right position of an element

Style definition	Controls
text-align	The alignment of a block of text
text-decoration	Additions to a block of text, such as underlines, overlines, or strikethroughs
text-indent	The amount of indentation in the first line of a block of text
text-justify	The justification setting of a block of text
text-transform	The capitalization style of a block of text
top	The top position of an element
visibility	The visibility of an element
width	The width of an element
z-index	The position of the element in the stacking order; elements with higher z-index values superimpose those with lower z-index values

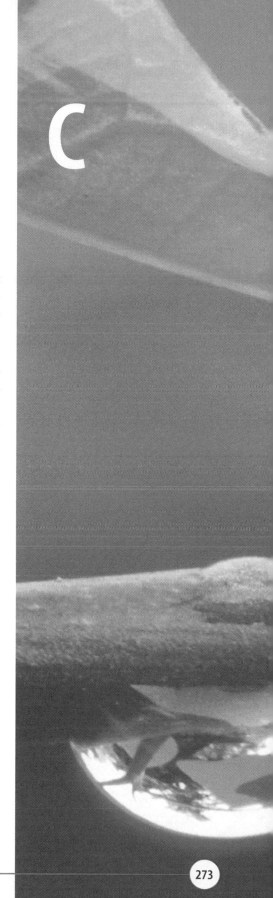

JavaScript Event Handlers

In the Behaviors panel, Dreamweaver lists the JavaScript event handler that controls the behavior's activation. To help you figure out exactly what is happening on your page and when, or to set the behavior to fire under different circumstances, please see the following table.

This table lists the most common and reliable JavaScript events—the ones that tend to work across browsers and devices. Depending upon your Dreamweaver settings, the Behaviors panel may offer a great many other JavaScript events from which to choose. You should probably avoid the ones that don't appear in this table, because they often lead to compatibility problems.

As always, be sure to test your behaviors in several different live browsers before you upload your pages, even if you pick from the safe choices. Not all browsers support all events under exactly the same set of circumstances.

Event	Fires when
onAbort	The visitor stops an image from downloading
onBlur	The element loses focus
onChange	The visitor alters a text field, text area, list, or menu
onClick	The visitor single-clicks with the left mouse button
onDblClick	The visitor double-clicks with the left mouse button
onDragDrop	The visitor drags an item and drops it on the browser window
onError	An image does not download correctly, usually because the path to the image is incorrect
onFocus	The element gains focus
onKeyDown	The visitor holds down a key
onKeyPress	The visitor presses a key
onKeyUp	The visitor releases a pressed key
onLoad	The browser loads the current web page
onMouseDown	The visitor holds down the left mouse button
onMouseMove	The visitor moves the mouse

Event	Fires when
onMouseOut	The visitor moves the mouse pointer away from the element
onMouseOver	The visitor hovers over the element with the mouse pointer
onMouseUp	The visitor releases the left mouse button after holding it down
onMove	The visitor moves a window or frame
onReset	The visitor resets a form
onResize	The visitor resizes the browser window
onSelect	The visitor selects text in a text field or text area
onSubmit	The visitor submits a form
onUnload	The browser begins to load a new web page

Glossary

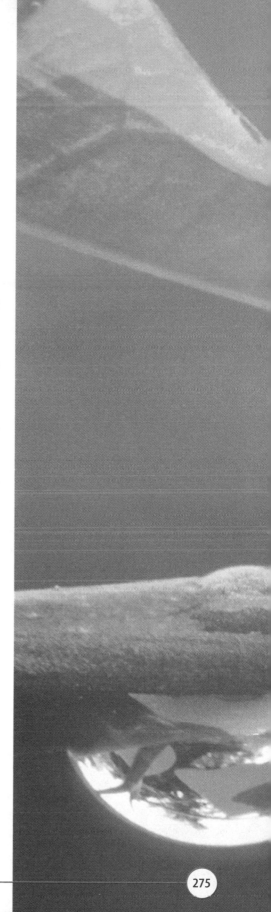

Above the fold

Pertaining to content that is visible without scrolling when the visitor first lands on a web page.

Access key

A keyboard key that the user presses in conjunction with the Alt key to select an interactive element on the page.

Accessibility

The degree to which the content of your site is available to your visitors, especially with regard to visitors who have special needs.

Active state

The appearance of a hyperlink when the visitor is currently clicking or tabbing onto the link.

Affordance

A visual cue that suggests the purpose or function of an element, such as the shape of a button graphic.

Alpha channel transparency

A type of image transparency that affords multiple levels of opacity, such as the kind in PNG images, rather than the all-or-nothing, palette-based method of transparent GIFs.

Animated GIF

A GIF image with two or more frames. The computer displays each frame in turn, creating the illusion of motion.

Appearance attributes

Styling options for a page element, such as a block of text.

Application server (app server)

Software that adds dynamic information to a web page before the web server sends the page to the client.

Autostretch

Dreamweaver terminology for a layout table or layout cell that changes width depending upon the width of the browser window.

Bandwidth

The amount of information that your web host pushes to your visitors over a given length of time, typically one month.

Behaviors

See *JavaScript behaviors*.

Below the fold

Pertaining to content that the visitor must scroll to see upon landing on a web page.

Bitmap

See *Raster graphics*.

Box

The (usually transparent) rectangle that contains a page element, such as a block of text.

Broken links

Links that can't find their destination pages.

Browser check

A troubleshooting procedure for finding code that a particular browser doesn't like.

Browser plug-in

See *Plug-in*.

Buttons

Clickable images on a computer screen, especially in the case of a web page.

Class style

A CSS style rule that applies to special instances of any element.

Client

In a computer network, the software that requests a file from a server.

Client-side behaviors

See *JavaScript behaviors*.

Client-side technology

Any technology, such as HTML, CSS, and JavaScript, that pertains to the requesting side of a network connection.

Code editor

Software for building web pages, of which Dreamweaver is a fine example.

Colspan

A table-cell attribute that allows the cell to straddle more than one column in the grid of the table.

Compression

A method for reducing the weight of a computer file, such as an image.

Content

The information that appears on a web page or web site, including text, images, and media.

Country-code top-level domain (ccTLD)

The suffix of a domain name that identifies the web site's country of origin, such as *.ie* for Ireland and *.de* for Germany.

CSS (Cascading Style Sheets)

A markup language that describes the presentation of structural elements on a web page.

Database server

Software that allows an application server to connect with an online database.

Data transfer

See *Bandwidth*.

Defining a site

Providing basic information about a project so that Dreamweaver can manage it more effectively.

Description (meta tag)

A short, one-paragraph summary of the content or purpose of a page.

Div

See *Layer*.

Domain name

The web address of your site.

Down state

The appearance of a button in a navigation bar when the visitor is on the corresponding page or section of the site.

Draw program

Software for creating and editing vector graphics.

Dreamweaver template

A document that locks down all the permanent elements of your page layout while providing editable regions for content that changes from page to page.

Dynamic site

A web site that mixes client-side and server-side technology.

Editable region

A place for variable content inside a Dreamweaver template.

Email link

A link that opens the visitor's default email program and creates a blank message.

Embedding

The practice of writing code, such as CSS, directly into an HTML page.

External link

A link that goes from your site to some other site.

Fields

See *Form fields*.

Fixed-width layout

A page layout that always keeps the same width, no matter the width of the browser window.

Flash button

A short, interactive Flash movie that works just like a rollover graphic.

Flash text

A short Flash movie that contains clickable text content.

Font

The typeface of a text element.

Form

An HTML structure for collecting visitor input.

Form fields, form objects

Interactive elements in a form that the visitor clicks or fills out, such as text fields, checkboxes, and radio buttons.

Format

In Dreamweaver parlance, the structural type of a block of text, such as a paragraph or a heading.

Get

To download a file from the web host's computer to your computer.

GIF (Graphical Interchange Format)

A type of web image that works well with large areas of flat color. GIF images contain a palette and support animation and transparency.

Grouping

The psychological tendency for humans to find similarity in things that happen to be in close proximity.

Home page

The page that loads when your visitor types your URL into the Address field of the browser.

Horizontal rule

A browser-generated line that runs from left to right on the page.

Hotspot

A clickable region in an image map.

Hover state

The appearance of a hyperlink when the visitor rolls over the link with the mouse pointer.

HTML (HyperText Markup Language)

A markup language that describes the content of a web page.

ID

A unique label to identify a particular page element.

Image editor

Software for creating and editing computer graphics, such as Macromedia Fireworks, Macromedia FreeHand, Adobe Photoshop, and Adobe Illustrator.

Image map

A graphic with one or more hotspots.

Inline image

An image that sits within its surrounding content.

Internal link

A link that goes from one page of your site to another.

JavaScript

A computer language for writing short computer programs that run in the visitor's web browser. Dreamweaver uses JavaScript to implement its set of client-side behaviors.

JavaScript behaviors

Prebuilt JavaScripts that come with Dreamweaver. Use JavaScript behaviors for helpful and interactive effects such as validating form submissions, setting the text of the status bar, creating rollover graphics, and controlling Flash movies.

JPEG (Joint Photography Experts Group)

A type of web image that works well with photos, wide ranges of color, and subtle shading. JPEG images do not have a built-in palette.

Justified text

Lines of text padded with space so that they all have the same length, except for the last line in a paragraph.

Keywords (meta tag)

The subject headings of a web page.

Layer

A logical division of a web page. You can use layers instead of tables to create standards-compliant page layouts.

Layout cells

Rectangular areas inside a layout table into which you place content.

Layout mode

In Dreamweaver, a special mode of Design view that offers table-drawing tools.

Leading character

The letter, number, or typographical mark that precedes an item in a list.

Line height

The amount of space between rows of type.

Linking

The practice of pointing to an external file, such as a CSS document, from an HTML page.

Liquid layout

A page layout that changes size to match the width of the browser window.

Local

Pertaining to the files and software on your personal computer.

Local root folder

The folder on your personal machine in which you store the files for your site.

Long description (longdesc)

An accessibility attribute of a clickable image, giving the complete URL of the page that loads when the visitor clicks the image.

Lossless compression

A method of compression that retains all the information in the file.

Lossy compression

A method of compression that jettisons some of the information in the file.

Mailto link

See *Email link*.

Main navigation

The primary method for getting around your site, such as a navigation bar.

Meta tags

HTML structures that provide high-level information about the content of a web page, mostly for the benefit of search engines.

MIME (Multipurpose Internet Mail Extension) type

The format or category for a particular computer file.

Multimedia (media)

Special kinds of web content like animations, audio, and video, usually requiring a browser plug-in or external application.

Named anchor

A specific link destination within a web page.

Navigation bar

A collection of links to the main content areas of a site, usually appearing in the same position on every page.

Nested table

A table that appears inside the cell of another table.

Ordered list

A list in which the leading character of the list items is sequential.

Orphaned files

Files in your local root folder that don't appear on any page of your site.

Out of synch

The state of a web site when its local and remote versions don't have the same content or structure.

Over state

The appearance of a button in a navigation bar when the visitor rolls over the button with the mouse pointer.

Over-while-down state

The appearance of a button in a navigation bar when the visitor hovers over a down-state image with the mouse pointer.

Padding

The amount of space between the margins of a box and the edge of the content inside it.

Page view

A common measure of web traffic; one person viewing one page of your site one time.

Paint program

Software for creating and editing raster graphics.

Palette

In a GIF or PNG image, the built-in color chart of up to 256 colors. The computer uses these colors to display that particular GIF or PNG image file.

Parked

The state of a domain name that has been reserved but doesn't yet point to an actual web site.

Path

In vector graphics, an outline formed from two or more points thus describing the shape of an object. The path is the most basic component of a vector graphic.

Pixel

Short for "picture element"; a very small, colored box. The pixel is the most basic component of a raster graphic. It is also the standard way to measure lengths and widths in web design.

Plug-in

A computer program that adds functionality to some other application, such as a web browser.

PNG (Portable Network Graphics)

A type of web image that, like GIF, works well with large areas of flat color. PNG images contain a palette and support alpha channel transparency.

POP3 (Post Office Protocol 3)

A standard for Internet email delivery that allows users to download their email to their personal computers through client software like Microsoft Outlook and Mozilla Thunderbird.

Primary preview browser

The browser that opens and loads the current page when you press F12 in Dreamweaver.

Put

To upload a file from your computer to the web host's computer.

Raster graphics

Computer images made up of pixels.

Registrar

A service for reserving a domain name.

Remote

Pertaining to the files and software on a computer other than your own, especially one that is part of the same network as yours.

Remote root folder

The folder on your web host in which you store your live site files.

Resampling

Fine-tuning the resolution and size of an image for a particular page of your site.

Reset button

In a form, a button that restores all fields to their default values.

Resolution

The pixel density of an image. In web graphics, the common measurement for resolution is pixels per inch (ppi). A typical Windows monitor screen displays at 96 ppi. A typical Macintosh monitor displays at 72 ppi.

Rollover graphic

An image that appears to change when the visitor hovers over it with the mouse pointer. What actually happens is that the browser swaps one image file for another in response to the position of the mouse pointer.

Rowspan

A table-cell attribute that allows the cell to straddle more than one row in the grid of the table.

Scope

The extent of a web site's content.

Scripts

Short computer programs that often run inside other pieces of software, such as a web browser.

Secondary navigation

An alternate navigation scheme that reinforces the main navigation of the site.

Secondary preview browser

The browser that opens and loads the current page when you press Ctrl-F12 or Command-F12 in Dreamweaver.

Second-level domain

The "name" part of a domain name, such as *amazon* and *ebay*.

Self-referential link

A link that points to its own page. In other words, it goes nowhere.

Server

In a computer network, the software that sends a file in response to a client's request.

Server-side technology

Any technology, such as CFML and PHP, that pertains to the sending side of a network connection.

Side-nav layout

A common layout in web design in which the navigation area runs down the side of the page.

Site definition

The collection of information that Dreamweaver uses to manage your web site.

Slicing

A technique by which you cut an image file into smaller rectangular areas, each of which you then save as a separate image file for reassembly on a web page, usually within a table structure.

Slide show

An interactive feature that steps through a sequence of static images.

Small caps (small capitals)

Smaller versions of uppercase letters that stand in for lowercase letters.

Spacer image

A 1x1-pixel transparent GIF that pads out a liquid layout table and maintains the widths of the fixed-width cells.

State

The appearance of an element like a hyperlink or an image based on what has happened (or is happening) in the browser window.

Static site

A web site that relies solely on client-side technology.

Status bar

The element of the browser interface that displays brief messages about what the browser is currently doing or where the selected hyperlink leads.

Structure (of a page)

Collectively, the elements that make up a web page.

Structure (of a site)

The way in which a web site organizes its content.

Style definition

An attribute/value pair in CSS that gives the appearance of a specific feature or aspect of the selector.

Style rule

In a Cascading Style Sheet, the collection of style selectors that together describe the presentation of a specific structural element.

Style selector

The structural element to which a style rule applies.

Submit button

In a form, a button that transmits the values of the fields.

Swap

In a rollover graphic, to switch one image for another.

Synchronized

The state of a web site when its local and remote versions have the same content and structure.

Tab index

The order in which the browser selects an element when the visitor presses the Tab key.

Table

An HTML structure for organizing rows and columns of data. You can also use it to build the layout of a web page, although standards bodies like the World Wide Web Consortium (W3C) strongly discourage the practice.

Tags

The markers in an HTML file that identify structural elements. For example, the <p> tag identifies its content as a paragraph.

Target browsers

In a browser check, the list of browsers against which you check the code of your site.

Targeting

With hyperlinks, identifying where the browser should load the destination page.

Text area

In a form, a multi-line text field.

Text equivalent

A literal, textual description of a purely graphical element. You use text equivalents to make content like images accessible to those with visual disabilities.

Three-click rule

A navigation ideal for web design, stating that your visitors should be able to find the content that they want within three clicks from anywhere on your site.

Title

The text that appears in the title bar along the top of the browser window when a web page loads.

Top-level domain (TLD)

The suffix of a domain name, such as *.com*, *.org*, and *.net*.

Top-nav layout

A common layout in web design in which the navigation area stretches across the top of the page.

Tracing image

A to-scale mockup of your layout upon which you draw in Dreamweaver's document window.

Transparent GIF

A GIF image in which all the pixels of a particular palette color become see-through on screen.

Type size

The length of the characters in a block of text.

Unordered list

A list in which the leading character is a bullet.

Unvisited state

The appearance of a hyperlink when the visitor has not yet been to the link's destination.

Up state

The default appearance of a button in a navigation bar.

URL (Universal Resource Locator)

The specific address of a page or file on the Web.

Validation (code)

Checking the code against official standards.

Validation (form)

Checking the fields of the form for technical errors before the browser submits them.

Vector graphics

Computer images made up of paths.

Visited state

The appearance of a hyperlink when the visitor has been to the link's destination.

Web host

The owner (or renter) of the computer that serves your web site to your visitors.

Web optimization

The practice of achieving the lightest possible image file while maintaining overall image quality.

Web-safe font

A typeface that most computer users have on their machines, such as Times New Roman and Arial on Windows computers.

Web server

Software for responding to client requests for HTML documents over a network connection.

Weight (border or rule)

The visual thickness of an element.

Weight (computer file)

The amount of disk space that a computer file requires.

Widgets

See *Form fields*.

Word wrapping

In a text area, the browser's moving of incomplete words from the end of one line to the beginning of the next.

World Wide Web Consortium (W3C)

The leading standards organization for web and web-related technologies.

Index

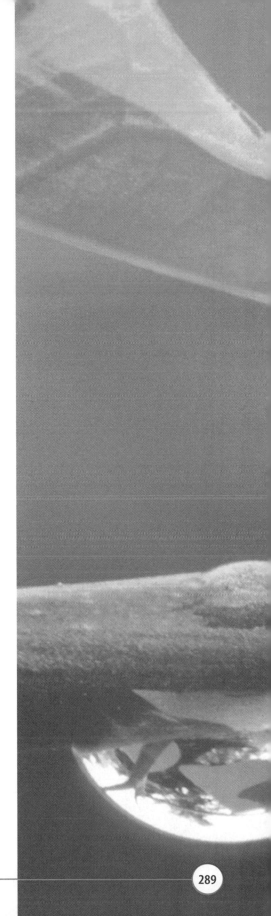

Marc Campbell has been building web sites since 1997 for everything from comic book fan communities to state government portals and e-commerce applications. A Macromedia Certified Dreamweaver Developer and beta tester, he has taught web design to students at all levels and has written eight books on the subject.

Colophon

The cover fonts are Birka, Syntax, and Trade Gothic. The text fonts are Birka and Syntax; the heading font is Myriad Condensed; and the code font is TheSans Mono Condensed.

Better than e-books

Buy *Dreamweaver 8 Design and Construction* and access the digital edition FREE on Safari for 45 days.

Go to www.oreilly.com/go/safarienabled
and type in coupon code KZF8-UBUE-VUZ3-W9EN-UTYQ

Search
thousands of
top tech books

Download
whole chapters

Cut and Paste
code examples

Find
answers fast

Search Safari! The premier electronic reference
library for programmers and IT professionals.

Related Titles from O'Reilly

Web Programming

ActionScript Cookbook

ActionScript for Flash MX: The Definitive Guide, *2nd Edition*

Dynamic HTML: The Definitive Reference, *2nd Edition*

Flash Hacks

Essential PHP Security

Google Hacks, *2nd Edition*

Google Pocket Guide

HTTP: The Definitive Guide

JavaScript & DHTML Cookbook

JavaScript Pocket Reference, *2nd Edition*

JavaScript: The Definitive Guide, *4th Edition*

Learning PHP 5

PayPal Hacks

PHP Cookbook

PHP in a Nutshell

PHP Pocket Reference, *2nd Edition*

PHPUnit Pocket Guide

Programming ColdFusion MX, *2nd Edition*

Programming PHP

Upgrading to PHP 5

Web Database Applications with PHP and MySQL, *2nd Edition*

Webmaster in a Nutshell, *3rd Edition*

Web Authoring and Design

Ambient Findability

Cascading Style Sheets: The Definitive Guide, *2nd Edition*

Creating Web Sites: The Missing Manual

CSS Cookbook

CSS Pocket Reference, *2nd Edition*

Dreamweaver 8: The Missing Manual

Essential ActionScript 2.0

Flash 8: The Missing Manual

Flash Hacks, *2nd Edition*

Flash Out of the Box

FrontPage 2003: The Missing Manual

Head First HTML with CSS & XHTML

HTML & XHTML: The Definitive Guide, *5th Edition*

HTML Pocket Reference, *2nd Edition*

Information Architecture for the World Wide Web, *2nd Edition*

Learning Web Design, *2nd Edition*

Programming Flash Communication Server

Web Design in a Nutshell, *3rd Edition*

Web Site Measurement Hacks

Web Administration

Apache Cookbook

Apache Pocket Reference

Apache: The Definitive Guide, *3rd Edition*

Perl for Web Site Management

Squid: The Definitive Guide

Web Performance Tuning, *2nd Edition*

The O'Reilly Advantage

Stay Current and Save Money